Higher Education in Emerging India

Higher Education in Emerging India

Problems, Policies and Perspectives

Foreword by

Jandhyala B.G. Tilak

Edited by

Abdul Salim. A

SHIPRA

(First Published in India in 2018)

₹ 1600; US$ 80

ISBN: 978-93-86262-78-3

2022 Impression

Higher Education in Emerging India: Problems, Policies and Perspectives

Published by:
SHIPRA PUBLICATIONS
LG 18-19, Pankaj Central Market
I.P. Ext., Patparganj, Delhi 110092, India
Tel.: +91 11 2223 5152/6152, 9650028065
info@shiprapublication.com
www.shiprapublication.com

Foreword

Higher education in India has been experiencing explosive growth during more than the last quarter century. The rate of growth of the sector accelerated mainly due to the expansion of private sector in higher education. With the phenomenal growth, the higher education system in India emerged as the second largest system in the world after China, producing the second largest stock of scientific and technical manpower. Higher education is regarded as an engine for equitable economic and social progress. Though some progress has been made, inequalities in higher education – particularly between rural and urban regions and the rich and the poor—are persistently high in India. Secondly, quality and standards in higher education are widely perceived to be poor and declining. Thirdly, despite being the second largest system, the gross enrolment ratio is only about 25 per cent, while it is felt that we need to raise it to about 40 per cent, to realise the goals relating to fast and sustainable economic growth. In addition, poor and inadequate infrastructure, absence of research environment, severe shortages of teachers, ineffective governance, outdated curricula and teaching-learning methodologies, inefficient evaluation mechanisms, plagiarism, unhealthy competition and stress among the students, and above all growing tendencies of commercialisation, have been some of the striking features of a large part of higher education system in the country. Taken individually, each of these aspects has been troubling enough; and together, they represent a gloomy scenario of higher education.

The government at the centre and also in states, has been taking quite a few important initiatives; but they are not adequate, some ill-conceived and many are designed as piecemeal short term solutions. For the development of a strong higher education system in a sustainable way and for it to contribute to socio-economic transformation of the nation, it is necessary that the system is expanded further, and at the same time it is inclusive, and is of high quality and standards. We need a proper perspective plan for the development of higher education. In the absence of a clear cohesive long term policy statement making a firm commitment to higher education, the growth of higher education has been unplanned and unregulated; it is subject to all kinds of vagaries, uncertainties, instability and related weaknesses. The system is characterised, like a bubble, by sudden pops and long slides.

A visionary perspective plan for the development of higher education, including a long-term financial plan of higher education, is critically needed. Government has to make a firm commitment to liberally allocate a steadily increasing flow of public resources to higher education to meet increasing challenges. Principles of adequacy, equity, excellence and steady growth should guide the process of allocation of resources to higher education. Higher education has to be seen as a major area of high priority in the nation's developmental efforts.

The Inter University Centre for Alternative Economics (IUCAE) is a recently initiated unit of the University of Kerala. The Center is engaged in promoting research and innovative studies in alternative economic streams that comprehensively address problems of the economy and society at large. It also tries to encourage interactions between institutions engaged in serious studies in alternative economics. The book '*Higher Education in Emerging India: Problems, Policies and Perspectives*', based on the papers presented in the International seminar organised by the IUCAE on 24-26 October 2016, is a valuable volume, critically analyzing a variety of issues afflicting the higher education sector in India and other developing economies. Major themes covered in the book include policies and strategies adopted by both developing and developed economies for massification of higher education, impact of globalization on higher education, liberatory and transformative role of education, diversity and discrimination in higher education institutions, autonomy and accountability, university governance, funding, sustainability of universities, privatization of higher education, gender inequalities, quality and excellence, and linkages between higher education and labour market.

Eminent scholars and highly experienced academicians have contributed to this book. I hope this book would attract the attention of academicians, policy makers, researchers and other scholars interested in various issues in higher education in India and other developing and developed countries.

Jandhyala B.G. Tilak
Former Vice Chancellor,
National Institute of Educational Planning and Administration
Distinguished Professor,
Council for Social Development, New Delhi

Introduction

Development of human resources is crucial for economic development of a country. Human resources can be developed by imparting skills and education. In fact, the relationship between education and economic development is mutually reinforcing. Higher education contributes to national development through dissemination of specialised knowledge and skills. India has one of the largest higher education systems in the world. However, Indian higher education sector faces several quantitative as well as qualitative challenges. Ensuring equitable access to quality higher education for students coming from various socio economic groups remains as a major challenge. The quality of higher education which can be assessed in terms of performance of students and employability of graduates is lower in India than the developed and the emerging economies in the world. Majority of graduates coming out of universities are not employable due to the lack of necessary skills. There exists a huge demand-supply gap in the higher education sector. Given the high demand, the expansion of higher education system appears to be slow. The privatisation of higher education sector is expected to fill the gap by bringing foreign universities and starting new institutions of higher learning. Gradual government withdrawal and the consequent under-investment in institution facilities makes it strenuous to provide quality instruction or engage in cutting-edge research.

Lack of adequate financial support from government has made it difficult for many institutions to attract qualified and talented teachers and have to run courses with sub-qualified teachers on ad hoc basis, which is a serious threat to quality of education. Most of the premier institutes in India face a faculty crunch with keeping nearly one third of the posts vacant. Further, with government funding in higher education receding over the years, many institutes themselves suffer, barely managing to survive. In such a scenario, employees are more focused on sustaining themselves rather than deliver quality education. Even as the woes of inadequate faculty remain, a major part of the ones who are present to impart higher education are woefully unequipped in terms of either qualifications or experience or proper training. Moreover the curriculum of most higher education courses is very infrequently updated even as the world sees a continuously changing scenario in industry manpower requirements. This has caused a crass divide between the industry expectations and the college pass outs who are poorly equipped with the right technical, business or social skills to be employed. The poor connectivity of higher education institutions with research centres and the poor education industry linkage are other issues.

The recent trend in higher education consists of the increasing role of private sector and gradual withdrawal of public sector. The expenditure on higher education as a percentage of GDP and as a proportion to total education expenditure are very low and declining over the years, compared to the developed countries and the emerging economies. The implicit policy pursued by central and state governments in general since the mid 1990s to promote elementary education at the cost of higher education affected the expansion of higher education institutions in the public sector. This trend reduces the relative size of public sector. Eleventh and twelfth five year plans promote public private partnership in higher education along with emphasising the role of private sector expansion. This policy has led to the proliferation of self financing education, which has serious implications for access, social equity and quality. Growth of for-profit institutions in higher education with a tradeoff between cost efficiency and quality raises serious menace to quality. Besides, there is a lack of effective regulatory framework to control private institutions. Uncontrolled private institutions already contribute towards vulgar forms of commercialisation. In public private partnership, very often profits are shared among private partners while costs and risks are for the public, raising questions against its effectiveness.

The book basically addresses the problems afflicting the higher education sector in India. N. V. Varghese, in his paper on 'The Changing Landscape of Higher Education: An Analysis of Changes in Developing and Developed Countries' discusses the strategies and policies adopted by developed countries for massifying higher education system. He observes that returns to higher education were higher than that of other levels of education. So the 21st century experienced massive expansion – enrolment more than doubled to 207.5 million in 2014. During the period 2000-2010, nearly 90 per cent of the increase in enrolment was in developing countries and that enrolment in developed countries were stagnating or declining. The developed market economies relied on public institutions to massify higher education while developing countries relied on markets to massify higher education. It is estimated that US needs to increase the enrolment of foreign students to 1.2 million by 2020 to maintain its competitiveness. Cross-border student flow is increasing. Student flow is from developing to developed countries. Also he rightly pointed out the need for Massive Open Online Courses (MOOC). The MOOC popularised learning without boundaries. Then, he spoke about the pressure from globalisation to improve quality through External Quality Assurance (EQA) and Internal Quality Assurance Cells (IQAC). Professor

Varghese concludes by stressing that higher education is becoming a global business rather than a global public good and the major challenge is how to manage massification. Professor Morshidi Sirat, Director of Common Wealth Education Facility, University Sains Malaysia, focused on the 'Role of Government in Higher Education of Emerging Economies: the Case of Malaysia'. The Malaysian economy is caught in middle income trap. The government has envisioned a plan, Vision 2020, to overcome the middle income trap and to acquire the tag of a growing nation.

The paper on 'Structure and Pattern of Higher Education Courses in Singapore' by N. Varaprasad, Adjunct Professor of the University of Singapore provides a lucid picture on the metamorphosis of Singapore from a third world nation to a developed nation and the role that educational policies played for achieving the same. He opined that the role of a university is to create, apply and disseminate knowledge and concluded his paper with policy lessons for developing economies. Radhakrishna Pillai in his paper on 'Impact of Denationalisation and Gobalisation on Science Education and Research in Developing Countries' explores the impacts of globalisation adopting India as a model for developing countries. He pointed out India's great tradition in education and the legacy of great universities like Nalanda. He noted that the role of education had changed; the prevalent ideology now is 'human capital'. The resource needed for the economy is that of highly skilled human capital. It also analyses the impact of the new trends in education due to globalisation on the traditional system of education and how a developing country can reap the benefits and overcome the negative impact of globalised education. The paper also suggests various strategies that the Universities in developing countries can adopt to enhance the quality of the staff and move the thrust of education from theoretical based to practical oriented one.

In the paper on 'Higher Education in the Context of Development', M. Kunhaman calls for a re-look at both higher education and development. He argues that higher education must provide the skill-kit required from time to time without, at the same time, compromising liberatory and transformative role of education. The author argues for repositioning the university needs in the context of the shift in development focus from the nation/ society to the individual, based on liberalism and individualism. 'While the state should follow a hands-off policy towards academic matters, strong state and social interventions are needed to eliminate social discrimination, inbreeding and nepotism'.

Malish C. M. and Nidhi S. Sabharwal in their paper on'Diversity and Discrimination in Higher Education Institutions in India: Case Study of Selected States' reveals that both individual and institutional discriminations exist in higher education. They conclude that the institutional receptivity towards socially disadvantaged groups is negative and that they are deprived of opportunities to integrate both academically and socially.

Aishna Sharma in her paper 'Autonomy and Accountability of Universities in India' identified the changing face of regulation in the autonomy and accountability of higher education in the liberalised era. She opined that the neoliberal discourse seeks to create rational individuals in the quest for improving quality through accountability and shared the caveat that this tendency might thwart the very objective of quality improvement. She concluded the paper by showing her strong remonstrance over the anomaly of policy framework which desisted the culture of an institution and reckoned only individualism.

Saumen Chattopadhyay in his paper on the 'Mode of Funding Higher Education and University Governance' argues for the input based funding with complete academic freedom. Further he finds that even the marketisation and increased private sector participation have not led to any improvement in the quality. C. Krishnan's paper on 'Are Our Universities Financially Sustainable? The Case of Four South Indian Universities' discusses the transition of Indian Universities from grant-depended institutions to self-sustaining universities by identifying their own resources. The additional resources can be mobilised by resorting to donations, enhanced fee, introducing more user charges and reducing the burden of state apparatus. The study points to the necessity of exploring alternative channels of resources mobilisation to offer quality education. Rajan Varughese in the paper on 'Government Withdrawal and Privatization of Higher Education in Kerala' focusses on student enrolment of higher education in Kerala, evolution of college finances, non-institutional and institutional sources of financing and the alternative to disinvestment in higher education. S. R. Sheeja's paper on 'Access and Equity: A Study on the Impact of Self- financing Colleges in Kerala' shows that though Indian higher education system has expanded substantially in the post-independence period, ensuring quality education based on the principles of access and equity still remains a challenge. More than three fourth of university eligible age group children do not have access to Indian higher education system. Despite several measures undertaken by the successive governments to enhance the participation of the disadvantaged groups of the society, growth of higher education was not inclusive in India. There exists considerable disparities based on gender, caste/community, region and economic status. Careful planning and policy framework are essential to eliminate different types of barriers prevailing in higher education and to revamp and upgrade this sector to meet the future challenges.

The paper by Christabell P. J. and Rajeev B. on 'Gender Participation in Science, Technology, Engineering and Mathematics (STEM) Education and Emerging Challenges to Innovation in India' argues that the top concern of industry, government and economic leaders in the globalised era is on the STEM workforce. They raise their resentment by arguing that India stands far behind in STEM investment, expending just 0.88 per cent of its GDP in science research compared to 7-8 per cent for the US and 3-4 per cent for South Korea. As a result, India is one of the countries with the most acute talent crisis globally. Asha J. V. in her study on 'Quality Issues and Trends in Teacher Education: An Alternative Perspective' emphasises the need for policies and strategies to strengthen teacher education. She argues that teachers' work is complex and demanding, and improvement in teacher quality requires a re-conceptualisation of how we prepare a new generation of teachers. G. L. Arunjilal in his study on 'Higher Education and Labour Market in India: Missing Linkages' stresses the necessity to move towards a student demand-driven system and the need for a globally relevant and competitive higher education system. P.S. Deva Kumar in his study on 'Bridging the Industry—Academia Gap: The Way Ahead for Higher Education in Kerala' points out the importance of university-industry tie-ups so that faculty members can be placed with industry openings by way of exchange programmes. Patent registration and commercial exploration options also need to be exploited.

This volume is a compendium of a few selected papers presented in the International conference on Higher Education organized by Inter University Centre for Alternative Economics (IUCAE) under the University of Kerala in 2016.The author is indebted to the University and the Government of Kerala which facilitated the activities of the centre through generous funding. It is also expected that this volume would be useful to the researchers, academicians, policy makers and those interested on various issues in higher education.

Abdul Salim. A

Contents

Foreword *v*
Introduction *xv*

SECTION I
Higher Education in India: A Comparative Perspective

1. The Changing Landscape of Higher Education: An Analysis of Changes in Developing and Developed Countries
N.V. Varghese 2

2. Role of Government in Higher Education of Emerging Economies: A Case Study of Malaysia
Dato' Morshidi Sirat 22

3. Structure and Pattern of Higher Education Courses in Singapore
N Varaprasad 38

4. Impact of Denationalisation and Globalisation on Science Education and Research in Developing Countries
Radhakrishna G Pillai 48

SECTION II
Policy Crisis in Indian Higher Education

5. Higher Education in the Context of Development
M. Kunhaman 71

6. Diversity and Discrimination in Higher Education Institutions in India: Case Study of Selected States
C. M. Malish and Nidhi S. Sabharwal 84

7. Autonomy and Accountability of Universities in India: A Critical Look at Policy since Independence
Aishna Sharma 99

SECTION III
Restructuring of Higher Education in India

8. Mode of Funding Higher Education and University Governance: A Critical Assessment of the Possibilities
Saumen Chattopadhyay 115

9. Are Our Universities Financially Sustainable? The Case of Four South Indian Universities
C. Krishnan 129

10. Government Withdrawal and Privatisation of Higher Education in Kerala
Rajan Varughese 142

11. Access and Equity: A Study on the Impact of Self-financing Colleges in Kerala
S. R. Sheeja 154

12. Gender Participation in Science, Technology, Engineering and Mathematics (STEM) Education: Emerging Challenges to Innovation in India
P. J. Christabell and Rajeev B. 164

13. Quality Issues and Trends in Teacher Education: An Alternative Perspective 181
J. V. Asha

14. Higher Education and Labour Market in India: Missing Linkages
G. L. Arunjilal 193

15. Bridging the Industry — Academia Gap: The Way Ahead for Higher Education in Kerala
P. S. Deva Kumar 207

Contributors *217*
Index *218*

List of Tables

1.1: Growth in Enrolment in Higher Education, 1980-2014 4
1.2: Gross Enrolment Ratio(GER) by Regions, 2000-2014 5
1.3: GER in Selected Countries, 2000-2014 6
1.4: Distribution of Foreign Students by Host Countries (%) 9
1.5: Share of International Students by Countries 9
1.6: Cross Border Institution Mobility in Enrolment, 2016. 11
1.7: Enrolment in MOOCs, 2015 12
2.1: Malaysian Government Expenditure for Education and Tertiary Education from 1971 to 2013 31
3.1: World University Rankings (Asia, selected universities), 2015/16 44
4.1: Indicators of Global Potential, Capacity and Engagement with respect to Student Enrolment in year 2014 54
5.1: SC/ST Population (2011 Census) and their Respective Shares in Faculty Positions in Higher Educational Institutions 76
5.2: Enrolment of Dalit and Adivasi Students in Higher Education 77
6.1: Relationship between Initial Days Experience and Social Group belonging 89
6.2: Invitation for Orientation Programme 90
6.3: Welcome party at the time of joining 90
6.4. Awareness about the cell / committee and its role (%) 91
6.5: Awareness about where and whom to contact in case of complaint (%) 92
6.6. Faculty involved in the Equal Opportunity Cell (%) 92
6.7. Awareness about Bridge / Remedial Coaching among the Students 92
9.1: Sources of Finance of Universities in Kerala during 2007-08 to 2011-12 133
9.2. Resource Generation in Kerala University 2005-06 to 2011-12 (%) 134
9.3: Components of Internal Resources in Kerala University 2005-06 to 2011-12 (%) 134
9.4: Resource Generation in Calicut University 2005-06 to 2011-12 (%) 135
9.5: Components of Internal Resources in Calicut University 2005-06 to 2011-12 (%) 136
9.6: Internal Resource Generation in M.G. University 2005-06 to 2011-12 (%) 137
9.7: Components of Internal Resources in M.G. University 2007-08 to 2011-12 (%) 137

9.8:	Resource Generation in Kannur University 2005-06 to 2011-12 (%)	138
9.9:	Components of Internal Resources in Kannur University 2005-06 to 2010-11 (%)	138
11.1:	Number of Higher Education Institutions in India, 2014-15	155
11.2:	International Comparison of GER, 2013	156
12.1:	Number of Institutions by Type 2013-14 (Provisional)	168
12.2:	Enrolment in Different Disciplines / Subjects at Under Graduate Level in Higher Education 2012-13 (Provisional)	168
12.3:	Gap in the Literacy rates of Males and Females over decades	169
12.4:	Gross Enrolment Ratio (GER)	169
12.5:	Number of Females per 100 Males in University Education in Major Disciplines	170
12.6:	Enrolment in different Programmes in Higher Education	170
12.7:	Girls' Enrolment at Different levels, 2015-16	171
12.8:	Research Scholars in STEM in Universities of Kerala	172
12.9:	Number of STEM Scholars in different Universities	173
12.10:	Academic publications of STEM scholars	174
12.11:	Participation of STEM scholars in various academic programmes	174
12. 12:	Academic performance of STEM scholars	175
12.13:	Scholars participation in STEM communication Activities	175
12.14:	Participation of STEM Graduates in Economic Contribution	178
14.1:	Country wise distribution of student enrolment in higher education (2012) and Number of higher education institutions (2013)	195
14.2:	Global Ranking of Indian Higher education Institutions	195
14.3:	India's Position in different ranking criteria	195
14.4:	Drivers of Change in the skill and employment front	197
14.5	Distribution of Unemployed Population aged 15-59 years across General Education	201
15.1	Criteria of Students Selection — Aptitude in the Relevant Discipline	211
15.2:	Mapping of Potential Employment Opportunities	212

List of Figures

3.1: Link between Economic Structural Change, Education and Employability 39
3.2: No. of Degree Programmes (NUS, 1982-2016) 42
3.3: No. of Multidisciplinary Programmes (NUS, 2006-2016) 43
4.1: Nationality of Foreign Students Enrolled in Indian Higher Education Institutes —2015 57
4.2: Research Carried Out by Scholars in India 62
7.1: Game Tree under Information Asymmetry 107
7.2: Collective Action Game: the Problem of Free-riding 110
8.1: Funding Systems in Academic Institutions 118
13.1: Rating on the Capacity of the Curriculum in Realising Self-directed Learning 185
13.2: Rating on the Capacity of the Curriculum in Providing Autonomy in Teaching 186
13.3: Rating of Teacher Educators on Incorporating Theory, Practicum and Internship within the Semester Framework 187

SECTION I

Higher Education in India: A Comparative Perspective

1.
The Changing Landscape of Higher Education
An Analysis of Changes in Developing and Developed Countries [1*]

N.V. Varghese

Knowledge is key to economic development and 'nations that ignore this fact suffer, while those that recognise it flourish' (Hanushek and Woessmann, 2015, p.1). In fact, knowledge has become the driving force of economic performance and enhanced growth (UIS/OECD, 2003) and human capital has been 'the single-most important engine of growth in OECD countries in the past three decades' (OECD, 2000: p.17). The higher education institutions are evaluated for their contribution to development based on their capacity to innovate and produce knowledge. It is increasingly realised that future economic growth and national competitiveness depend on investments made in research and development (R&D) activities. A realisation of the economic value of knowledge and the role of higher education institutions in producing knowledge has increased the economic interest and investment in higher education. This is an important reason for the massive expansion of the sector in the recent past. Countries are competing to massify and further to universalise higher education and to achieve global standards through establishment of world class universities. This paper will examine the reforms leading to the changing landscape of higher education in the developing and developed world in this century.

Revival and Massification of Higher Education

One of the distinguishing features of higher education development in this century is its global revival. The revival of the sector is reflected in terms of a favourable public policy environment, enhanced public funding support, increased household investment, multiplication of providers and diversification of study programmes leading to proliferation of institutions (private and public) and an explosion in student numbers (Varghese, 2012). While expansion of the sector was mostly a phenomenon experienced in the developed countries in the earlier decades, it became a global phenomenon in this century with the developing countries accounting for a larger share of the global expansion.

1 The opinions and views expressed in this paper are of the author and hence should not necessarily be attributed to the institution where he is employed.

The higher education sector experienced expansion across countries in the decades of 1960s and 1970s. This was followed by a decade of decline of the sector in the 1980s reflected in terms of slow growth in student enrolment, declining or stagnating gross enrolment ratios (GER) and reduced share of public expenditure. Between 1975 and 1985 the global GER declined from 14 to 13 per cent. The GER declined in East Asia and Pacific region and in Europe and Central Asian region, stagnated in low and middle income countries and experienced very low rates of growth in the high income countries. The resources allocated to higher education as a share of public expenditure also declined in the 1980s in low and middle income countries from 18.5 per cent to 15.7 per cent and in high income countries from 20.3 to 18.2 per cent (The Task Force, 2000).

The global enrolment in higher education increased from around 100 million in 2000 to 207.5 million in 2014 (UIS, 2016) accounting for an average annual increase of around 7.7 million students. As of now, the developed countries have universalised higher education, the middle income countries have massified, if not universalised, their higher education sector while it is a fast expanding sector in the less developed countries of Asia and Africa. The developed countries experienced higher rates of growth of higher education in the 1970s and 1980s. The growth rates show a consistent trend of decline in developed countries from the 1980s and becoming negative in the current decade (Table 1.1). On the other hand, higher education growth rates have been consistently increasing in developing countries.

While the system expanded in all regions, the expansion was faster in the developing world (Altbach, et al. 2009) in the first decade of the present century and the expansion was entirely in the developing world in the current decade (Varghese, 2016). Nearly 90 per cent of the total increase in enrolment between 2000 and 2014 was in developing countries. However, if we compare the first and second decades of this century, one can notice a changing trend in growth in enrolment. In the first decade (between 2000 and 2010) the total increase in enrolment was 82.1 million and the developing countries accounted for more than 80.0 per cent of the increase in enrolment. During the current decade (2010-2014), the total increase in global enrolment was 26.0 million. During this period, the enrolment in the developed countries declined by around 3.5 million students and that in the developing countries increased by 29.4 million. In other words, unlike in the decades of the past century, the expansion of higher education is a phenomenon confined mostly to the developing countries in this century. Since developing countries experience low GERs and a bulge in youth population, the possibilities are that these trends in surge in enrolments led by the developing countries may continue more vigorously in the coming years.

Table 1.1: Growth in Enrolment in Higher Education, 1980-2014

Year	*Enrolment in millions*	*Rate of growth in enrolment (global)*	*Rate of growth in developing countries*	*Rate of growth in developed countries*
1980	50.8	-		
1990	68.3	3.0	3.3	2.7
2000	99.7	3.9	5.5	1.5
2010	181.5	6.2	7.7*	1.3
2014	207.5	3.4	4.7*	-ve

*Includes countries in transition
Sources: Calculated based on: i) The Task Force 2000; and ii) UIS 2004, 2012 and 2016

Gross Enrolment Ratios (GER)

At the school level, net enrolment ratios (NER) are relied on to assess expansion and progress of education. NER is not estimated at higher education level and therefore, the gross enrolment ratio (GER) is considered as a reliable indicator of expansion of higher education. It took nearly 30 years to double the global GER in higher education —the GER increased from nine per cent in 1965 to 18 per cent in 1995. However, the global GER almost doubled in the next 20 years from 18 per cent in 1995 to 34 per cent in 2014. While all regions gained from growth in enrolments and improved their GERs, the inter-regional disparities widened over a period of time. For example, in 2014 the GER varied between eight per cent in sub-Saharan Africa and 76 per cent in North America and Western Europe. The corresponding figures for 2000 were four per cent and 60 per cent respectively (Table 1.2).

Between 2000 and 2014 the gain in global GER was more due to the expansion of the higher education system in the developing countries than in the developed countries. The GER, on average, more than doubled (2.4 times) in developing countries. The increase in the Asia Pacific region, South and West Asia was 2.6 times, and it doubled in Latin America and African region. The slowest growth and lowest gains in GER were made by the Central Asian region. While East Asia and Pacific was the region with slowest expansion in higher education in the past century, it became the fastest growing region in this century (Table 1.2). While expansion of higher education was faster in the less developed countries in the first decade of this century, it became almost entirely their contribution in the current decade. Between 2010 and 2014 the GER declined in developed countries in general and also in the North American and Western European countries.

Table 1.2: GER by Regions, 2000-2014

Regions	*2000*	*2010*	*2014*	*GER Female 2014*
World	19.0	29.0	34.0	36.0
Developed countries	56.0	75.0	74.0	83.0
Developing countries	12.0	22.0	29.0	29.0
Countries in transition	43.0	58.0	58.0	62.0
Arab states	19.0	25.0	29.0	30.0
Central and Eastern Europe	43.0	69.0	74.0	80.0
Central Asia	22.0	25.0	26.0	27.0
East Asia and the Pacific	15.0	28.0	39.0	41.0
Latin America and the Caribbean	22.0	40.0	44.0	50.0
North America and Western Europe	60.0	77.0	76.0	86.0
South and West Asia	9.0	17.0	23.0	22.0
Sub-Saharan Africa	4.0	8.0	8.0	7.0

The disparities in GERs were the widest between Eritrea with three per cent and countries such as Finland, Spain and Belarus with a GER of 89 per cent. In fact, the GER was 100.0 per cent in the Republic of Korea in 2010. The widening disparities are the result of varying rates of growth in GER among countries. A more disaggregated analysis at the country level may be useful to understand this trend. For example, between 2000 and 2014, while the GER increased by eight times in Ethiopia, five times in Lesotho, more than three times in Vietnam, more than doubled in Chile, Columbia, India, Indonesia, etc., the increase in GER was less in all the developed countries which already have universalised higher education (Table 1.3). A general trend one finds is that countries which have massified or universalised higher education, there the GER of females is higher than that of males giving a gender parity index of more than one. There are only few exceptions to this general trend such as Lesotho which has a higher GER for females even when the system is at an elite stage. In Republic of Korea and Japan, on the other hand, the female GERs are consistently lower than that of males even when the system is universalised. One of the sources of fast growth of the sector is the emergence of private higher education institutions and expansion of enrolment in these institutions. The emergence and expansion of the private higher education institutions was more in the developing world than in the developed world.

Table 1.3: GER in Selected Countries, 2000-2014

Regions	*GER 2000 Total*	*GER Male 2000*	*GER Female 2000*	*GER 2014 Total*	*GER Male 2014*	*GER Female 2014*
World	19.0	19.0	19.0	34.0	33.0	36.0
Ethiopia	1.0	2.0	1.0	8.0	11.0	5.0
Lesotho	2.0	2.0	3.0	10.0	8.0	12.0
Bangladesh	5.0	7.0	4.0	13.0	15.0	11.0
Vietnam	9.0	11.0	8.0	30.0	30.0	31.0
India	10.0	11.0	18.0	23.6*	24.5*	22.6*
Indonesia	15.0	16.0	14.0	31.0	29.0	33.0
Colombia	23.0	22.0	24.0	51.0	48.0	55.0
Chile	37.0	39.0	35.0	87.0	89.0	92.0
Portugal	48.0	41.0	55.0	66.0	61.0	70.0
France	54.0	49.0	60.0	64.0	58.0	71.0
Spain	58.0	53.0	63.0	89.0	82.0	97.0
UK	59.0	54.0	63.0	56.0	49.0	64.0
Sweden	67.0	55.0	80.0	62.0	49.0	76.0
USA	68.0	58.0	78.0	87.0	73.0	101.0

Source: UIS several years; *MHRD (2016)

Privatisation and Private Sector

The State funding and public institutions played a dominant role in the development of higher education in most countries. The period of 'state monopoly on tertiary education' (World Bank, 2002) came to an end by the turn of this century. The political shift to the right, the embracement of market ideology and the results of the rate of returns to investment in higher education provided the rationale for the shift. The rate of return studies in recent decades showed higher returns to higher education than to other levels of education (World Bank, 2002; DBIS, 2011). 'The gap between the earnings of students with a college degree and those without one is bigger than ever' (Porter, 2015, B1). Further, the returns to investments in higher education in some of the least developed countries were, perhaps, the highest with 27 per cent in Ethiopia and 25.1 per cent in Kenya (World Bank, 2009).

All these factors contributed to a policy of moving away from a total reliance on state to markets in financing of higher education. The move from state to markets led to two phenomena: the privatisation of public institutions and the promotion of the private sector in higher education (Varghese, 2006).

Privatisation implies applying market principles in the functioning of public institutions of higher education even when ownership and management of institutions remained with the public authorities. The cost recovery, income generating, and for-profit activities in public universities are instances of privatisation of public institutions. The private sector represents the non-State sector in higher education where institutions are owned and operated by private individuals or agencies and they do not receive funding from the government.

Public institutions in many countries — developed as well as developing countries — introduced cost recovery measures and income generating activities. The cost-recovery measures were common among many developed countries. Needless to add, public institutions in the UK and the USA were leaders in this process. The revival of higher education in Africa started with privatisation of public institutions. The reforms initiated in the Makerere University in Uganda are perhaps the best example of this phenomenon in Africa which soon spread to other countries in the region. The least developed countries such as Cambodia and Vietnam in South East Asia implemented privatisation measures very successfully. A closer examination will reveal that growth of enrolment in public higher education institutions in many countries was mostly in the market / private segment of the public institutions.

The other phenomenon contributing to higher growth of the sector is private higher education. Private higher education has traditionally been common in countries such as Japan, Indonesia, Philippines and Malaysia in South East Asia and countries such as Brazil, Chile, Costa Rica, El Salvador, Peru, etc. in Latin America (Bjarnason *et al.*, 2009). The emergence of market process and private higher education in Central and Eastern Europe was a phenomenon of the post-Soviet Union period. Although there was a spurt in private enrolment, the enrolment shares still continue to be less than one-third of the total even in the most privatised countries such as Estonia, Georgia, Latvia, and Poland (Slantcheva and Levy, 2007). Sub-Saharan Africa experiences fast expansion of private higher education institutions and enrolment. Two-thirds (around 70) of the new universities founded in the Arab states since 1993 are private, and at least 50 of them are branches of Western, mostly American universities (Varghese, 2013).

Private higher education institutions are of two types — not-for-profit and for-profit institutions. These two categories of private institutions co-exist in many countries. In some countries the private nonprofit institutions became entrepreneurial and acquired the characteristics of for-profit institutions' (Levy, 2005). The for-profit institutions are at times labeled as 'pseudo universities' since they do education as a business (Altbach, 2005, p.23). Many of the private higher education institutions are religious based. While the Catholic church dominated in the provision of private higher education in Latin America, Evangelical and Islamic faiths are common in Africa (Levy, 2006). Religious institutions are the fastest growing type of private higher education institution in almost every African country, perhaps, with the exception of South Africa (Varghese, 2006). This is partly due to the fact that many of the religious-based private higher education institutions are not-for profit, especially in Africa, and at times they not only levy low fees, but also provide financial support to students.

One of the interesting features of these developments is that private higher education institutions emerged and expanded in countries that have less developed markets while countries with developed and matured markets relied on their public institutions to expand higher education. For example, contrary to general belief, the private sector surge is experienced mostly in the developing countries and privatisation efforts are seen more in OECD countries. In fact, OECD countries relied more on public institutions and privatisation measures than private higher education institutions to massify, and later to universalise, higher education.

New Forms of Globalization: Education Hubs and MOOCs

The growing importance of knowledge in production contributed to an expanding demand for higher education degrees from universities of the developed world. The world ranking of universities further aggravated the demand for foreign degrees in the developing world. Globalisation of higher education has become a market-driven activity and a major global industry attracting billions of dollars and millions of students. Globalisation of education takes place under the GATS (general agreement on trade in services) through four modes of trade (Knight, 2002). They are cross border mobility of programmes, students, institutions and teachers.

Traditionally, the most visible form of cross border mobility in education was student mobility. The student flow has mostly been from developing to the developed world. In 2000 more than 70 per cent of the cross border students were hosted by nine countries (Table 1.4). These countries hosted less than 60 per cent of the students in 2012. One can notice that between 2000 and 2012 the number of students crossing borders more than doubled from 1.9 million to 4.1 million (UIS, 2016) while the share of top four countries hosting them declined from more than 50 per cent to less than 40 per cent (Table 1.4). The share of USA declined from 25 per cent to 18.1 per cent. The largest sending countries in 2012 were China (694 thousand), India (182 thousand), and the Republic of Korea (121 thousand). These three countries together accounted for nearly one-fourth of the total international students in 2012. Of these countries, 22.5 per cent of Chinese students, more than half of the Indian students and 56.6 per cent of the Korean students were hosted by the USA in 2010.

Table 1.4: Distribution of Foreign Students by Host Countries (%)

Host country	*2000*	*2010*	*2012*
USA	25.0	19.2	18.1
UK	12.0	10.9	10.4
Germany	10.0	5.6	5.1
France	7.0	7.3	6.6
Australia	6.0	7.6	6.1
Canada	6.0	2.7	3.0
Japan	4.0	4.0	3.7
New Zealand	0.0	1.1	1.0
Russian Federation	3.0	3.6	4.2
Others	27.0	38.0	41.9
Total (millions)	1.9	3.6	4.1

Source: UIS various years

Table 1.5: Share of International Students by Countries

Country	*1995*	*Country*	*2012*
China	6.8	China	17.3
Korea	4.0	India	4.7
Japan	3.7	Korea	3.1
Germany	2.7	Germany	2.9
Greece	2.6	S.Arabia	1.6
Malaysia	2.4	France	1.6
India	2.3	USA	1.4
Turkey	2.2	Malaysia	1.4
Italy	2.1	Vietnam	1.3
Hong Kong	2.1	Iran	1.3
Total (millions)	1.7 mn	Total (millions)	4.1 mn

Source: UIS several years

Emergence of Education Hubs

One of the new trends in the context of globalisation is institutional mobility. Institutional mobility takes place in different forms such as branch campuses, franchising or twinning arrangements. Franchising denotes the delivery of course of a foreign university within the country by an authorised domestic institution and twinning denotes the joint ownership and delivery by institutions in the home and host countries. The branch campuses are of two types — branch campuses established by a foreign university mainly to attract the students from the host country or education hubs to attract students seeking cross-border education within the country and abroad. The education hubs represent branch campuses of universities located in foreign lands which offer courses of a foreign university through face-to-face instruction leading to award of a degree from the parent institution or jointly with a partner institution (ACE, 2009; Cao, 2011). The emergence of 'education hubs' or the 'new global regionalism' (Knight, 2014) is a fast expanding segment of institutional mobility. Several countries are actively promoting globalisation of higher education through education hubs.

Malaysia is developing an international education hub targeting the undergraduate education market. Dubai Knowledge Village (DKV) established in 2003 has several international universities from Australia, India, Pakistan, Iran, Russia, Belgium, the UK, the USA and Canada. Dubai International Academic City (DIAC) attracts a large number of branch campuses from several counties and hosts more than 20,000 students. Over the last two years, there has been a 37 per cent increase in the number of students studying for UK qualifications in Dubai (Fox, 2015). Qatar has established an education hub attracting academic programmes from US universities with a view to reduce the out-flow of Qatari students. The Education City has six branch campuses from international institutions. Singapore's Global Schoolhouse (GS) initiative, launched in 2002, houses over 16 leading foreign tertiary institutions. It is estimated that the GS has already attracted over 86,000 international students. Hong Kong is emerging as a regional education hub. Mauritius has already developed collaborations with prestigious foreign universities of the USA, the UK, France, India, South Africa, etc., to establish a 'knowledge hub'.

According to CBERT (2016), there are a total of 232 international branch campuses (IBCs) in operation as of January 2016. There are a total of 32 IBC exporting countries and 76 importing countries. The largest exporters of branch campuses are USA (82), UK (38), Russia (20), France (16), and Australia (15). The largest importers of branch campus are United Arab Emirates (32), China (27), Singapore (13), Qatar (11), and Malaysia (9).

Three institutions accounted for more than 90 per cent of all UK branch campus enrolments in 201213. These were the University of Nottingham, in Malaysia and China; Middlesex University in Dubai and Mauritius; and Heriot-Watt University in Dubai and Malaysia. The Xiamen University of China plans to establish a branch campus in Malaysia, so also Soochow University of China in Vietnam (Lane and Kisner, 2013).

Table 1.6: Cross-border Institutional Mobility in Enrolment, 2016

Export Country	*% of total*	*Host Country*	*% of total*
USA	35.3	China	11.6
UK	16.4	UAE	13.8
Russia	8.6	Singapore	5.6
Australia	6.5	Qatar	4.7
France	6.9	Malaysia	3.9

Source: Based on CBERT (2016)

Many private universities from India are establishing branch campuses in other countries. Amity has branch campuses in the USA, the UK, China, Singapore, the UAE, Romania and it plans to have branch campuses in 50 countries by 2025. The Manipal group has campuses in Malaysia (2), Dubai, and Antigua, Nepal. The JSS Academy of Technical Education has established an independent institution in Mauritius. DY Patil Post-Graduate School of Medicine has established partnership with University of Technology in Mauritius (UTM) in 2009. Four Indian private institutions are represented in the Dubai International Academic City.

The ACE survey (ACE, 2009) showed that business programmes continue to dominate in Asia and Europe. IT courses occupy the second position followed by international courses common in Europe and Computer courses in Middle East. The field of international relations was common in Europe but not in other regions. Almost half of all degree programmes in the Middle East were offered in STEM fields.

There are views in favour and against branch campuses. It is argued that competition from branch campuses will negatively impact on domestic institutions (Lester, 2013). Others argue that education hubs arrest out-flow of students and money from developing countries. These debates are live in India too. Some estimates indicate that India can save to the tune of US $4 billion on foreign exchange if branch campuses were established and cross border students in India study in India instead of seeking degrees abroad (Tilak, 2008).

Programme Mobility through MOOCs

The most recent new trend in the globalisation of higher education is programme mobility through MOOCs. While online courses and online universities came into existence in the past decades, the emergence of massive open online courses (MOOCs) is a phenomenon of this decade. MOOCs has become an event changing the landscape of global higher education provision and some argued that MOOCs will replace the traditional brick and mortar system and will mark the "end of university as we know it" (Harden, 2013). The fast growth in enrolment in MOOCs gave further affirmation of these views. Within a year of its launch, the MOOCs attracted 3.1 million users from around the world (Washington Post, 6 April 2013). The enrolments in 2012 for the courses offered by Coursera, EdX, and Udacity together were around four times (2.4 million) that of the OLI, Open University and Phoenix put together (0.66 million). The expansion potential through MOOCs seemed to be large and wide.

The enrolments in MOOCs were found to be unbelievably high within two years. According to ICEF Monitor, the user base for MOOCs in 2015 almost doubled that of 2014 to reach an enrolment figure of 35 million students. In absolute terms the enrolment in 2015 was around 16-18 million more than the enrolment in 2014. Those enrolled in MOOCs were following 4,200 MOOCs courses offered by more than 500 universities. Coursera is again the clear leader and offered more than a third of all available MOOCs as of 2015 (Table 1.7). EdX is the second-ranked provider with over 18 per cent of all courses. The UK-based FutureLearn which grew by 275 per cent in 2015 (with an estimated user base of 3.0 million) is the fourth largest provider of MOOCs (Table 1.7).

Table 1.7: Enrolment in MOOCs, 2015

MOOCs Platforms	*Share of Enrolment (%)*
Coursera	35.6
EdX	18.1
Canvas.net	6.9
FutureLearn	5.7
Miriada	3.7
France Uni.Numerique	3.3
Udacity	3.0
Others	23.7
Total enrolment	35.0 million

Source: ICEF Monitor, 05 January 2016

It seems that MOOCs have tremendous potential to change the higher education scene not only by enrolling large numbers but also by relying on MOOCs to improve teaching and learning. Many institutions avail of these courses to reinforce their own courses, explore new pedagogical practices, business models and flexible learning paths in the provision (Yuan and Powell, 2013). In fact many universities are compelled to rethink how to make their curriculum delivery models and courses truly flexible and accessible (Carr, 2012). The blending of virtual classrooms with real classrooms will be a process of reinventing education and changing the landscape of globalisation of higher education.

The MOOCs are penetrating the higher education markets in the developing world. The developing countries such as Brazil (Veduca) and China (XuetangX and Ewant), Rwanda (Kepler from Generation Rwanda) are examples of countries relying on higher education provisions through MOOC platforms. Several institutions from India are joining the MOOCs platform providers to offer courses. For example, the Indian Institute of Technology (IIT), Bombay has joined hands with EdX to train engineering teachers. IIT, Delhi is offering a course on web intelligence in partnership with Coursera. COL in collaboration with IITs offered a course on MOOC on a mobile application which attracts a majority of its enrolees from poor socio-economic groups. The Udacity in collaboration with Georgia Tech and AT&T offers an online MOOCs Master's degree in India.

Do MOOCs mean end of traditional universities? Some strongly believe so. For example, Professor Sebastian Thrun, the founder of Udacity predicts that, as a result of MOOCs, by 2060 there will only be 10 universities in the world. Harden (2013) argues that MOOCs mark the beginning of the end of traditional universities. These may be exaggerated views given the limited evidence on the nature of enrolment in MOOCs. The MOOCs at present serve relatively well among the Anglophones. The University of Madison Wisconsin and University of Edinburgh both report (Gebel, 2014) that around 70 per cent of MOOC participants already possess a university degree. Another study conducted on 35,000 MOOC participants of Pennsylvania University also indicates that MOOC enrolees already have a university degree. Many of them are young professionals who are already employed. Many of them see MOOCs as an opportunity to gain additional knowledge and skills for their professional advancement from world's top universities.

The MOOCs are seen by educational leaders in the developing world more to reinforce learning rather than as a substitute for traditional universities. If these efforts are successful, the MOOCs will be playing an indirect, but important role in enhancing quality of higher education and teaching learning process in the universities of the developing countries. It seems that hybrid courses and blended courses may become more widespread and hence MOOCs need not necessarily be a threat to existing brick and mortar universities. The MOOCs can be seen as providing opportunities for the brick and mortar universities to restructure their academic activities, pedagogical practices and to transit to new ways of offering and organising their study programmes.

Diversity and Concern for Quality

As discussed in the previous sections, higher education systems expanded in countries across the world. State policies play a significant role in expanding the system and in promoting equity in access to higher education. The progressive state policies under democratic regimes, in general, follow an egalitarian approach to promote fairness in the distribution of opportunities. The fairness principle of democracy may imply redistribution of resources if the existing distribution is not fair. This redistributive dimension of democracy stems from the belief that equality in the political arena will be followed by equality in the economic and social domains (Sirowy and Inkeles, 1990).

The expansion of higher education was accompanied by diversification in terms of providers, students, programmes of study and sources of funding. In an expanding system, students belonging to different religious orientations, caste backgrounds, rural areas and poor families with illiterate parents study along with those from the privileged social and economic background (Sabarwal and Malish, 2016). Student diversity can be seen as an indicator of success in expanding access to higher education.

Many institutions of higher education, especially the administrators and teachers in institutions of higher education, have not yet reached a level of maturity to see diversity as an asset and an extension of democracy. Many of them fail to manage student diversity in the campuses leading to contested decisions and complaints of discrimination. At times increasing student diversity is seen by some groups as an important factor influencing a decline in the quality of higher education. Therefore, the concern for quality in an expanding system of higher education assumed new urgency in the decades of the 2000s.

The other pressure to focus on quality has been the globalisation process which enhanced the demand for production of skills for global markets. The accreditation of institutions and programmes became necessary for academic survival of institutions of higher education to remain competitive in the globalised world of higher education. Many countries created external quality assurance (EQA) mechanisms and accreditation became a common practice across academic systems. While EQA facilitates periodic assessment and evaluation of quality, it was increasingly felt that periodic accreditation processes alone may not help monitoring quality and student learning. Consequently, many countries established internal quality assurance (IQA) mechanisms at the institutional level. The IQA Cells are expected to carry out monitoring and review of academic programmes, conduct student surveys on teaching effectiveness, student and staff satisfaction surveys and analyse student progression. Remedial measures for those who need additional help are also organised in some of the systems.

The quality and accreditation movements are very strong in Africa. Most countries have not only established accreditation agencies but also that the national initiatives and experiences are shared among policy makers and practitioners in the region. The largest number of conferences and seminars in higher education organised by the countries in the region may be on issues related to quality and accreditation. The region has also developed training modules and has been organising orientation programmes for senior managers on quality of higher education. There are regional networks created for quality assurance.

Global Ranking and World Class Universities

This century witnessed another important development, namely, global ranking of universities and higher education institutions. The position of national universities in the global ranking is one of the most discussed topics in many countries. The first effort towards ranking was the ARWU (Academic Ranking of World Universities) published in Shanghai in 2003. This was followed by Times-QS (Quecqurely Symonds) ranking of world universities (WUR) in 2004 and others followed. The most recent ranking effort is World University Ranking by Centre for World University Ranking in Jeddah, Saudi Arabia in 2012.

The most important ranking systems are WUR by Times Higher Education, QS World University Ranking and Academic Ranking World Universities which are inexistence for more than a decade. Many of the parameters considered for ranking of universities are similar, even when the weights and methodology of data collection vary among these different systems of ranking. While QS ranking gives 50 per cent of the weights to reputation as perceived by academics and employers, only 33 per cent of the weights depend on opinions on teaching and research in the Times ranking and ARWU rarely depends on opinion surveys.

All the three ranking systems give priority for research, publications and citation index. Therefore, it is not surprising that most of the top ranking institutions are research universities. In spite of different ranking systems rely on varying parameters and their weights, the top universities in all rankings are common. For example, one may find Harvard, MIT, Stanford, Caltech, Cambridge, Oxford, Imperial, Princeton, etc. appear among the top ten institutions according to all the three rankings. Although the top ranking universities are mostly in the US and the UK, the discussions on rankings and absence of their national universities in the global ranking list, is a point of heated debate. This debate often has led to three types of outcomes — either to establish world class universities or to move towards national ranking of universities or both.

Although there is no universal recipe or magic formula for "making" a world class university, international experience shows that all top ranking universities have: a) high concentrations of talent; b) abundance of resources; and c) flexible governance arrangements (Salmi, 2009). The move towards creation of research universities is a necessary step in the creation of world class universities with concentration of talents, resources, and institutional autonomy (Altbach, 2011). Many of the reforms initiated in several countries have some of these elements included in the reform measures. The Chinese reforms of Project 985 or Project 211, the Centers of Excellence (COE 21) in Japan, Brain Korea 21 (BK 21), and the Accelerated Programme for Excellence (APEX) in Malaysia are good examples of developing excellence and world class universities.

India does not have world class universities. Some of the institutions in India are of high quality and are moving towards world class institutions of higher education (Jayaram, 2011). The government of India in its recent budget announced its intention to create twenty world class universities (10 public and 10 private universities). It seems that many of the members of the academic community are not excited about the idea of developing world class universities in India. "The academia, particularly belonging to the public sector universities, expressed disdain for world class university as an irrelevant concept, and global ranking as an improper method of measuring performance of universities" (Tilak, 2014, p.9). Whether or not India succeeds in creating world class universities within a short period of time is debatable. However, the pressure on universities to enhance their level of performance to achieve excellence is continuing with greater vigour.

National Qualification Frameworks (NQFs)

Employment and employability of higher education graduates have come to the centre stage of discussions in many countries. These discussions led to a conclusion that graduates of higher education are unemployed because they do not have necessary skills for being productively employed. The reliance on education for screening and recruiting prospective employees is based on the assumption that those who do well in education will also do well on the job. Studies show that there exist at least two types of mismatches — a mismatch between degrees and the skills and competencies they certify and a mismatch between skills developed during education and skills demanded in the labour market.

Employers started losing confidence in the qualifications and degrees awarded by institutions and there developed a 'crisis of legitimacy' of the existing qualification systems. The employers argued for greater participation in skill formation and to shape the content of education and training programmes. This was an attempt to shift the balance of power away from provider-defined qualifications and curricula to user-defined qualifications and curricula. The QF is seen as a mechanism to regain confidence on the education and training systems by employers. The move towards NQF started in the UK with the introduction of competency based qualification reforms in the 1980s (Jessup, 1991; Young, 2005). This was immediately followed by similar efforts in Australia, New Zealand, and South Africa. In the recent decades it spread to other countries.

The development of NQFs is supported by international agencies such as OECD, ILO, the World Bank and the European Union and it a major international trend in reforming national education and training systems. A parallel development to the NQFs is the Regional Qualification Frameworks (RQFs) in many regions. The RQFs are being developed in the Caribbean, European Union (EU), Southern African Development Community (SADC) and in Asia. The Qualification descriptors called the Dublin descriptors which are general statements of the typical achievement of learners who have been awarded a qualification on successful completion of a cycle was adopted, with necessary modifications, in most countries in their efforts to develop NQFs.

A competency based education is education based on learning outcomes and predetermined standards (Gonczi and Arguelles, 2000). The QF classifies qualifications according to a set of criteria (using descriptors) applicable to specified levels of learning outcomes. It is expected that the QFs will provide: (a) quality assured nationally recognised and consistent training standards; (b) recognition and credit for all acquisition of knowledge and skills (Tuk, 2007). India developed a national vocational education qualification framework (NVEQF) in 2012, a national skill qualification framework (NSQF) in 2013 and is in the process of developing national higher education qualification framework (NHEQF).

Economic Crisis and Higher Education

One of the dramatic developments in this century is the economic crisis of the 2008 which became global in its coverage and impact. This had serious impact on higher education development in several countries. The effect of the East Asian crisis of 1998 showed that the government allocations to higher education declined, staff recruitments were deferred, cross border student mobility declined and private universities faced insolvency situations (Varghese, 2001). The effects of economic crisis of 2008 were different from that of the 1998 crisis. The budget cuts for higher education were mostly limited to Commonwealth of Independent States (CIS). In fact, several countries increased allocations to higher education during the crisis period. These included countries least affected as well as severely affected by the crisis (Varghese, 2010). Countries in Africa and Asia, in general, were less affected by the crisis and allocations to higher education did not decline. Unlike during the East Asian economic crisis, the cross border student flow increased during the global economic crisis of 2008. During the period of 2009 and 2010, India with an increased flow of cross border students at 9.2 per cent and China with a rate of 21 per cent increase helped retain the level of cross border flow of students.

One of the important implications of the crisis and policies followed during the crisis period is a shift in the mode of financing higher education from financing institutions to supporting students. Student support systems and scholarships increased considerably during the crises periods. This was a direct way of supporting students and an indirect way of saving many private institutions from bankruptcy and closure. The crisis changed the ways of thinking about higher education at least in two ways. First, the fast expanding private sector and market forces in higher education need to be better regulated. Second, with the crisis of 2008 the world moved from a situation of viewing higher education as part of the problem to a situation of viewing it as part of the solution (Varghese, 2010).

Conclusion

The increasing realisation of the economic value of knowledge in production promoted expanding enrolments in institutions producing knowledge. At present countries are competing to massify and further to universalise higher education. This paper analysed reforms leading to the changing landscape of higher education in the developing and developed world. This paper showed that the present century experienced a revival of higher education worldwide. The global enrolment in higher education more than doubled and the developing countries benefitted the most and they accounted for nearly 90 per cent of the total increase in enrolment.

While higher education has been a state sponsored sector, the market friendly reforms helped in expanding the domestic and cross border segments of the higher education sector. Privatisation of public higher education institutions and encouragement of private institutions reduced reliance on public funding for domestic expansion of the sector. Similarly, market reforms led the globalisation process in higher education. While student mobility has been an important mode of trade in the context of globalisation, this century saw the emergence of education hubs and MOOCs.

The concern for quality is global in nature. The national authorities established external quality assurance (EQA) mechanisms and internal quality assurance cells (IQACs) to ensure quality is not compromised in the context of massification. The most recent move is towards establishing world class universities and to get into top positions in the global rankings of universities. Globalisation also demanded standardised skills for the global markets. The higher education institutions are seen as yet another opportunity to invest in globally acceptable skills to maximise profit. The national qualification frameworks help production of standardised skills since they certify learning outcomes and competencies according to global standards.

Although the economic crises affect higher education sector in a big way, the paper shows that the negative effects of global economic crisis on higher education were low. More significantly, most of these reforms that helped revive the higher education sector took place despite the global economic crisis of the past decade.

References

Altbach, P.G. 2005. "The rise of the pseudo-university". In Altbach, P.G.; Levy, D.C. (eds.). *Private higher education: A global revolution* (pp.23-27). Rotterdam: Sense Publishers.

Altbach, P.G.; Reisberg, L; Rumbley, L.E. 2009. "Trends in Global Higher Education: Tracking an Academic Revolution. A Report Prepared for the UNESCO 2009 World Conference on Higher Education", Paris, UNESCO.

Altbach, Philip G. 2011 "The past, present and future of World University" in Altbach, Philip G and Salmi, Jamil (eds.). *The Road to Academic Excellence: the making of World Class Research Universities*, Washington D.C., the World Bank, pp. 11-32.

ACE: American Council of Education. 2009. "U.S. Branch Campuses Abroad", ACU Brief, September.

Bjarnason, S.; Cheng, K.; Fielden, J.; Lemaitre, M.; Levy, D.; Varghese, N.V. 2009. *A new dynamic: Private higher education*. Paris: UNESCO.

Cao, Yi. 2011. "Branch Campuses in Asia and the Pacific: Definitions, challenges and strategies", *Comparative International Higher Education*, Vol.3, pp. 8-10.

Carr, Nicholas. 2012. "The crisis in higher education", In: *MIT Technology Review*, 27 September.

C-BERT: Cross-border education research team 2016. *Research and news about transnational higher education*, January, University of Albany, New York.

DBIS: Department for Business, Innovation and Skills 2011. "The returns to higher education qualifications", BIS Research Paper No.45, London, London School of Economics.

Fox, Warren, 2015. "Are international branch campuses misleading students?" *Voices*, 02, June.

Gebel, Michael. 2014. MOOCs: *Massive online open courses*, Brussels, European University Association

Gonczi, A.; A. Arguelles. 2000. "Introduction". In Arguelles and Gonczi (eds). *Competency based education and training: a world perspective*. Mexico City: Group Noriega.

Hanushek, Eric, A. And Woessmann, Ludger 2015. *Knowledge capital of nations: Education and Economics of growth,* Massachusetts, MIT Press growth.

Harden, Nathan 2013. "End of the University as We Know It", *American Interest* January/February

Jayaram, N. 2011. "Toward World Class Status? The IIT system and IIT Bombay" in Altbach, Philip G and Salmi, Jamil ed. *The Road to Academic Excellence: The making of World Class Research Universities*, Washington D.C.: The World Bank pp.167-194.

Jessup, Gilbert. 1991. *Outcomes. NVQs and the Emerging Model of Education and Training*, London: The Falmer Press.

Knight, Jane. 2002. *Trade in higher education services: Implications of GATS*. London: Observatory of Borderless Education.

Knight, Jane 2014. "*International Education Hubs: Student, Talent, Knowledge–Innovation Models*", Springer.

Lane, Janson and Kisner, Kevin. 2013. "Five models of international branch campus facility ownership", *International Higher Education,* No. 0, 9-11.

Lester, Simon. 2013. "Liberalizing cross-border trade in higher education: The coming revolution of online universities", *Policy Analysis* No.720, 5 February

Levy, D.C. 2005. "Private higher education's surprise roles". In: Altbach, P.G. and Levy, D.C. (Eds), *Private higher education: A global revolution* (pp.33-36). Rotterdam: Sense Publishers.

Levy, D.C. 2006. "The unanticipated explosion: Private higher education's global surge". In: *Comparative Education Review*, 50(2), 218-40.

Ministry of Human Resource Development (MHRD) AISHE 2016

OECD. 2000. *Knowledge management in the learning society: Education and skills.* Paris: OECD

Porter, Eduardo. 2015. "Education Gap between Rich and Poor is Growing Wider", *The New York Times*, 22 September, pp.B1.

Sabarwal, Nidhi and Malish, C.M. 2016 *Student diversity and civic learning in higher education in India*, CPRHE Research Papers series no.3, CPRHE/NUEPA, New Delhi.

Salmi, J. 2009. *The challenge of establishing world-class universities.* Washington DC: The World Bank.

Sirowy, Larry, and Alex Inkeles. 1990. The Effects of Democracy on Economic Growth and Inequality: A Review. Comparative International Development 25 (1):126-157.

Slantcheva, S.; Levy, D.C. (eds.). 2007. *Private higher education in Post-communist Europe: In search of legitimacy.* New York: Palgrave-Macmillan.

The Task Force: *The Task force on Higher Education and Society 2000 Higher education in Developing countries: Peril and Promise,* Washington D.C., The World Bank.

Tilak, J.B.G. 2008. "Higher education: A public good or a commodity for trade? Commitment to higher education or commitment of higher education to trade". *Prospects,* 38, pp.449-466.

Tilak, J.B.G. 2014 Global ranking, "World class universities and dilemma in higher education policy in India" (Krishna university public lecture series 2014), Machilapatanam, Krishna university.

Tuk, Ron. 2007: *Introductory Guide to National Qualifications Frameworks: Conceptual and Practical Issues for Policy Makers,* Geneva, Skills and Employability Department, International Labour Office (ILO)

UIS. (Various years) *Global Education Digest: Comparing education statistics across the world.* Montreal: UIS.

UIS/OECD. 2003. *Financing education – Investments and returns: Analysis of the World Education Indicators* 2002 Edition. Paris: UNESCO/OECD.

Varghese, N.V. 2001. "Impact of the Economic Crisis on Higher Education in East Asia: Country Experiences", Paris: IIEP/UNESCO

Varghese, N.V. 2006. *Growth and Expansion of Private Higher Education in Africa.* Paris: IIEP/UNESCO.

Varghese, N.V. 2010. "Running to stand still: Higher education in a period of global economic crisis", IIEP Research Papers, Paris, IIEP/UNESCO.

Varghese, N.V. 2012. "Higher education reforms and revitalization of the sector", *Higher Education Forum,* (Hiroshima University), vol. 9, 2012, pp. 45-59.

Varghese, N.V. 2013. "Globalization and higher education" *Analytical Reports on International Education,* vol. 5, no.1 2013, pp. 7-20.

Varghese, N.V. 2016 "What changed after the 'Peril and Promise'? An analysis of higher education in developing countries", *International Journal of African Higher Education,* (forthcoming)

World Bank. 2002. *Constructing knowledge societies: New challenge for higher education.* Washington, D.C.: The World Bank.

World Bank 2009. "Accelerating Catch-up: Tertiary Education Growth in Sub-Saharan Africa", Washington, D.C. The World Bank.

Yuan, L and Powell, S. 2013. *MOOCS and open education: Implications for higher education – A white paper.* UK: Centre for Educational Technology and Interoperability Standards (CETIS).

Young, M. 2005. *National Qualification Frameworks: their feasibility for effective implementation in developing countries,* Geneva, ILO.

2.
Role of Government in Higher Education of Emerging Economies
A Case Study of Malaysia

Dato' Morshidi Sirat

The upward trend of emerging economies in Asia is more pronounced than any other regions in the world. In this respect, there is no denying of China's role and dominant position in the narratives of emerging economies in Asia. Notably, between 1981 and 2012, China's gross domestic product (GDP) grew on average 9.7 per cent a year and this swift expansion along its secondary effects on other nations is rapidly changing global dynamics (Hidalgo, 2013, p. 10). It was reported recently (Tee & Zainul, 2016) that the Chinese are not only keen to invest in Malaysia but also in other ASEAN countries such as Indonesia, Thailand and to some extent in Cambodia and Lao People's Democratic Republic. Malaysia is highly regarded by Chinese corporations and investors as Malaysia's currency (Ringgit) is undervalued but the country well governed. However, while China's growth has a positive contribution towards Asia's development, it is also crucial to note that any deceleration of China's growth would present serious challenges for many emerging economies in Southeast Asia, which have been propped up by the commodity boom propelled by China's growth. Arguably, with the rise of China, East Asia has gained prominence in that the region was before this the home to the late 20th century's most celebrated success story of Hong Kong, Taiwan, Singapore and South Korea. Malaysia, Indonesia and Thailand are three emerging economies in Southeast Asia which are benefiting from the growth of the West in late 1980s and recently from China's commodity boom (Hidalgo, 2013; Fleming & Søborg, 2014). Fleming and Søborg (2014) report that before the 1997/1998 Asian financial crisis, these emerging South-East Asian economies experienced high yearly growth rates of 7-8 per cent. Since the crisis, however, the growth rates have fallen to 4-5 per cent per annum and after the 2008 financial crisis, the growth rates have not returned to the previous levels. The slowdown in the growth rates has sparked off caution among the upper middle-income countries such as Malaysia and Thailand. Following recent unfavourable scenarios as far as China's growth and global oil and gas sector are concerned; analysts are of the opinion that Malaysia would be caught in a middle-income trap, unable to reach the high-income level according to the target year set. However, the Malaysian government appears to be very confident in achieving its high-income nation status, with higher education being one of the contributing factors, and it is precisely because of this very optimistic view that it is pertinent to examine the role of higher education. A state centrism approach to higher education development was considered as failing to push this sector to deliver what is expected of it in the next 15 years. Thus, the widespread adoption of neoliberal ideology in as early as 2000 trusted the market forces with the government receding to play a facilitating role. The neoliberal discourse painted a picture whereby the government and the market could work in tandem in order to achieve set objectives. It is further argued that the public universities as agent of the government should use the market to benchmark their progress and contribution to the national objectives. The argument to be proven here is that the adoption of neoliberal ideology has resulted in observable government retreat from its primary responsibility for higher education. Further, it will be proven that Malaysian public higher education institutions, with the ascendancy of neoliberalism, have shifted in the way they define and justify their institutional existence in the context of the market and national interest.

Malaysia: Towards a High-income Status Nation

Since Malaya has gained its independence from the British on 31 August 1957 and subsequently together with Singapore[1], Sabah and Sarawak formed Malaysia on 16 September 1963, the federal government of Malaysia has been leveraging on the power of education and later higher education for national economic and social development. Notably, education was the primary vehicle for the restructuring of the Malaysian society between 1970 and 1990. The *Vision 2020*, which was introduced in 1990, has also adopted education as an important foundation for the emergence of a Malaysian society: a diverse society which is united and progresses on the basis of racial harmony through an equitable socio-economic framework. More importantly, beginning from mid 2000s, Malaysia was leveraging on higher education as a tool of diplomacy and profiting from it as an important source of national income, particularly through the internationalisation of higher education and the inflows of foreign students to Malaysia.

Malaysia is an emerging Southeast Asian economy but one caught in the middle-income trap (Fleming & Søborg, 2014). Admittedly, being in the middle-income trap is not a desirable situation as it means that the country on the one hand is unable to compete against advanced economies with high levels of innovation and value-adding activities, and on the other hand, unable to compete with less developed economies which could offer relatively cheaper labour (The Asia Foundation, quoted in Kok, 2014). This phenomenon holds true for Malaysia's neighbours, Thailand and Indonesia. Based on the report by The Asia Foundation (TAF), Malaysia's economy shows signs of being in the "middle-income trap" and this reflects the Malaysian situation in which despite numerous bold policy measures and long-term plans introduced by the Malaysian government since 1990s, economic progress continues to be hampered by innovation and skills development that is lagging behind, low level of investments in technology, standard of education that is still playing a "catch up game" with that of the world education benchmark (based on Programme for International Student Assessment scores, for instance), relatively high labour cost and sluggish productivity growth. Indeed, the TAF's report maintains that despite the government policy focus and increased investment to address constraints and weaknesses related to this predicament, progress has been, at best, modest in relation to targets set. While political economists would most likely explain this scenario by relating it to the difficulties of Malaysia's political structure (*see* The Asia Foundation report), analysts who are familiar with the openness of the Malaysian economy and its high dependence on manufactured exports would explain Malaysia's predicament as due to its integration with the global economy. About a decade ago, the World Bank (2007, p. xiii) reports that the progress of the Malaysia economy in recent decades has been nothing short of impressive, a reflection of strong macroeconomic management and political stability. That was the decade when Malaysia was performing rather well in terms of economic growth. But this is no longer true presently, which is largely attributable to declining oil prices and stiff competition from other low-cost production locations.

Malaysia's bold vision to pull itself out of the middle-income trap is encapsulated in the national *Vision 2020*, which is to transform itself from an upper-middle income nation into a high-income nation through shifting the mode of economy from an efficiency-driven to an innovation-driven economy" (Fleming & Søborg, 2014). This moving-up the income ladder is benchmark against high-income status as defined by the World Bank in 2012, as one with a Gross National Income (GNI) per capita of more than US$12,615. However, it is acknowledged that the shift cannot be expected to be seamless as there are serious constraints in the provision of highly skilled workforce, in particular, those compatible with the needs of economic sectors designated as the drivers of growth in Malaysia's Economic Transformation Programme.[2]

The government's current assessment is that Malaysia is no longer stuck in the middle-income trap, as its GNI is now progressively growing towards the high-income benchmark as defined by the World Bank (Kok,

2016). Kok (2016), quoting government sources, reported that this favourable situation is attributable to the positive development from the various reforms undertaken via the multi-year Economic Transformation Programme. Despite the difficult national and global economic climate, it is reported that Malaysia's GNI at US$10,570 (RM42,340) per capita in 2015 is now only 15 per cent away from the high-income-economy benchmark of US$12,475 per capita and factored in its published historical global inflation rate of two per cent until 2020. The gap of 33 per cent between Malaysia's GNI of US$8,280 per capita in 2010 and the then high-income economy threshold of US$12,276 per capita was closing up. But, the considerable gap before 2010, and the difficulty in closing this gap for many years, led many economists and financial experts to conclude that Malaysia is still stuck in the middle-income trap, and would not be able to become a high-income nation by 2020 unless Malaysia could 'unstuck' (Kok, 2016).[2] Among other sectors, higher education was regarded as a strategic enabler to get Malaysia out of the middle-income trap. Factually, Malaysia has not only made remarkable investments in expanding higher education in recent years, but it has also been concentrating on becoming a high-income economy by way of development of the education sector (Fleming & Søborg, 2014). The National Key Economic Area (NKEA), for instance, seeks to leverage Malaysia's strategic location and accessibility throughout Southeast Asia and sound infrastructure to make the country a regional education hub. Top tier foreign universities continue to be welcomed to the Malaysian shores to be located in areas identified as education clusters.

Following the preceding discussion, but viewed from a different perspective, however, meeting the GNI according to the World Bank's definition can only be a small milestone of a bigger agenda as the ability to manage the process of achieving the GNI target and subsequently to maintain its position as a high-income nation in the context of rapid societal change is more critical. This paper will therefore critically examine the roles of the government in pushing for higher financial allocation and investments into the higher education sector, first, as a vehicle to restructure the Malaysian society and second, as part of the strategy to get Malaysia out of the middle-income trap. It is argued in this paper that the government has and continues to invest heavily in this sector to meet Malaysia's human capital need and to fulfil government's responsibility for the development of education. It will be argued that even though the government has not retreated from its responsibility with respect to primary and secondary education, the same cannot be said for higher education. There are indications that the government has relied on the market forces in ensuring the sustainable development of the higher education sector. It is, therefore, pertinent to establish at the outset the shift of emphasis on the part of the government with respect to higher education provision and funding. What are the policies and initiatives that have been introduced to strengthen the role of higher education in national development process and what are the outcomes? Are these policies based on conventional interventionist approaches or are we seeing novel approaches in the manner the government influences higher education development, especially in relation to funding for public higher education institutions? In what sense is Malaysia's *Vision 2020*— an agenda for high-income developed status — a significant departure from the conventional growth theory? In this respect, the introduction of neoliberal approach to the development of the higher education sector in Malaysia requires close examination. The argument in this paper is premised on the idea that while the Malaysian government has continued to play a critical role in the development and growth of the higher education sector in Malaysia, in line with *Vision 2020* and the ambition to be a high-income status nation, the widespread adoption of neoliberal ideology in early 2000s has given priority to market forces with the government playing a facilitating role. It is further argued that Malaysian higher education institutions, with the ascendancy of neoliberalism, have produced a fundamental shift in the way these institutions define and justify their institutional existence in relation to the market and national interest.

Higher Education and Neoliberalism Discourse

Mainstream economic theory is evolving fast (Colander, Holt, Rosser, 2004; Krugman, 2009; *The Economist*, 2009). Economic theories are moving away from a strict adherence to the holy trinity — rationality, selfishness, and equilibrium — to a more eclectic selection which includes examination of purposeful behaviour, enlightened self-interest and sustainability (Colander, Holt, Rosser, 2004). Indeed, the old established economic orthodoxy, based on notions of rational utility maximisation, perfect information, stable preferences and market equilibrium, is being heavily contested by various new research programmes such as behavioural economics, experimental economics and complexity economics (Davis, 2006, cited in Gilead, 2016).

In positioning, higher education as an instrument for enhancing both personal and social productivity, human capital theory conceptualised in the 1950s had opened the door for discussion of a relationship between higher education and economic growth via higher education's influence on productivity (Gilead, 2016). Following the development of new growth theory in the late 1980s, it has been recognised that economic growth is highly reliant on the production, circulation and diffusion of knowledge that contributes to technological and scientific advancements (Peters, 2003). Within this theoretical framework, knowledge is significant because of its correlation to economic growth, and unlike other commodities, it does not have diminishing returns and is non-rivalry, as one can have more of it without others having less (Stiglitz, 1999). With regards to new arguments regarding the role of the government in the development of higher education, Olssen & Peters (2005, p. 315) argue that whereas classical liberalism represents a negative conception of state power in that the individual was taken as an object to be freed from the interventions of the state, neoliberalism, on the contrary, represents a positive conception of the state's role in creating the appropriate market by providing the conducive conditions, laws and institutions necessary for its operation. But, Giroux (2002) also warns that one consequence is that in so far as higher education is concerned, civic discourse has given way to the language of commercialism, privatisation, and deregulation. In addition, individual and social agencies are now defined largely through market-driven notions of individualism, competition, and consumption. In terms of the human capital desired, particularly in the more developed economies, classical liberalism characterised the individual as having autonomous human nature and can exercise freedom. In neoliberalism, the state seeks to create individuals who are enterprising and competitive entrepreneur, with the state facilitating the production of such individuals via higher education. It is a challenge to shift from classical economics to neoliberalism in emerging economies such as Malaysia especially in the manner the government deals with human capital. The government, to a great extent, has been curtailing autonomous human nature and freedom through various government circulars governing the conduct of academics, for instance.

In a knowledge-based economy, it is argued that education makes an indispensable contribution to economic productivity by disseminating knowledge, developing research capacity, enhancing creativity, teaching higher order thinking skills and providing adequate grounding in science and technology to the mass. All which are prerequisites for the production of enterprising and competitive entrepreneur. Comaroff and Camaroff (2001) argue that neoliberalism works to "displace political sovereignty with the sovereignty of 'the market', as if the latter had a mind and morality of its own". (Giroux, 2002, p. 428). Following the principle of neoliberalism, policies are market driven and the claims of democratic citizenship are subordinated to market values (Giroux, 2002, p. 428). Crucially, in the context of higher education and the role of the government, Bauman (2001) observes the manner the private overcomes the public via private interests and pursuits.

The Role of Government in the Development of Higher Education in Malaysia

Following the preceding discussion, the roles of government in the development of higher education in Malaysia are necessarily focused on two major areas: providing resources, and creating the conducive environment for the development of higher education within the context of a shifting philosophy from state centrism to neoliberalism with *Vision 2020* as the guiding principle. With reference to productivity, the role of the government is a contested terrain in the discussion on finding ways out of the middle-income trap (Fleming & Soborg, 2014). The World Bank in its Malaysia Monitor report recommends a much restrained government intervention approach in the Malaysian economy. Nonetheless, the Malaysia's Economic Planning Unit of the Prime Minister's Department through its Five-year Malaysia Plans has been consistently presenting an inclination towards governmental intervention in supporting productivity development, for instance in the area of education and human resource development. From a wider theoretical perspective, the first approach as recommended by the World Bank is based on the neoclassic approach in which the role of the state is primarily to limit or amend market failures, while the second developmental state approach reflected in Malaysian policy emphasises a more state-active intervention to set up objectives and measures for productivity development (Lauridsen, 2007).

It is important to note that neoliberalism approach as proffered by the World Bank to Malaysia in their report on knowledge economy and the Malaysian higher education sector was quickly adopted in the *National Higher Education Strategic Plan, 2007* and the *Tenth Malaysian Plan, 2010-2015.* The ever increasing deficit budget of the government has also, in part, prompted the government to adopt a different approach towards national economic development. But the idea that education as a means to increase economic productivity can easily come into conflict with other key educational goals such as producing holistic graduates with a well-balanced mix of skills, competencies and spirituality. This is clearly demonstrated in the current *Malaysia Education Blueprint, 2015-2025 (Higher Education).* Notably, neoliberal discourse vocabularies clashed with vocabularies typically related to equity and distributional justice. In this regard, Darder (2012) sketches the social decay of our neoliberal movement as follows:

"In the efficient, cost-effective, and competitive neoliberal world, questions of difference have been neatly conflated and diffused by a hypocrisy fuelled by racism, elitism and a tenacious disbelief in the equality of those who exist outside the narrow rationality of its profit logic. As a consequence, 'deficient' subjects of difference, unable to march to the homogenizing and boot-strap neoliberal refrain, are conveniently tossed aside or criminalized and held behind iron bars, without concern for their numbers or their fate (2012, p.413)."

The *Malaysia Education Blueprint, 2015-2025 (Higher Education)* as the main document which charts the way forward for the development of higher education in Malaysia for the next 10 years exemplified such contradictory tendencies in its proposed implementation of the strategic intent.

Resources for Higher Education

In recent decades, Malaysia has been transforming its economy from one based on mass production and relatively unskilled labour to one based on knowledge, creativity and high productivity, and a shift from state-centrism to one that is based on the market. In implementing the transformation agenda in the higher education sector, the government has made substantial allocation for higher education. For instance, in terms of Gross Domestic Product (GDP), on an average the government allocates about 2.7 per cent of its GDP to higher education. This relatively high percentage is due to the subsidisation of tuition fees and on-campus accommodation (World Bank, 2007).

From the *Fifth Malaysian Plan, 1986-1990* to *Eighth Malaysian Plan, 2001-2005*, development expenditure for higher education averaged at about 34 per cent of the total educational development expenditure, reaching an all-time high of 43.5 per cent in the *Sixth Malaysian Plan, 1991-1995*, only to fall to 25 per cent in the *Seventh Malaysian Plan, 1996-2000*. This was largely because of the fiscal contraction triggered by the 1997 Asian financial crisis. In the *Eighth Malaysian Plan, 2001-2005* and *Ninth Malaysian Plan, 2006-2010*, the spending on developing the higher education sector was raised back to 35.3 per cent and 39.8 per cent respectively. In absolute terms, government development expenditure for higher education increased from RM1.7 billion in the *Fifth Malaysian Plan, 1986-1990* to RM5.0 billion in the *Seventh Malaysian Plan, 1996-2000* and RM16.1 billion in the *Ninth Malaysian Plan, 2006-2010* (Lee, 2014). The *Eleventh Malaysian Plan, 2016-2020*, laid emphasis on reducing dependency on government funding, and as have been illustrated earlier, funding higher education sector has become a burden for the government.

Based on UNESCO, Institute of Statistics and the World Bank data, government commitment to the development of education and in particular higher education in Malaysia, government expenditure on education (current, capital, and transfer), as total (% of GDP) in Malaysia was 6.3 per cent as of 2013. Its highest value over the past 42 years was 7.7 per cent in 2002; while its lowest value was 4.0 per cent in 2008 (*see* Table 2.1). The global financial crisis in 2008 has affected the education sector in terms of public funding. Education expenditure (education expenditure refers to the current operating expenditures in education, including wages and salaries, but exclude capital investments in buildings and equipment) in Malaysian current USD was 19,896,030,000 as of 2014. Over the past 44 years, the value for this indicator has fluctuated between 19,896,030,000 in 2014 and 165,016,500 in 1971. With declining oil prices, there are indications that Malaysian government's expenditure for higher education for 2016 will show a dip in term of percentage of GDP.

Although public funding has rightly remained the main source of support for higher education, new financing strategies have been put in place in recent years in the public universities to generate revenue from institutional assets, mobilise additional resources from students and their families, and encourage donations from third party contributors (World Bank, 2007). In the *Malaysia Education Blueprint 2015-2030 (Higher Education),* strategies to achieve sustainability in financing higher education were identified. These strategies focus on financial sustainability of the higher education system and in particular higher education institutions stems in part from the contradiction "where the need to trim government spending runs smack into the fact that more education equals better employment chances and significantly boosts financial returns over an individual's lifetime" (Hauptman, 2014, p. 1).

Public universities in Malaysia have to diversify their sources of income in order to be financially sustainable and reduce their reliance on government funding. Arguably, based on the arguments in the blueprint, public universities have to be entrepreneurial by creating products and services that generate income while ensuring operation costs remain optimum (that is, optimisation of resources). New funding mechanisms from the government will no longer be in the form of fixed operating and development budgets or block grants but will be based or linked to performance level. New mechanisms are in place to link allocation to performance for specific outcomes, such as production of employable graduates and the number of postgraduates who graduate on time (GOT), the number of international students, research projects and commercialised products. The government is determined to connect the output, outcome and impact of higher education with resources allocated, which will be monitored closely by the Project Delivery and Management Office (PMO) of the Prime Minister's Department and the Economic Planning Unit in addition to the Ministry of Higher Education. Project implementation and monitoring of all public universities are measures that will directly stimulate higher productivity and increase accountability of public universities (Economic Planning Unit, 2015).

Table 2.1: Malaysian Government Expenditure for Education and Tertiary Education from 1971 To 2013

Years	*Expenditure on primary as % of government expenditure on education*	*Expenditure on tertiary as % of government expenditure on education*	*Expenditure on education as % of total government expenditure*	*Expenditure on secondary as % of government expenditure on education*	*Government expenditure on education, total (% of GDP)*
1971	..	..	..	..	4.3
1979	..	..	..	..	5.0
1980	..	..	..	..	5.6
1981	..	..	..	..	6.6
1982	..	..	..	..	6.9
1984	..	..	..	..	5.6
1985	..	..	..	..	6.0
1986	..	..	..	..	7.1
1987	..	..	..	..	6.3
1992	..	..	..	..	5.1
1993	..	..	..	..	4.7
1994	..	..	..	..	4.7
1995	..	..	..	..	4.3
1996	..	..	..	..	4.9
1997	..	..	19.0	..	4.6
1999	..	..	21.2	..	5.7
2000	27.2	32.1	21.4	34.5	6.0
2001	27.8	34.3	24.3	33.4	7.5
2002	31.2	33.3	25.9	33.5	7.7
2003	29.3	35.0	24.5	34.1	7.5
2004	29.6	33.4	21.0	35.1	5.9
2006	27.7	36.1	16.7	29.6	4.5
2007	29.8	33.0	16.1	29.5	4.4
2008	39.1	..	14.0	28.2	4.0
2009	27.7	35.9	18.5	32.8	6.0
2010	28.6	34.5	18.4	33.7	5.1
2011	29.3	37.0	21.0	30.6	5.9
2013	30.3	34.0	21.5	34.1	6.3

Source: Economic Planning Unit, 2015

Environment for the Development of Higher Education

In response to the increasing demands for higher education and the changing higher education landscape, the state has introduced and amended several legislations, such as the Education Act 1996, Private Higher Education Act 1996 (Act 555), National Council of Higher Education Act 1996, National Accreditation Board Act 1996 (a precursor to the Malaysian Qualifications Agency) and the Universities and University Colleges (Amendment) Act 1996. The Private Higher Education Act 1996 (Act 555) was amended in 2003 in response to new challenges in the provision of private higher education, providing the legal framework governing those private colleges upgrading into private universities and the operation of branch campuses of foreign universities in Malaysia. In 2014, Act 555 was again amended to take into account the requirement of the World Trade Organisation (WTO) with respect to trade in services. The Universities and University Colleges Act (UUCA) 1971 was also amended in 2012 in order to take into account the local and global changes that have important implications for the development of higher education. Arguably, the old higher education governance model based on the state-control model and later the state supervising model hardly prepare public universities for the present and not to mention, future challenges in terms of securing own funding. The idea of 'steering from a distance' is widely received especially when it is an agenda championed by agencies such as the World Bank. The corporatisation of public universities, a notable change in moving away from state-control model, was meant to make public tertiary education institutions more proactive to changes, underpinned by ideas from new public management and neoliberalism tendencies in the tertiary education system regionally since the early 2000s. Empowering public universities to be more accountable for some areas of their operations and making universities more entrepreneurial are central objectives set out by the Ministry of Higher Education to transform its university system in the current globalising world. This was a major agenda then in 2007 with the *National Higher Education Strategic Plan* and remains an important government agenda now for the future.

As far as corporatism and the emerging corporate culture in the Malaysian higher education system is concerned, starting from January 1998, University of Malaya, the oldest university in Malaysia, was corporatised along with eight other public universities. According to the original policy's objectives, corporatised public universities would become more self-financing especially when they are allowed to source for external development fund, venture out into business, establish companies and consultancy firms, as well as acquire and hold investment shares. Under the revised Universities and University

College Act (UCCA amendments), corporatised universities are expected to raise funds through diverse channels (Lee, 1999), but these rooms for manoeuvre were subjected to various interpretations of the public universities management. Allowing universities to engage in business activities relates specifically to the commercialisation of research *outcomes*, which is generally known as 'academic capitalism' (Slaughter and Rhoades, 2004).

The roles of the government in steering the development of higher education have evolved via the above mentioned legislations to form a regulatory and supervisory framework for the development of higher education in Malaysia. The Private Higher Education Act 1996 (Act 555) was amended in 2003 in response to new challenges in the provision of private higher education, and it provides the legal framework to govern the operation of private colleges, private universities and branch campuses of foreign universities in Malaysia. With reforms of higher education in place, the *National Higher Education Strategic Plan* was launched in 2007. Later, the *Tenth Malaysia Plan, 2011-2015* ushered in a period where national economic development became very much guided by the desire to reach high productivity via higher education. In recent years, a series of high-profile government initiatives has been undertaken to renew the structural change agenda, including the *Economic Transformation Programme* in January 2010 and the *New Economic Model for Malaysia* in March 2010, culminating in the *Eleventh Malaysian Plan, 2016-2020*. For Malaysia, education reforms were introduced in mid to late 1990s and they were all set to move on the high-income agenda based on neoliberal philosophy and approach. The *Malaysia Education Blueprint 2015-2025 (Higher Education)* yet again reveals the dilemma of the state in relation to its role in the development of higher education. While there are initiatives towards introducing a self-regulation model for public higher education institutions and offering more autonomy in several areas of governance, the state cannot be seen by the public as completely retreating from funding higher education for doing so will generally be perceived as abandoning "national interest", one agenda which has been embedded in the public higher education system since 1963.

Neoliberalism and the Role of Government in Higher Education

The higher education initiatives noted earlier do not lack sources of inspiration. Success stories of Singapore, South Korea and Taiwan, which have been high-income economies for a longer period, deliver recipes of growth and change. A common ingredient in these recipes is educational reforms that aim to underpin provision of a well-educated and creative workforce. In this connection, The *Eleventh Malaysian Plan, 2016-2020* further emphasised a neoliberal approach towards national and higher education development as the deadline 2020 for Malaysia to be a high-income status nation draws nearer. Malaysia's success and experiences will be a beacon for countries such as Lao PDR and Cambodia in moving up the ladder. Sharing of good practices within ASEAN is a much encouraged agenda.

The neoliberal discourse as it relates to Malaysia can be summarised as follows. One of the major objectives of the reforms in higher education has been to install relations of competition among universities as a way of increasing productivity, accountability and control of all components of the higher education ecosystem. This strategic intent is based on the assumption that increased competition will bring improved quality in the provision and delivery of the higher education system, a major argument within neoliberalism discourse. Marginson (1997) supports this argument, pointing out that increased competition is meant to increase responsiveness, flexibility and rates of innovation in the higher education system. In terms of the governance of higher education system and institutions, strategic intents as expressed in the Blueprint are based on the belief that neoliberalism could introduce a new mode of regulation or form of governmentality. In this respect, Burchell (1996, pp. 23–24 cited in Olssen & Peters, 2005) argues:

> "while for classical liberalism the basis of government conduct is in terms of 'natural, private-interest-motivated conduct of free, market exchanging individuals', for neoliberalism, the rational principle for regulating and limiting governmental activity must be determined by reference to artificially arranged or contrived forms of free, entrepreneurial and competitive conduct of economic-rational individuals."

Indeed, from neoliberal perspectives, the techniques of auditing, accounting and management are thus a prescription for rule, which becomes both the ethos and technique of government in the development of higher education.

In this sense, Barry, Osborne & Rose (1996, p. 8) argument appears to illustrate Malaysian government stand on the future role of the state with respect to governance arrangement of public higher education institutions in Malaysia as follows:

> "Liberalism is understood not so much as a substantive doctrine or practice of government in itself, but as a restless and dissatisfied ethos of recurrent critique of State reason and politics. Hence, the advent of liberalism coincides with discovering that political government could be its own undoing, that by governing over-much, rulers thwarted the very ends of government."

Following these observations, and in the context of neoliberal governmentality and higher education in Malaysia, higher education is increasingly viewed as "an input–output system which can be reduced to an economic production function" (Olssen & Peters, 2005). From the Blueprint, the core dimensions of new governance as applied to public universities are: flexibility (via regulated autonomy), clearly defined objectives (for public universities), and result-oriented (measurement of and managerial responsibility for achievement of objectives for both public universities and their staff). But increasingly, 'public service ethic' whereby public universities were governed according to norms and values derived from assumptions about the 'idea of the university', the 'role of higher education' and 'common good' or 'public interest' are slowly being replaced with a new set of principal-agent, performance-based rules. Arguably, when public universities are ruled by the new governance arrangements and models based on neoliberal ideology, notions like accountability and trust that academics as public servants are familiar with will be recast in the market mould and higher education will be eroded of its 'public good' essence and character.

Conclusion

The neoliberal discourse painted a picture where the government and the market work in tandem in order to achieve set objectives. It is argued in this paper that neoliberal ideology insisted that public universities as agent of the government should use the market to benchmark their progress and contribution to the national objectives. The adoption of neoliberal ideology has resulted in the government retreat from its responsibility for higher education, giving more opportunities for the market to come in while the government focuses on providing the infrastructure and regulatory framework to enable the entry of the market. Malaysian public higher education institutions, with the ascendancy of neoliberalism, have also shifted in the way they define and justify their institutional existence more in relation to the market despite still serving national interest. This can be seen through strategic intents of public universities such as producing employable graduates and commercialisation of research products as important income-generating activities and yet still can argue that they are serving national agenda / interest.

In conclusion, the rise of neoliberal economics over the past three decades has affected the public university sector, in both positive and negative ways. What is happening in Malaysian higher education sector is reminiscent of Slaughter and Rhoades's (2004) argument that neoliberalism focuses "not on social welfare for the citizenry as a whole but on enabling individuals as economic actors." Undoubtedly, this kind of neoliberal ideology has become the basis for the current development trajectory of the Malaysian higher education and many saw the income proposition to academics as they are allowed to undertake consultancy.

Notes

1 Since the formation of Malaysia on 16 September 1963, Singapore and Malayan leaders were fully aware of the wide differences in their political approach and aspirations. Thus, on 9 August 1965, Singapore separated from Malaysia to become an independent and sovereign state.

2 The Malaysian Prime Minister's Budget 2017 Speech to the Malaysian Parliament on 31 October 2016 gave an indication that *Vision 2020*will not be achieved in view of the slow rate of growth of the Malaysian economy. At the Parliament budget presentation the Prime Minister, also the Finance Minister, introduced his 30-year development program "Transformasi Nasional 2050" or National Transformation 2050, which is undoubtedly an alternative to Mahathir's *Vision 2020*, launched in a landmark speech in 1991.

3 Launched on 25 September 2010, the Economic Transformation Programme (ETP) was formulated as part of Malaysia's National Transformation Programme. Its goal is to elevate the country to developed-nation status by 2020, targeting GNI per capita of US$15,000. This will be achieved by attracting US$444 billion in investments which will, in turn, create 3.3 million new jobs.

References

Barry, A., Osborne, T., & Rose, N. (Eds.). (1996). *Foucault and political reason: liberalism, neoliberalism, and rationalities of government.* London and New York: Routledge.

Bauman, Z. (2001). *The individualized society.* London: Polity Press.

Colander, D., Holt, R. P. F., & Rosser, B. (2004). The changing face of mainstream economics. *Review of Political Economy.* 16(4):485–499. doi:10.1080/095382504 2000256702

Comaroff, J., & Comaroff, J. L. (Eds.). (2001). *Millennial capitalism and the culture of neoliberalism.* Durham, NC: Duke University Press.

Darder, A. (2012). Neoliberalism in the academic borderlands: An on-going struggle for equality and human rights. *Educational Studies: A journal of the American Educational Studies Association.* 48(5), 412-426. doi: 10.1080/00131946.2012. 714334

Economic Planning Unit. (2015). *Eleventh Malaysian Plan, 2016-2020.* Retrieved from http://rmk11.epu.gov.my/book/eng/Elevent-Malaysia-Plan/RMKe-11%20 Book.pdf.

Fleming, D., & Søborg, H. (2014). Are emerging south-east asian economies caught in a middle-income trap? case: Malaysia. paradoxes in provision of higher skilled labour, *Forum for Development Studies*, 41(1), 115-133. doi:10.1080/08039410. 2014.889035

Gilead, T. (2016). Education's role in the economy: towards a new perspective, *Cambridge Journal of Education*, 1-17. doi: 10.1080/0305764X.2016.1195790

Giroux, H. (2002). Neoliberalism, corporate culture, and the promise of higher education: the university as a democratic public sphere. *Harvard Educational Review*, 72(4), 425-464. doi: http://dx.doi.org/10.17763/haer. 72.4.0515nr62324n71p1

Hauptman, A. (2014, October 16). Making higher education financially sustainable. *University World News*. Retrieved from http://www.universityworldnews.com/article.php?story=20141016131012558

Hildago, J. C. (2013). *The rise of emerging economies, challenges and liberal perspectives.* Berlin: Liberal Institute.

Kok, C. (2014, January 11). Is Malaysia in middle-income trap? *The Star Online.* Retrieved from http://www.thestar.com.my/business/business-news/2014/01/11/is-msia-in-middleincome-trap-underlying-political-dynamics-a-major-barrier-to-economic-reform/

Kok, C. (2016, August 18). M'sia no longer stuck in mid-income trap. *The Star Online*. Retrieved from http://www.thestar.com.my/business/business-news/2016/08/18/ msia-no-longer- stuck-in-midincome-trap/

Krugman, P. (2009, September 2). How did economists get it so wrong? *The New York Times Magazine*. Retrieved from http://www.nytimes.com/2009/09/06/magazine/06Economic-t.html?_r=0

Lauridsen, L. S. (2007). *State, institutions and industrial development. Industrial deepening and upgrading policies in Taiwan and Thailand compared, vol. 1.* Denmark: Shaker Verlag.

Lee, H. G. (2014). Malaysia's funding system for higher education not sustainable. *ISEAS Perspective*, 2, 1-11.

Lee, M. N. N. (1999). Education in Malaysia: towards vision 2020. *School Effectiveness and School Improvement,* 10(1), 86-98.

Marginson, S. (1997). Competition and contestability in Australian higher education, 1987–1997. *Australian Universities' Review*, 40(1), 5–14.

Olssen, M., & Peters, M. A. (2005), Neoliberalism, higher education and the knowledge economy: from the free market to knowledge capitalism. *Journal of Education Policy*, 20(3), 313-345. doi: 10.1080/02680930500108718

Peters, M. A. (2003). Classical political economy and the role of universities in the new knowledge economy. *Globalisation, Societies and Education*, 1, 153–168. doi: 10.1080/1476772032000105483

Slaughter, S., & Rhoades, G. (2004). *Academic capitalism and the new economy: markets, state and higher education.* Baltimore, MD: Johns Hopkin University Press.

Stiglitz, J. (1999). *Public policy for a knowledge economy*. Retrieved from http://akgul.bilkent.edu.tr/BT-BE/knowledge-economy.pdf.

The Economist. (2009, July 16). The state of economics: the other-worldly philosophers. *The Economist*. Retrieved from http://www.economist.com/node/14030288.

Tee, L. S., &Zainul, I. F. (2016, September 10). The china factor in Malaysia's growth. *The Star Online.* Retrieved from http://www.thestar.com.my/business/business-news/2016/09/10/the-china-factor-in-malaysias-growth/.

World Bank. (2007). *Malaysia and the Knowledge Economy: Building a World-Class Higher Education System*. New York: EPU and the World Bank.

3.
Structure and Pattern of Higher Education Courses in Singapore

N. Varaprasad

Universities, which emerged as great institutions of higher learning even before the advent of formal schooling for young people, were seen as both creators as well as preservers of knowledge and culture. The earliest universities in the Indian subcontinent arose from the need for highly formalised methods of Vedic learning which promoted the establishment of large teaching institutions such as Takshila, Nalanda, and Vikramashila which are often characterised as India's earliest universities. These centres of learning attracted scholars from different parts of the world to study there and return to their homes with new knowledge to propagate, a feature of present-day universities.

Initially religion-based universities (e.g. Nalanda, Al-Azhar in Cairo, and later Christian monastic), adopted the English Oxbridge model and expanded to become centres of intellectual debate and thought in philosophy, science, economics, history and so on. Universities today perform very similar roles as they did before, except that they have been subject to the democratisation process of expanding intakes and becoming more socially relevant. Higher education now exists in a variety of forms, such as public, private, community colleges, Liberal Arts College, polytechnic universities, on-line universities, etc. in order to cope with the increase in demand from students. Inevitably, the emergence of such diverse forms and vehicles of delivery has led to a wide range of quality in the HE landscape of each country.

As the demands of a knowledge-based economy grows, so too does the demand for tertiary education. Statistics from UNESCO[1], for example, show that advanced nations have higher tertiary participation rates than less developed ones. S Korea has a Bachelor's gross participation rate of 67.5 per cent, while Bangladesh has a rate of 10 per cent, China 11 per cent and India 14 per cent. It is not surprising that given the high bachelor participation rates in S Korea, youth unemployment there is also among the highest in the OECD countries at 10 per cent. This then has a domino effect on graduate studies as students decide that if they cannot secure a job, then the next best thing is to remain in the university, or to seek other options such as acquiring new skills

1 http://www.uis.unesco.org/Library/Documents/higher-education-asia-graduate-university-research-2014-en.pdf

that are needed in the labour market are also available. The investment in university education will need to be set aside for the time being.

Education and Employability

The Singapore Government placed its educational priority post-independence on the fledgling nation's immediate economic needs and by extension, graduate employability. Periodic reviews of the economy lead to changing economic structures, targeting specific industries and growth areas are identified together with the professional and technical manpower that is needed. This is then directed towards the various training institutions. As skills and knowledge advance, wages climb up, and hence new business models and market sectors have to be developed in tandem to maintain competitiveness. Figure 3.1 shows this close relationship graphically.

Each economic restructuring cycle is led by the government with the participation of business, industry, unions, small enterprises, entrepreneurs and relevant government agencies. Currently, there is such a committee called the Committee on the Future Economy active, engaging all sectors of the economy, including education. The membership and terms of reference may be sighted here: https://www.gov.sg/microsites/ future-economy

The recommendations of such a consultative committee will have repercussions on the nature of education itself and the different skill-sets needed. Such competency gaps are identified and educational policies, curricula and

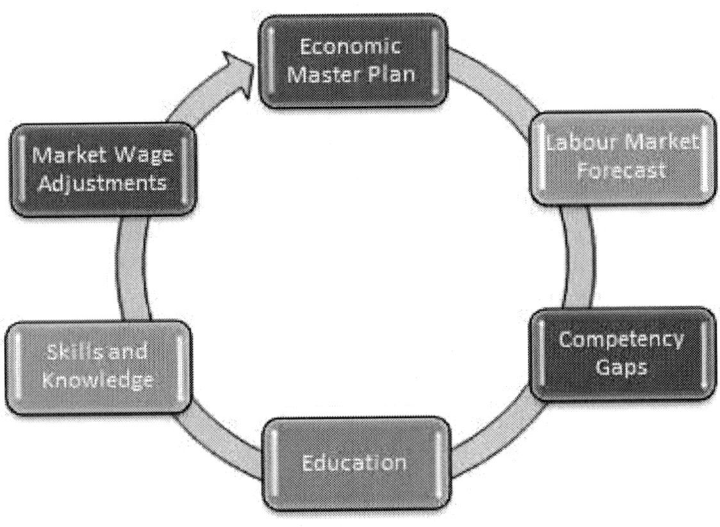

Figure 3.1: Link between Economic Structural Change, Education and Employability

pedagogies are adjusted accordingly. These new skills and knowledge result in changes to the wage structure, national productivity as well as immigration policies. At some stage, these changing demographic characteristics and competitiveness will require to be re-adjusted with changing circumstances. The economy and the educational landscape, therefore, work in tandem in a feedback loop and not independently.

Singapore Experience

Singapore's educational policies, especially in higher education were driven by the reluctant independence that was thrust upon it suddenly in 1965. With limited and finite land resources, diverse ethnicities and languages, no domestic market and high unemployment, the policy solutions were based on pragmatic problem-solving, rather than ideology.

In higher education, the split between nations led to the division of campuses between Singapore and Malaysia. What remained in Singapore were a few colleges and universities. While the politics of language, identity and opportunity raged on the streets, large numbers of young people were in schools going into a non-existent job market. Sensing the danger and needing to grow the economy, the government launched a massive industrialisation programme with the start of the very first integrated industrial estate to house factories, ship-yards and steel-mills. As a matter of urgency, the Singapore Polytechnic's programmes were revamped and re-prioritised to meet immediate skill gaps. Professional diplomas in Engineering, Accountancy and Architecture were launched (in lieu of a university counterpart degree). These were later to be upgraded and transferred to the University of Singapore.

The necessary deep two-way relationship between higher education and economic priorities were structured through the Council for Professional and Technical Education (CPTE), chaired by the Ministry of Trade and Industry. The CPTE set intake targets for all state-funded tertiary bodies and the institutions were funded to grow accordingly. As an outcome of the projected need for more engineers, for example, a new engineering college was established in 1981. Initially called Nanyang Technological Institute (NTI), it later became a full-fledged university, Nanyang Technological University (NTU) and later a comprehensive research university. To ensure relevance to industrial needs, the emphasis was placed on applied engineering and it was situated on the industrial heartland of Jurong on the grounds of the earlier Nanyang University, which was merged with the University of Singapore to become the National University of Singapore (NUS). The growth of the HE sector was carefully calibrated so as not to create an excess of graduates in areas of little or low demand.

Multiple Pathways to Higher Education

One key differentiator in the Singapore HE landscape is the strong presence of polytechnics, which absorb about 40 per cent of each school cohort after grade 10, leading to a 3-year diploma. This provides an alternative pathway to university but with a prior qualification, and even some work experience. Polytechnics in Singapore are similar to Community Colleges in North America, providing work-related programmes in a wide range of areas, not just engineering and technology, but also ICT, healthcare, design, applied social sciences, business, retail, media, culinary arts, tourism and hospitality, veterinary sciences, fashion and logistics. This ensures that while HE gross participation ratios are growing from 25 per cent to 30 per cent, the increase is a mix of direct entry to university from school but also from the polytechnic graduate cohorts with a strong practical bias. Polytechnics in Singapore are well-resourced, staffed by competent and trained lecturers and have strong links with business and industry creating authentic learning environments for students.

Spending on Education

According to the World Bank database, there is not a significant difference in per cent of GDP spent on education. In 2011 for example, Singapore spent 3.1 per cent of GDP while India spent 3.7 per cent of GDP on education as a whole. Expenditures on education rose from SGD1.8Bn in 1984 to SGD3.3Bn in 1994, SGD6.2Bn in 2004 and SGD11.7Bn in 2014. In terms of government budget, in 2013, Singapore spent 18.1 per cent of its annual budget on education, including capital expenditure as well as operating expenses and manpower. This was third after defence and infrastructure development. Therefore, the yield per dollar spent on education is high, with 100 per cent participation in primary education with no compulsory education.

Introducing Diversity and Autonomy into Higher Education

The economy continued to evolve from a manufacturing base driven by technology to one driven by knowledge-based services, such as financial and IT services. A new breed of graduates to address these developments was identified, innovative and not risk-averse. Rather than modifying the existing universities directly, the government's approach was to do this indirectly through a new kind of university. In 2000, American-style business education was introduced into Singapore through a collaboration with the Wharton Business School. The Singapore Management University (SMU) became Singapore's 3rd public university with a focus on management, business, accountancy and IT. It has lately added a law school to its portfolio of schools.

These three universities continued to grow the participation rate in HE rising from a low of 7-8 per cent to something closer to 25 per cent, across a multitude of disciplines. At around the same time, the CPTE was no longer instrumental in determining courses and intakes, but allowed the universities to make their own decisions. However, since the university sector was overwhelmingly public, university administrators were always aware of the need to ensure relevance. The Government also appointed an International Advisory Panel (IAP) to advise it on future directions. As an outcome of such recommendations, new models of governance and autonomy were devised, giving the universities more freedom to offer courses, but held to deliver quality and results.

The Universities came under the Quality Assurance Framework for Universities (QAFU), under which the government provided block budgets, but gave the Universities significant autonomy to manage themselves as long as they remained responsive to the labour markets as measured by graduate employment. In return for autonomy, universities are required to submit themselves to QAFU. An independent panel of experts is appointed by government to undertake an assessment of performance against goals which had been agreed and to recommend improvements and new directions. This happens at 5-year intervals. The findings are used to assess performance of the university management against goals and outcomes that had previously been agreed between them and the government, and would affect future directions of funding. This autonomy and freedom can be seen in the sudden surge of new degree courses offered at the Universities. For example, Figure 3.2 shows the rapid growth of degree programmes at the National University of Singapore.

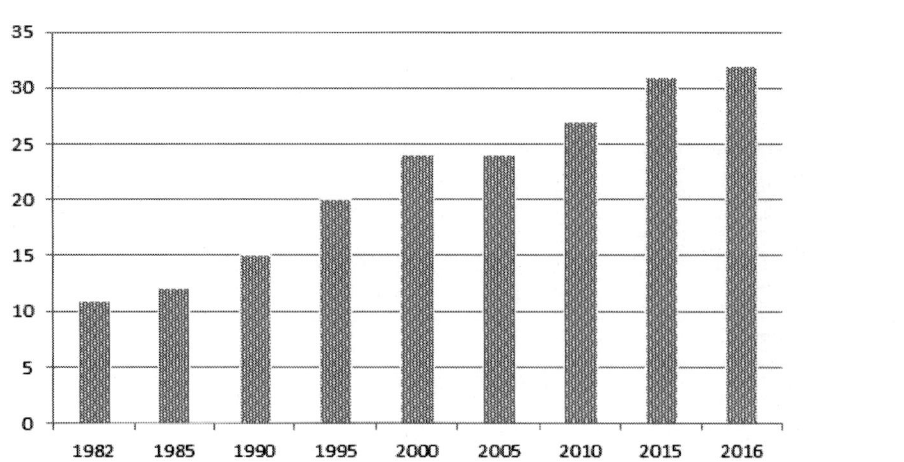

Figure 3.2: No. of Degree Programmes (NUS, 1982-2016)

Even more interesting is the explosion of multi-disciplinary courses as shown in Figure 3.3.

At the same time, one could observe the introduction of many new hybrid degree programmes, with a major and minor, and later as dual degrees, for example, Law and Economics or Engineering with Business, IT and Law and so on. These hybrid degrees were made possible by increased modularisation and cross-modules within faculties as well as with other faculties. The rationale for these was to cater to a broader range of interests of students as well as attracting students to specific faculties. It was also thought that graduates would have broader employment opportunities in more diverse fields and also be better prepared for changes in the workplace. The growth of multi-disciplinary degree programmes at NUS can be seen in Figure 3.3

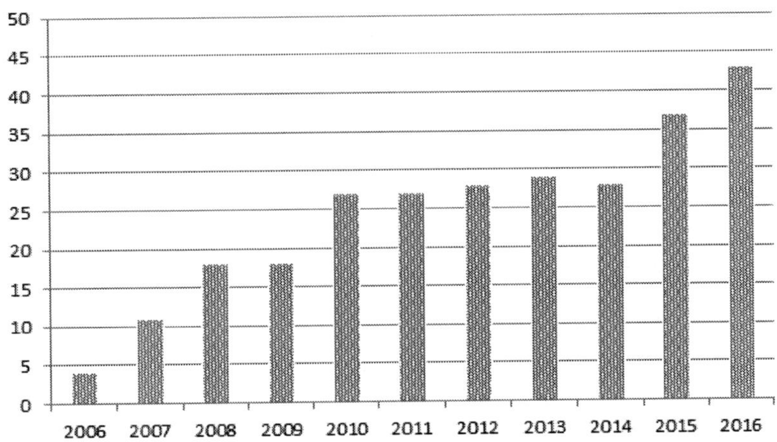

Figure 3.3: No. of Multidisciplinary Programmes (NUS, 2006-2016)

Some of the more interesting combinations are Computer Science and Entertainment Technology, Life Sciences and Psychology, Life Sciences with Law, Law and Public Policy. Recently the Nanyang Technological University (NTU) announced a Renaissance Engineering degree combining Engineering, Business and Humanities (For details of various hybrid courses which can be replicated in India, visit university website.

International Benchmarking

As a result of the very focused and targeted approach to higher education in Singapore, the international rankings for both NUS and NTU have been climbing steadily.

Table 3.1: World University Rankings (Asia, selected universities), 2015/16

World Ranking Quacquarelli Symonds (QS)	*World Ranking Times Higher Education (THES)*	*University*
12	26	National University of Singapore
13	55	Nanyang Technological University
25	47	Tsinghua University
28	59	Hong Kong Univ. of Science & Technology
30	44	University of Hong Kong
36	85	Seoul National University
39	43	University of Tokyo
41	42	Peking University

Private Higher Education

No survey of HE in Singapore would be complete without mention of the vibrant private sector in higher education. Private HE can be classified under the following categories:

(a) *State-sponsored or assisted:* Under an ambitious Global School house initiative of the Economic Development Board (EDB), several high-end institutions were incentivised to establish branches in Singapore. Among them were the French graduate business school INSEAD, the Chicago Graduate School of Business, University of New South Wales from Australia, the Tisch School of the Arts from New York, Essec Business School, Johns Hopkins University, the University of Nevada Las Vegas, Digi Pen Institute of Technology, and the SP Jain School of Global Management from India. Of these, only INSEAD and the SP Jain School have continued to grow in enrolment and reputation. The others have either closed or reduced their footprint. In addition, there are some indigenous Singapore brands which have developed with some state support. These are Lasalle College of the Arts and Nanyang Academy of Fine Art, both with long histories.

(b) *Twinning programmes*: A more common arrangement is for a foreign university to collaborate with a local player to offer its degrees here. Among the large players in this space are SIM Global Education, Kaplan, MDIS, PSB Academy, with a number of mid and smaller institutes such as TMC, Auston, and EASB. Most of them are affiliated to 2nd and 3rd tier UK and Australian universities. Most of the campuses are not purpose-built, and lessons are conducted in former schools or renovated commercial spaces.

The Singapore Institute of Technology (SIT) has collaborative arrangements with a number of Tier 1 overseas universities to offer their degree programmes at its campuses but these are specialised courses which would not be otherwise commercially viable.

(c) *Branch campuses*: These are few in number, and James Cook University (JCU) is the most prominent and successful of these. Private Universities and institutions are regulated by the Committee for Private Education (CPE) which ensures that facilities, lecturers, curricula, assessments, academic and student support systems, graduate employment, fees and advertisements are of high standards. Over time, the number of smaller players is expected to be squeezed out of the market, leaving only the major players left. At last count, there were 626 Bachelors programmes, 96 Masters Programmes and 28 post-graduate certificate and diploma qualifications available at private educational institutions. In the future low-growth environment, this will reduce as the lower end of the quality spectrum is gradually sifted out by a tighter regulatory framework.

Widening Opportunities

More recent developments include the establishment of universities with special courses and purposes. SIM University was established in 2005 for adult-learners to come back to university to continue their learning. It now offers 84 degree programmes in part-time mode, seven in full-time mode and 15 graduate programmes, all designed and tailored for working adults. It is expected that the full-time mode courses will increase over time.

A new Duke-NUS medical school was opened in 2005 in collaboration with Duke University to prepare clinical scientists and medical officers using the US model of medical education, where one starts to study medicine after completing a basic degree. This is to provide an alternative training model to the existing one. The Singapore University of Technology and Design (SUTD), in collaboration with MIT in Boston USA and Zhejiang University in China was established in 2011 to drive innovative multi-disciplinary problem-solving using technology for issues that Singapore and the world are facing.

Similarly, the Yale-NUS Liberal Arts College was opened in 2012 to emphasise the multi-disciplinary study of the arts and humanities. Over at NTU, the third medical school was established in collaboration with Imperial College London. By tying up with renowned, best of class institutions overseas, these new colleges are able to establish a brand and reputation early and be able to attract good students. Much of the emphasis has been on producing globally-competitive students with a significant overseas student component and the recruitment of distinguished faculty for all over the world. Finally, a new Singapore Institute of Technology (SIT) has also been established to provide opportunities for diploma holders to receive quality degrees as part of their career upgrade. This is also to encourage them to stay within their particular field and deepen their knowledge and skills.

All of these have served to widen the gross tertiary participation rate closer to 30 per cent of the birth cohort. This is an underestimated figure as there are various other routes for higher education both within and outside Singapore. The actual figure could be closer to 70 per cent since diploma holders are quick to upgrade themselves as soon as they are able to, primarily through a large number of twinning programmes with overseas universities. One concern arising from this is that in an economic downturn, the segment to be most affected are likely to be those termed PMETs, or those in Professional, Managerial, Executive and Technical positions. These are the middle-level positions which are easiest to close or replace with cheaper staff. The Singapore Government's response is a long-term programme called Skills Future.

Skills Future

Skills Future is designed to develop a long-term upskilling attitude among the working population, while ensuring greater connectivity and line of sight between training and employment. Skills and skills deepening can only be enhanced when one works hard at it, like the Germans and Japanese. Hence the emphasis is on ensuring constant topping up of knowledge and skills throughout one's lifetime. A Skills Future account for every individual citizen which is topped up annually, provides the financial support for continual learning. A Life Long Learning Institute (LLI) has been established as well as an Institute for Adult Learning (IAL) to provide age-appropriate training pedagogies.

Lessons for Developing Nations

This brief survey of the evolution of the Singapore Higher Education landscape is not intended to be presented as best practice, nor something to be emulated in any way. There are, however, some key success factors in the system which can be highlighted.

(a) A strong (though weakening) linkage with business and industry. Although initially the numbers and types of graduates in the professional and technical fields were prescribed, these restrictions have been replaced by a governance framework that is based on accountability and results, with employment being a key measure.

(b) Maintenance of high academic standards by limitations on participation ratios. The public university sector has taken many years to expand to its present level of 30 per cent of each cohort. The remaining 70 per cent went through the technical and vocational education and training route (TVET) to employment and further education.

(c) Private higher education was generally seen as an economic service sector, creating an education business hub in Singapore, and less as a vehicle for local students. However, private HEIs were able to attract those who were going abroad to study to take their courses. Recent reports indicate that these graduates find difficulty in finding suitable employment.
(d) Modularisation of courses and curricula have led to many innovative combinations and approaches to undergraduate studies. Courses combining engineering, economics and humanities can be offered; students are able to mix and match modules to suit their interests and talents. This shift from a British-type to a more US-type of degree configuration is seen as more appropriate in preparing for a more complex and dynamic future. These hybrid courses have seen a high growth rate, and helps graduate to cope with rapid disruptive changes in the economic landscape, new business models and labour mobility (with the emphasis on entrepreneurship, services and continuous learning).
(e) Entry into certain courses like medicine are highly competitive and intakes restricted. There are no private players in this market.
(f) Finally, the K-12 school system is of a uniformly high standard with high achievements in Mathematics and Science and hence prepares students well for tertiary study at technical institutes, polytechnics and universities. A system of bridges and ladders allows good performers to reach their maximum potential over time.

Conclusion

In this brief survey of the Singapore experience in the course offerings in the tertiary sector, several key ideas stand out. These are (a) a strong public higher education sector, well-funded and resourced; (b) a culture of continual accountability to deliver excellence for the student; (c) employability as a key measurable outcome, and (d) variety and diversity in the HE landscape, all different but of the highest quality. Over time, institutions have come up with a number of innovative courses, responding quickly to the needs of business and industry, and closely monitoring the economic pulse of the country.

Although the numbers of state institutions are not many, they all operate competitively and cooperatively, several under the same umbrella. The Government supports the competitive spirit and branding efforts as long as they keep to their mission and do not get mission-drift. Unlike in India and other countries, the private HE market is complementary and is tightly regulated. Private education is not the first choice, given the quality and resources in the state institutions. The government is in the process of tightening private education even further and the number of players will reduce even more in the next decade.

4.
Impact of Denationalisation and Globalisation on Science Education and Research in Developing Countries

Radhakrishna G Pillai

Globalisation is a phenomenon that is characterised by the massive growth in communication, trade, cultural exchange, information flows, etc. around the world with 'decreasing restrictions' in a complex and integrated global society (Crawford, 2003). The globalisation of education, especially higher education, has spread to all parts of the world and in different levels. This has been forcing universities and colleges around the world to compete in a global capitalist market and engage in activities to help them sustain in an increasingly uncertain world. Beerkens (2004) defines globalisation as "a process in which basic social arrangements within and around the university become disembedded from their national context due to the intensification of transnational flows of people, information and resources". The reality is that higher education institutions are becoming and will become "disembedded" from their national contexts as forces of globalisation exceed the strength of national factors. The computer and Internet based communication technology is an important driving force towards globalisation. Projects such as Massive Open Online Courses (MOOC) speed up the processes of globalisation in education (Kim *et al,* 2015).

Influence of Human Capital Theory in Globalising Education

Increased prominence in education of human capital theory (Erosa, 2010) has led to the revamping of education for the creation of high-skilled individual to suit the forthcoming high skilled economies throughout Europe in light of new realities of the global economy. Economic development and role of education coupled with technocratic model of evolutionary social change helped change in the nature of industrialisation through the use of science and technological innovation. This demanded change in the education (Brown et al 2008). This has led to the transformation of the education system from the mass elementary to mass higher education due to the high demand for skilled workers (Brown *et. al,* 2006, 2006a). New technologies led to the elimination of certain jobs and the creation of some new high skilled employment which had led to a change in the relationships between the employer and the employee and the employees had become a new asset of the companies. Availability of suitably skilled employees determines the profitability of the companies. In the present scenario, it is the competition for ideas, knowledge and skills that define the new economy (Drucker 1993). Now the prosperity of individuals, companies and nations depends on human and intellectual capital rather than on issues of ownership (Brown *et.al*, 2008).

The new political equation of high skills leading to high wages has changed the investment pattern in education. This has led to the introduction of 'user pays' models for the funding of higher education. This has resulted in the starting up of many "self financed" educational institutions even in developing countries. Here the institutions need to generate the fund for their functioning and the profit for the investors. The education system has become a lucrative business opportunity for the business fraternity. High skilled workers are more productive and have greater market worth and are able to earn high wages and that forced people to pursue education in expensive institutions and become employable in a technocratic society. This has further led to the blooming of "new generation" education institutes which impart high skills and provide an international face to education. Institutions started providing education and skills that the employers needed. The character of education was thus changed from the society oriented to job oriented which led to competitions among educational institutes and less competent organisations are getting wiped out of the scenario.

Globalisation Weakens Power of Nations

Technological innovations of the 21st century reduced the whole world to a global village integrating economy and society around the world and on the outskirt it looks attractive. It was noted that globalisation necessitated a particular standard which often emerges unintentionally (Grewal, 2008) which led to a kind of competition by nations to meet the global standard. Global standard is defined in par with what is in existence in developed western countries. In effect globalisation can be considered as 'an emergent form of Western imperialism carried through cultural institution such as education' forcing each nation to establish their position in relation to capitalist West (Henry *et.al*, 2008). Some writers are of the opinion that globalisation is not as global as the developed countries make the rest of the world to believe. It has rather divided the world into 'the haves' and 'the have nots'. The 'have nots' are destabilised. They become vulnerable making their boundaries porous (Stiglitz, 2002, Singh, 2001).

The impact of the new Information and Communication Technology (ICT) has significantly changed the speed of production, use and distribution of knowledge economy depending on how much it can generate and share knowledge. International competition made it impossible even for powerful nations to protect their employees. Workers acquired freedom to sell their skills, knowledge and insights in the global job market and to grab a salary to suit their abilities irrespective of their nationality. Incomes of the top 20 per cent have pulled away from the rest because of their ability to break free of the constraints of local and national labour markets (Reich R, 1991). Quality jobs offered by advanced economies like the UK, the USA and France have made them magnet economies attracting highly skilled employees from all over the world (Brown & Lauder, 2006). Along with this, trade liberalisation offered an opportunity to both the developing and developed nations to exploit the changed education scenario.

The accelerated pace of technological development has made access to knowledge a requirement for participation in the global economy. Nations start competing for ideas, skills and knowledge and this led to knowledge wars an evolutionary shift from blood-shed wars. Those who are ahead of generating knowledge and making use of it have the advantage of 'out-smarting' their economic rivals who are slow or lethargic in advancing with knowledge and skills (Brown & Lauder, 2006). Various institutions of international status emerged and that led to the development of comparative measures of academic quality and performance along with a system for global ranking of higher education institutes (Marginson, 2006). In the current century the success *mantra* is 'offshoring' and the nations with resources and determination had come forward to exploit the opportunity (Brown & Lauder, 2006).

African countries are in debt and poverty partly due to the policies of international institutions like the International Monetary Fund (IMF) and World Trade Organisation (WTO) (Okoli NJ, 2008). It has been pointed out that 'globalisation creates rift within the nations, between what they called globalised and globalising elites, and those who have been adversely affected by globalisation through unemployment, job insecurity and growing inequality' (Henry *et.al*, 2008). The society experiences fragmentation and differences, with serious socio-economic and educational inequalities and inequities. This leads to change in educational policies or what Henry *et.al* (2008) called reframing of educational policies (Okoli NJ, 2012). Financial liberalisation has contributed to financial crises in various nations, and had created social, economic, political and educational inequality in the entire continent (Okoli NJ, 2012).

Over the years there are two types of human capital flow from India. First took place before globalisation where knowledge workers moved to western countries to feed their job market. This involves training students in India by western education institutes established through a system of franchising. These institutes coach Indian students in western curricula so that they could find employment anywhere in the world. Negative issues about this are high fee, use of curricula completely oriented for western needs and generates human resource completely identified by the lifestyles and needs of western countries which lead to subversion of the nationalised goals of higher education. There are three pertinent issues on globalisation: whether it is inevitable, who are the beneficiaries and who are the losers. The second started after the new trade regimes of WTO and GATS. Certain articles in GATS can ensure participation of developing countries on an equal footing, but the developing countries failed to evolve a coherent policy and programme to deal with the challenges of GATS and to control the institutions of higher learning.

Supra-national and trans-national political entities (like World Bank, UN, WTO and IMF), may affect the ability of nations to form effective national policies independent of any influence. They emphasise nation states (especially underdeveloped nations) to align their educational policies in favour of global citizenship. This pressure in turn leads to devising the curriculum in favour of globalisation which seriously curtails the limits of national sovereignty and national education policy. Nations that work against the globalisation policy will lose the support and funding crucial for its own existence and if it tries to work for globalisation it will soon be left impotent as in the cases of Papua New Guinea (PNG) and Malaysia (Taylor *et.al* 2000 and Ali S, 2005). The market forces shaped the Malaysian higher education policy and the IMF and the World Bank conditionality manipulated the educational policy of PNG against the wishes and needs of local authorities. The study of PNG and Malaysia presents a case typical of many underdeveloped nations (Ali S, 2005).

Knowledge Emerging as Key Asset of New Economies

As knowledge turned out to be the key asset of new economy, companies try to pay less for knowledge and skills. Companies decrease cost by accessing the increased supply of graduates from across the globe and by employing graduates from developing or under developed economies who work for less. The second way of reducing cost is by standardising knowledge work through processes that we call Digital Taylorism. Talents were paid extra by companies and this made employees to increase the market value of their knowledge. Offshoring had reduced the cost of employers as the cost of hiring an employee in India or China is far less than hiring an equally talented employee in the USA or the UK (Brown *et.al*, 2006). The national governments in the developed economies see educational development as a way of increasing prosperity which is not as easy in developing economies.

After the collapse of communism, development in ICT and economic integration led developing countries into a competition for knowledge creation and use which removed the distinction between 'head' and 'body' nations. For example, the nature of China's exports had changed from cheap low-margin goods to more value-added goods offering much higher profits. The educational revolution had increased the share of Asian countries in contributing graduates and postgraduates in Engineering, Science, Maths and Computer Science. In the US, more than half of those gaining a doctoral degree in engineering, mathematics and computer science are foreign students (NSB-USA, 2014; Stuen *et.al*, 2012). Now more than 90 per cent of all scientists and engineers in the world will be living in Asia (*Time*, 2006). The World Bank also estimates that Russia has the third-highest numbers of scientists and engineers per capita in the world and the other Eastern European countries also have a growing proportion of well-educated scientists and information technology specialists (Brown P, *et.al* 2008). Globally education is deemed important for the competitive advantage of nations, but the financial constraints has affected the quality, quantity and performance (Okoli, 2012).

The greatest destabilising influence of globalisation on the nation state is the global knowledge economy. Graduates from Africa, India, Korea, etc. seek employment abroad. As of 2002 estimated 30,000 Africans holding Ph.D were working outside the continent while 130,000 then were studying abroad, in various countries of the world (Okoli, 2012). Brain-drain took a toll on the talented experts who would have developed Africa (Loveland, 2007). Education institutions in Africa suffer a reverse in the recruitment of staff today as the top achieving graduates opt for high quality job across the border or in private institutions and the low achievers flock the government job and universities. In the present scenario the value of corporate brands are not restricted to the quality of the goods and services they sold, but to the workforce also. As the more corporate value is 'embodied' in the people who work for it, the more companies want to be seen to recruit 'the best' (Brown & Hesketh, 2004) which enhance cross border movements of persons of special skills.

Need to Redesign Education

Different companies in different sectors had entered into a system of build-to-order where products will be built according to the specification suggested by the customer, which necessitates developing ideas to compete with the rivals as well as to introduce innovations. For companies in states like the USA, it is essential to reduce the cost to match with that of Asia. This drive will lead to innovations as companies are increasingly experimenting with research, design, marketing, product development and human resource development. This is leading to innovative education and experiences to enhance skill settings. Educational institutions are redesigning education in such a way that it could go in par with employment (Hall & Soskice, 2001). Through high-performance management practice by making use of the highly educated and low-cost labour force, Chinese companies are able to produce high value-added goods at much lower costs (Venter *et.al*, 2002).

Henry et al. (2001) emphasise that the globalisation has created the spirit of managerialism in the governance of education. This spirit is concerned more with the goals, strict regulations, competition and devolution. The welfare-state is now being conceived as competitive-state, which should steer from distance and regularise the services to ensure three E's: Economy, Effectiveness and Efficiency (Mok & Lee, 2000). When this spirit of new public management is applied to the underdeveloped countries for education policy and implementation it meets a half-hearted response and may fail.

Elite Universities Attract the Best Talents

Elite universities around the world attract the best graduates and this gravitational pull is more towards the universities in developed countries like the USA, the UK, Australia, France, etc. (Cantwell B, 2015). The brand of the university as well as the calibre of its faculties is integral to the organisation of top quality education facilities. The universities claim world-class standards by attracting 'the best' academics or by forming alliance with other world-class universities elsewhere in the world. This game of achieving elite status is removing the parity of esteem between universities as seen in German universities. Until recently there was no difference in market value of degree between universities in Germany. But the 'excellence' reforms led to the channelisation of resources to certain universities to make them elite before the world and lift the profile of German higher education. We have seen the effect of creating elite institutions at the expense of others at least in Germany. The ranking of universities by reputation is forcing the students to study at a leading national university with an international reputation. This often reduces diversity among students. Universities found a short cut for having diversity by recruiting elite students from various nationalities which created a global war for talents where the have-nots in Universities failed.

Effect of Globalisation on Progress of Universities

High quality in both teaching and research is central for success of universities in the emerging knowledge economy. The developed world understood much earlier the fact that individuals with higher education have an edge over their counterparts. They are the ones who always believed that any amount of investment in higher education was justifiable. It is, therefore, imperative for developing countries too, to give due importance to both the quantitative and qualitative expansion of higher education (Prakash V, 2007).

In the networked global environment each university is visible to everyone and no nations or individual higher education institutions could completely seal themselves off from global effects. Universities with strong research base and vocational course are establishing their position as international course providers. This study had shown that Universities in developing countries are failing to establish a research base due to the poor infrastructural facility and the procedural delays prevalent in those countries. In developing countries, scientists are found to spend a lot of time in non-academic matters compared to their counterparts in the developed countries, which affect the progress of research by the faculty members of the Universities. In India University Professors in Science or Technology during the initial part of their professional development spend an average of five years to set up a basic research laboratory. Even in countries like China the initial time lag is far less than in India. In China the seed money provided by the Government helps a Professor in quick setting up of research facility. Scientists of India strongly feel that the call for modernisation and increase of research spending stay as huge cries of administrators and is far from reality. This will keep the research in Indian Institutions lethargic and the country will be left even behind some of the developing countries and will be paying the price in diminished effectiveness. Agenda for global exchange as well as cross-border flows varies between nations. The data in Table 4.1 shows that the higher education institutions of the United States enjoy a higher share of global exchange as a greater percentage of students enrol in US institutions than in any other country. At the same time the student flow out of the country is comparatively very low.

Table 4.1 Indicators of Global Potential, Capacity and Engagement with Respect to Student Enrolment in year 2014

S. No.	*Country*	*Gross National Income per Head*	*% of GDP spent on Tertiary Education Institutions*	*% of Foreign Students in Tertiary Education*	*% of Students Enrolled Abroad to Total Students*
1	*United States*	*>54960*	*1.2*	*5.5*	*0.2*
2	*United Kingdom*	*>43340*	*0.8*	*14.0*	*1.2*
3	*Germany*	*>45790*	*1.0*	*11.0*	*3.0*
4	*Japan*	*>36680*	*0.6*	*2.0*	*4.0*
5	*Israel*	*>35440*	*1.2*	*3.6*	*1.3*
6	*Malaysia*	*>10570*	*2.7*	*5.6*	*3.2*
7	*China*	*>7820*	*na*	*4*	*1.9*
8	*India*	*>1590*	*1.4*	*2*	*0.1*

Sources: OECD, World Bank, Country wide data

In addition to the technological advancement as well as the enhanced global visibility of US institutions, the job prospects for US educated graduate also contribute to the success (Currie 2005). Institutions everywhere are made to believe that it is necessary be like US universities to become successful. Global capacity and potential to recruit students from other countries is directly proportional to gross national income as well as spending on higher education.

Role of Research in Institutional Success

US institutions outperform others and almost all successful US institutions have got a powerful doctoral sector. This enhances the profile of the institutions through increased publications, generation of funds for research which will also enhance the infrastructural facilities. A survey by our group among scientists of US institutions and other developed and developing countries had revealed the fact that the US Scientists spend far less time on non-academic administrative duties compared to their counterparts in developed as well as developing countries. In India scientists spend more than 25 per cent of their time on unimportant administrative chores which could easily be avoided and that may enhance the research output. In India administrative staffs in Universities are far higher in number compared to research staff and they are well organised under the umbrellas of different political parties. This makes it difficult to change the administrative system in Universities. Some brave actions were successfully initiated by vice chancellors of certain modern Universities started recently and that attracted strong opposition by unions of employees. A commendable approach at the newly formed APJ Abdul Kalam Kerala Technological University (KTU) in Kerala is proving successful. In KTU 100 or so employees are managing the activities of the University whereas in other Universities in Kerala the staff numbers are more than one thousand and still administrative processes are happening at "tortoise speed". Thus brave decisions by the higher officers in Universities could help us to reduce non-academic costs and to channelise the money to research and development and that will definitely lead to success as in US Universities.

More than 45 per cent of the top 500 research institutions in the world are from the USA. Again 16 of the top 20 research universities in terms of research performance and 51 per cent of the top 100 universities are in the USA (Thomson Reuters, 2015). This attracts and holds talented doctoral students, postdoctoral researchers and world-class faculty from everywhere in the world. The distinctive American approach to competition and social markets in higher education is found successful and nations like India had started adopting this approach, though not fully successful yet. The US has shown us that a high aid mixed public/private system is a suitable alternative to the fully funded public system. At present the public sector commands more than 80 per cent of enrolments in India. We are realising the fact that as in the UK, non-profit and for-profit private sector models are important. Many developed countries like Australia, the UK and New Zealand appreciate the American tradition and are making changes in system-organisation and financing to move closer to the system in the United States. Control of government over US institutes is virtually nil, but the institutions themselves engage in cross-border dealings and let engage the faculty members to collaborate with institutions all around the world. Self restraint and the innovative proactive approach made them successful and is a good model to follow with suitable modifications to suit the cultural and socio-economic demands for institutions all over the world.

Globalisation and Government Policy

It was reported that member countries of the OECD account for 85 per cent of total investment in research and development. China, India, Brazil and the newly industrialised countries of East Asia (Malaysia, Singapore, etc.) account for 11 per cent, while the rest of Africa account for 4 per cent. Marginalisation of Africa in the global competition is clear from the above figures (Okoli 2008, 2012). It has already been said that globalisation pressures produce fragmentation and differences. These translate into unemployment, job insecurity and growing inequalities in access to education in developing countries. The children from both the rich and the working class and even from poor background face serious competition to gain access into the universities. It was pointed out that the clamour for access to university education is rather intense and has given rise to various facets of examination malpractices which are damaging to education (Okoli, 2008).

Government Free Approach for Success: In India the University Grants Commission (UGC) and related government agencies control most of the activities at tertiary education level. UGC being the major funding agency for Universities impart indirect strict control over the Universities. This in effect retards the progress of Universities. They could implement modernisation only by remaining within the limits set by UGC, which at most of the times is hindrance before the Universities in adopting a world class system of teaching-learning. Indian education system is the result of a policy matter of the governments, so the adoption of American system as model is not easy. Another key problem is that the success of American system is due to the high global flows of students, which cannot be treated as a stable arrangement. Even if it is stable for the USA it may not come true in case of India as India could not offer similar facilities that the USA offers to students. High unemployment and other inadequate physical facilities make India less attractive to students from developed nations. India normally attracts students from developing or underdeveloped nations (Figure 1).

In the USA, the proportion of doctoral graduates who are foreign-born has grown from 13.5 in 1977 to more than 30 per cent on an average for all subjects, whereas in Mathematics, Engineering and Computer science it rose to around 50 per cent, (Guellec & Cervantes 2002). For postdoctoral fellowship, the USA offers the majority of posts worldwide. India could not do this due to the high rate of unemployment in India and the Indian researchers with low esteem will not be able to compete with the western doctorates or even with the Chinese peers. Having faculty of world reputation and standard are important. Making use of the expertise of visiting faculty is an option before us as we can not afford offering long term positions to senior professors from developed countries. The recent "Erudite" program of the Kerala Higher Education Council, though not able to achieve the expected objectives is a good initiative.

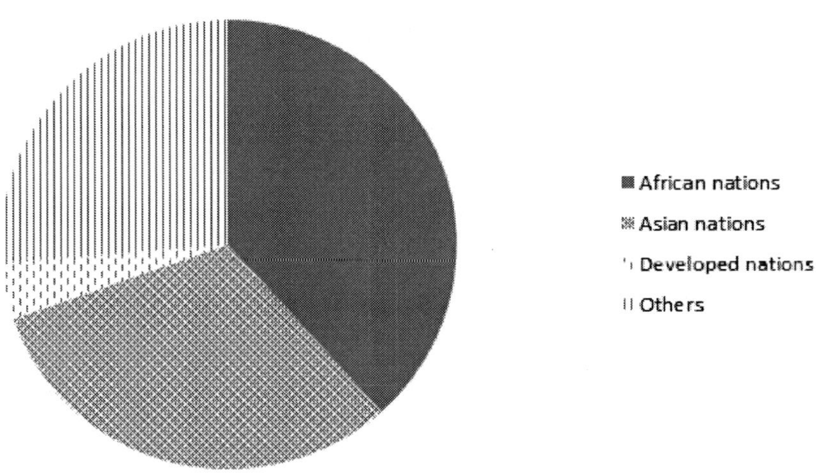

Figure 4.1. Nationality of Foreign Students Enrolled in Indian Higher Education Institutes —2015

Effect of Government Policies

Government policies, governance and management affect globalisation a lot especially in a democratic system like that in India. Keeping away from international systems of higher education should not be a strategic choice for a nation with forward thinking as this will be detrimental to the genuine interests of its citizens and force them to be a part of this knowledge revolution. A comparative study of the internationalised system of education shows that the United States is the number one beneficiary and the percentage of international students enrolling in the US institutions are far greater than many other developed countries. It may be noted that in many of the US institutions of higher learning a greater part of their resource generation is through the tuition fee of international students. This also resulted in brain drain from many countries including the developed nations like the UK.

India failed to realise the fact that the international student community could be used as catalysts for the development of educational system in India. A survey among the stakeholders of the higher education institutions in India had shown that 72 per cent of them are in favour of welcoming foreign students whereas 23 per cent was not in favour due to a fear of it removing some of the facilities of domestic students and five per cent was undecided. Those who are in favour of welcoming international students felt the benefits as:

1. Generation of financial resources for the development of the institutions.
2. Enhanced facilities to an international standard to attract international students which will also be open to the domestic students.
3. Examination systems will be streamlined and made efficient.
4. Interaction with international students will help in cultural exchanges and reframe career goals.
6. Curriculum in tune with the latest development in the respective fields.
7. Teaching-learning process will change with a student-oriented approach.

Information and Communication Technology and their Use and Misuse

American universities are relatively sophisticated in data retrieval technologies with the USA constituting the world's largest single pool of broadband Internet subscribers (Drache & Froese 2005). The American research system is remarkably insular and American researchers do not often cite works by scholars or researchers in other countries in their research. The American system accepts and absorbs scholars and scientists from other nations if only they conform to American academic and scientific norms (Altbach 2005, 2009). This pattern of insular globalisation and one way cross-border flows stands as a hindrance to the educational advancement of many developing nations.

Advancement in ICT provided the USA and other developed western countries an edge in the globalised education market. ICT has created the realistic possibility of developing global standards that reduce technical complexity and diversity (Davenport, 2005). The advancements in communication technology is achieved by the input from the scholars from developing countries especially India. In many of the multinational American companies, the Indians form more than 50 per cent of the employees. Countries like India should make use of the expertise of the workforce members, who have got commitment to the development of their mother nation. The quicker we make use of the expertise and develop ourselves, the faster we will come close to the American standard of educational development. This will help us to employ our youths in the country itself and reduce brain drain. The brain power of the country could be made use of its progress. This will reduce the uneven global knowledge flow.

Effect of Large Population

In China a state-driven development of higher education during the period 1998-2004 made profound changes which multiplied graduate admission by four times and this made Chinese higher education the largest system in the world. The changes were not just in quantity, but the quality of education was also improved. This increased the research activities, number of publications and the doctorate degree holders (Liu, 2005). Funding for research was also increased based on strategic plans put forward by Universities (Vincent-Lancrin, 2004). Admission to doctoral degree was increased to multiple times and this has reduced China's dependence on Ph.D training abroad and is increasing its own role as a global centre of research activity. This also resulted in the increase in the number of postdoctoral researchers recruited by the USA and other developed nations which in turn lessened the opportunities for doctoral degree holders from countries like India. For this success the Chinese Government used foreign educational providers mostly through a partnership model to open competition between local and foreign providers.

India has 1.2 billion people and participation in tertiary education is also expanding rapidly. The enrolment ratio which was only 8.1 per cent in 2001-02 increased to 20.4 per cent in 2011 (MHRD, 2011). Chinese success could be taken as a model for India, but there are inherent difficulties for India like cultural and regional diversity and lethargy in speeding up the research activities. Advancement in ICT enabled education and use of English as medium of instruction in tertiary education provide India certain advantages. Considerable autonomy enjoyed by Institutes of Technologies, state funded universities and the deemed-to-be-Universities is another positive character to be exploited (Natarajan, 2005). Success of IITs through research and proper funding (Bhushan, 2006) could be a model.

Factors Affecting Disembedding and Globalisation of Education in India

Initiatives of the Government of India through UGC to attract cross-border students have achieved some success. Institutions in India are able to attract students from underdeveloped countries or from certain Asian countries. The cultural diversity of India could also be used to attract international students, but the universities need to make certain changes to the mode of their functioning. A survey among the cross-border students in India revealed the following facts that are antagonising India's desire to attract more cross-border students:

1. Lack of student-friendly administrative system
2. Inordinate delay in admission and examination processes
3. Poor quality accommodation
4. Reluctance of Indian students to integrate freely with the international students
5. Lack of flexibility in the system and non-availability of bridge courses to rectify the skill and knowledge shortage
6. Lack of innovative courses — for example, India is the birth place of Yoga, but we took decades to start courses in Yoga
7. Lack of interdisciplinary approach
8. Cultural rigidity in Indian Society and the false propaganda about India's religious beliefs.

India needs to accept the fact that international students provide an easy source of income when public investment and fees do not cover the cost of teaching. Another factor that needs to take into account is that the population control in India is being successfully implemented and the impact of low birth rate on education system is going to be profound as observed in the USA, the UK and other countries of the European Union. Like them we may have to depend on cross-border students for gaining enrolment for certain courses. Life styles of people are also affecting the demand for courses and have to either adapt to the changing situations in the country or aim for cross-border students. India needs to see these two threats ahead and plan to overcome this through attracting cross-border students. A thorough revamping of the higher education system in India is warranted to achieve this goal.

International rankings affect the profile of institutions. International rankings favour universities that use English as the main language of instruction and research, have a large array of disciplines and programmes and substantial research funds from government or other sources. These rankings have methodological problems but they are widely used and influential, and show no signs of disappearing (Altbach *et al,* 2009).

University Grading and Globalisation

World University Rankings by various agencies provide a yardstick for assessing the competency of universities (Reena, 2010). The ranking of universities are made considering various factors like academic peer review, employer review, publication in global journals, citations per faculty, high citations, Nobel prize winners, presence of top researchers, international faculty ratio, faculty output, international student ratio and student / faculty ratio. As per the ranking data American research universities have 3614 high citation researchers compared to 224 in Germany, 221 in Japan, 162 in Canada, 138 in France, 101 in Australia, 94 in Switzerland, 55 in Sweden, 20 in China and none in India (ISI, 2006). Educational planning in developing countries should reflect on this data which may help their higher education institutes to excel.

Economic Stability of Nations and Academic Performance

The performance of the universities is relative to the economic capacity of the nations. In nearly all cases, superior national performance relative to economic capacity is due to high public investment in research in higher education. In nations like India, the dependence of research capacity on the meagre public investment is the major reason of under performance. Noticeable information is that the United States performs very well in its share of the top 100 research universities but its performance is not that good in its share of the top 500. This points to the fact that resources and status are being concentrated in globally leading research universities at the expense of the potential of regional knowledge economies. On the other hand, Germany does well in its share of the top 500. This indicates the effectiveness of a broad-based research capacity and funding across the national system. India should adopt the German model by supporting the institutions at different parts of the country with equal importance.

India has to climb uphill to build a national research cadre which is sufficiently strong in depth and breadth. This should be done with the realisation that the returns are low and the costs will be high. Singapore built a research base through a multi-locational system whereas Malaysia and Thailand adopted a system which depended on foreign training by offering fellowships to its citizens to meet the expenses of carrying out doctoral research in countries like the USA. Along with producing doctorate holders, India should find ways to retain them in India to avoid expensive brain drain effectively by overcoming the gravitational pull of the US institutions.

As in China, the long-term academic policy of India should adopt certain measures to foster research and collaborations. These include incentives to publish in leading international journals, financial support to researchers for participation in cross-border research partnerships, networks and other kinds of collaborative projects, enhancing the potential for knowledge transfer from other nations through exchange of doctoral students and by longer-term collaborations. In a country like India, large share of research is carried out by doctoral students (Fig 4.2). Adopting a policy that supports strong doctoral research base is important for India to excel in research and show an international presence in tertiary education. Researchers and students in Indian universities feel that the recent regulations by the University Grants Commission (UGC) are detrimental to research and the universities. To avoid such thoughts participatory decision making is to be practised. Certain conditions are essential to research universities to be globally effective and they include: strong resource base, full state support for academically controlled basic research, steering capacity of executives to concentrate resources in key strategic fields and projects, presence of emerging researchers of high calibre across a range of fields of research, institutional autonomy and academic freedom including the license to develop cross-border collaborations, better ICT systems and competency in English language. In addition to that,

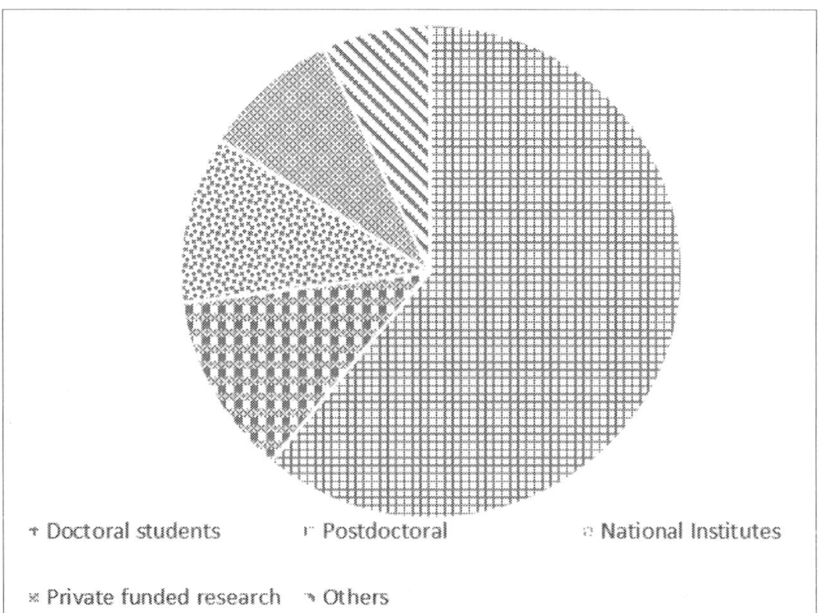

Figure 4.2: Research Carried Out by Scholars in India

conditions of work and life should be attractive at least to own citizens and flows of faculty, long-term or sort-term and students in both directions. The length of time taken to achieve this will affect the educational progress of nations.

Mobility of the Programmes

National borders could be crossed through the establishment of own campuses in foreign nations, or through open learning courses. A model to follow is the University of Phoenix in the USA which has opened campuses in various parts of the world including India, Mexico, the Latin America and Europe. They established a solid international presence in on-line education also. Good investment capital, proper executive steering, well developed courseware and business systems, and sufficient local knowledge made the Phoenix University successful. Phoenix offers a teaching-only form of higher education and hence is not requiring research capacity and many highly qualified and expensive academic staff. They offer short-term programmes in leased premises, twinning programmes in fields such as Medicine in partnership with local and foreign providers. Use of a profit partner is another way to impart cross border long term courses. Interactive online courses are also in offer. Development of global e-learning courseware in English with delivery into nations such as China where demand for tertiary education is outstripping supply is a potential area for developing countries like India to tap.

In 2008, the Organization for Economic Cooperation and Development identified several key demographic trends for the period to 2030 (Reena R 2010). Some of the key elements are: increased student participation, increased percentage of women students, varied student population including international students, older students, part-time students, and other types, change in social base that will reduce inequality, access policies in favour of disadvantaged sections, internationally oriented academic professionals, more diversified and specialised academics and ever-expanding need of university teachers.

SWOT Analysis of Indian Higher Education System

SWOT analysis of Indian Education System based upon the data collected from the various stakeholders including students, parents, teachers, administrators was carried out and the results are given below.

Strengths and Weaknesses of Indian Higher Education System

The low cost of education in India and the quality education that the statutory bodies ensure when compared to developing countries are our major strengths. The diversity in environment, social and cultural heritage, high ethical values and rich traditions also make us unique. Moreover, the consultancy service offered to international students and the unique courses like the Ayurveda, Sanskrit, Yoga and Hindi developed by the traditional knowledge system enthuses many international students.

Even though there are plethoras of strengths, the existence of weakness in the Indian higher education system can never be left unnoticed. The complex and vague Faculty Regulatory Framework is one of the important issues. Decreasing public expenditure on education is another problem. The Indian first post-independence Education Commission recommended 6 per cent of the national income to be allotted as government expenditure on education. But now it lies between 1-2 per cent. Moreover, infrastructural and other facilities are not enough for research work at international level like very low level of Ph.D enrolment and lack of high quality researchers. Averse to interdisciplinary and multidisciplinary working, lack of early stage research experience, weak ecosystem for innovation and low levels of industry engagement are other pitfalls.

In addition to that, the capacity of India's institutions is very much limited to meet the growing demand for postgraduate education in emerging fields viz., Bio-technology, Oceanography, Nano Science, etc. Theoretical based education rather than practical based and the insufficiency of competent faculties in universities, colleges and professional institutions to meet the global challenges also remains as an obstacle. Caste reservation even in case of appointment of senior faculty members is another issue.

Opportunities to Indian Higher Education System

1. Core values which include contribution to national development, fostering global competencies among students, inculcating a value system among students, promoting the use of research and technology, and quest for brilliance.
2. Increased priority in research with research funding, top priority for government to drive innovation, supporting technology transfer, encouraging impact-driven research, institutions establishing bond with the industry, tie up between government and private sectors which create jobs and enhance employability across the globe.
3. Higher education sector with an immense opportunity for local and foreign investors.
4. Plan of central government to increase the quality of teaching and learning.

Threats of Higher Education System

1. Fake university syndrome with absence of accountability and lack of quality control.

2. Restrictions in the contributions of academic institutions for national development, research relevant to the local needs and for participation in strengthening of civil society.
3. Differentiation among the same degrees obtained from foreign universities, from costly private domestic institutions and from government funded institutions.
4. Incompetent faculty especially in the private sector.
5. Increasing interest of parents to get their children admitted to foreign educational institutions.

Positive Impact of Globalisation on Indian Education System

The major impact includes increased competition among educational institutions which will ensure better service at a low cost. It also reduces brain drain and graduates with specific skills ensure the development of better industry. It leads to rapid developments in technology and communications. Possibility of continuing eduction also ensures personnels with up to date knowledge and skills. Competition between foreign institutions with the local institutes enhances facilities and service standards. This also ensures sharing of knowledge and skills between institutes from different nations.

Negative Impact of Globalisation on Indian Education

Globalisation may help money minded private organisation to make education a lucrative business. High fees leading to poor access to quality of education adversely affects the education system. Social agenda of the welfare state will be lost and the education institutes guided by profit and market. This would result in commodification of education. Investment in technical courses aiming at more profit will increase at the expense of quality education and research which is important for creating and developing human resources. Corruption due to competition, false degrees and taking bribe to clear the examination may increase. Local institutes with limited capital could not face tough competition as certificates of foreign universities are valued more than locally available ones.

Conclusion

Globalisation in education at present is in favour of developed countries, of which USA is benefited the most. Absolute freedom enjoyed by the institutes and the surplus fund availability offer a positive edge to the US institutes. The US institutes attract students from all over the world due to their innovative attitude, excellent facility and better employment opportunities provided by the US environment. The US institutes are up to date in their curricula and they respond quickly to the market needs and less inclined to social commitments. German institutes adopted a mid path with social commitments as well as liberalisation to attract cross-border clients. India being highly populous could adopt the path shown by the US institutes to achieve quality in education in the highly liberalised global education market and at the same time need to adopt a path similar to the institutes in Germany. UGC in India need to brush up its policies and regulations to aid the growth of tertiary education in India with importance to research. Enhanced research funding may help the institutes in India to find a place for in lead tables.

With the tradition of social commitments and high population, well distributed educational institutes in India could overcome China and even the USA and attract a great number of cross-border students. There is an urgent need to address the deficiencies faced by our higher education institutes. If India could not manage the institutes in India with proper funding and support, it is not advisable to allow foreign universities to open campuses in India. Presence of foreign universities in India will increase competition with local institutes which are less equipped and with low esteem. This will wipe away our educational institutes in the flood created by well funded and well managed foreign institutes who do not have a social commitment to Indian population.

When institutions in India like *Takshasila, Vikramasila, Pallavi and Nalanda Vishvavidyalaya* were radiating the rays of higher education among the nations of home and abroad, there were no such institution elsewhere in the world. India needs to act quickly and undergo a thorough reform to bring our system of education to its past glory. National goals of education in India include 'Education for All and Life Long Learning', offering wider choice, flexibility, competition, democracy, equity for all, and higher standards to improve performance and efficiency. Our aim should be to reap the benefits of globalised education without moving from our national goals. Moving the thrust of education from theory based to practical oriented, reducing red tape, and speeding up official process to induce faculties to explore funding through nontraditional means will help the universities to enter into the lead tables through world class research publication. The universities are also required to make use of the benefits of advancements in the information and communication technology.

References

Ali, S. (2005). The influence of globalisation on the national education policies of developing countries. *Journal of Educational Research*, 8(1), 14-21. Available at: http://ecommons.aku.edu/pakistan_ied_pdck/121

Altbach, P. (2005) Academic challenges: the American professoriate in comparative perspective, A. Welch (ed.) *The Professoriate: Portrait of a profession*, Springer, Dordrecht, pp. 147-165.

Altbach, G. Philip, Liz Reisberg and Laura E. Rumbley (2009) Trends in Global Higher Education: Tracking an academic revolution, A Report Prepared for the UNESCO 2009 World Conference on Higher Education, Paris: UNESCO available at http://unesdoc.unesco.org/images/0018/001831/183168e.pdf

Beerkens, H.J.J.G. (2004) Global Opportunities and Institutional Embeddedness: Higher education consortia in Europe and Southeast Asia. Center for Higher Education Policy Studies, University of Twente. Accessed at http://www.utwente.nl/cheps/documenten/ thesisbeerkens.pdf

Bhushan, S. (2006) Foreign Education Providers in India: Mapping the extent of regulation. The Observatory on Borderless Higher Education. Accessed at www.obhe.ac.uk

Brown, P. & Hesketh, A. (2004) *The Mismanagement of Talent*. Oxford: Oxford University Press.

Brown, P., Lauder, H., Ashton, D. & Tholen, G. (2006) Towards a High-Skilled, Low-Waged Economy? A Review of Global Trends in Education, Employment and the Labour Market, in S. Porter and M. Campbell, (Eds) *Skills and Economic Performance*, 55-90. London: Caspian Publishing.

Brown, P. and Lauder, H. (2006) Globalisation, Knowledge and the Myth of the Magnet Economy, Globalisation, Societies and Education, 4(1), 25-57.

Brown P, Lauder H and Ashton D, (2006) Education, Globalisation and the future of Knowledge Economy, *European Educational Research Journal*, 7: 131-140

Brown, P., Lauder, H. and Ashton, D., (2008), Education, Globalisation and the Future of the Knowledge Economy, European Educational Research Journal, 7(2), 131-156

Cantwell B, (2015) Are International Students Cash Cows? Examining the Relationship Between New International Undergraduate Enrollments and Institutional Revenue at Public Colleges and Universities in the US, Journal of International Students, 5(4): 512-525
http://jistudents.org Volume 5•Issue 4 Peer-Reviewed Article ISSN: 2166-3750 Online

Crawford, P. J. (2003). Captive of the system: why governments fail to deliver on their promises- and what to do about it. Sydney: Richmond.

Currie, J. (2005) Globalisation's impact on the professoriate in Anglo-Amercian universities, in A. Welch (ed.) *The Professoriate: Portrait of a profession*. Springer, Dordrecht.

Davenport, T.H. (2005) The Coming Commoditization of Processes, *Harvard Business Review*, June, 101-108.

Drache, D. and Froese, M. (2005). Globalization and the Cultural Commons: Identity, citizenship and pluralism after Cancun. Research paper. Department of Political Science, York University, Canada.

Drucker, P. (1993) *Post-Capitalist Society*. Oxford: Butterworth-Heinemann

Erosa A, Cantos, T. and Koreshkova, T.A. (2010), How Important is Human Capital? A Quantitative Theory Assessment of World Income Inequality, Review of Economic Studies, 01: 1–32

Fisher, S. (2001). 'Remarks at IMF Summit in Yaoundé, Cameroon' Accessed at http://portal.org/ev.php.

Grewal, D.S. (2008). The World isn't Flat--It's networked http://www.guardian.co.uk/ commentisfree/2008/july/29/globalisation.globaleconomic/print p1

Guellec, D. and Cervantes, M. (2002) International mobility of highly skilled workers: From statistical analysis to policy formulation, in OECD, International Mobility of the Highly Skilled. OECD, Paris.

Henry et al.(2008).*The OECD Globalisation and Education*, Emerald Publishing Limited p 21

Kim B, Ying W, Pushnaham K et al (2015), *MOOCs and Educational Challenges around Asia and Europe*, KNOU Press Edr. Bowon Kim, Richmond.

Liu, N. and Liu, L. (2005) University rankings in China, Higher Education in Europe, 30 (2), pp. 217-227.

Loveland, E (2007) On a Learning Curve In: Robinson, S and Whitelaw, T.2007. Global Education A Complete Guide to Studying worldwide, pp. 1-4

Marginson, S. (2006) National and Global Competition in Higher Education, in H. Lauder, P. Brown

Ministry of Human Resource Development, Government of India 2011-12, Al India Survey of Higher Education, http://mhrd.gov.in/sites/upload_files/mhrd/files/statistics/ AISHE2011-12P_1.pdf

Natarajan, R. (2005) The role of technical education in enabling the creation of a knowledge economy and society: The Indian experience, in G. Jones, P. McCarney and M. Skolnik (eds.) *Creating Knowledge: Strengthening Nations: The changing role of higher education.* University of Toronto Press, Toronto, pp. 155-166.

National Science Board. Science and engineering indicators 2014. National Science Foundation. 2014; 1: 600 Available: http://www.nsf.gov/statistics/seind14/content/etc/ nsb1401.pdf.

Nigeria: Issues and Implications. *African Journal of Historical Science in Education.* Vol. 4 Nos 1&2

Okoli, N.J (2008) Globalisation and Inequality of Access to University Education in Nigeria: Issues and Implications. *African Journal of Historical Science in Education*. Vol. 4 Nos 1&2

Okoli NJ (2012), Effects of globalisation on education in Africa1983-2008, *Academic Research International,* Vol. 2, No. 1

Mok, K. H. and Lee, H. H. (2000). Globalisation or re-colonization: Higher education reforms in Hong Kong. Higher Education Policy, 13, 361-377.

Organization for Economic Cooperation and Development, OECD (2005). Education at a Glance. OECD, Paris.

Planning Commission,"12th Five Year Plan 2012-2017", Planning Commission, Government of India, Vol.-3, (2013).

Prakash, V. (2007) Trends in Growth and Financing of Higher Education in India, *Economic and Political Weekly* (August 4): 3249-3258.

Reena, R. (2008) Financing Education and Development in Eritrea – Some Implications,

Manpower Journal, 43(1):73-97.

Reich, R. (1991) *The Work of Nations*. New York: Simon & Schuster.

Raveender, R. Emerging trends of higher educaion in developing countries, ANALELE STIINTIFICE ALE UNIVERSITATII "ALEXANDRU IOAN CUZA" DIN IASI, Numar special Stiinte Economice 2010

Robertson, S.L. (2012) *Teachers' Work, Denationalisation, and Transformations in the Field of Symbolic Control: A Comparative Account*, published by the Centre for Globalisation, Education and Societies, University of Bristol, Bristol BS8 1JA, UK at: http://susanleerobertson.com/publications/

Singh, K. (2005). *Questioning Globalisation*, Madhyam Books, Delhi & Zed Books, London and New York.

Stiglitz, J. (1999). Knowledge as a global public good, in I. Kaul, I. Grunberg & M. Stern (eds.), *Global Public Goods: International cooperation in the 21st century*. Oxford University Press, New York, pp. 308-325

Stuen, E.T. Mobarak, A.M. Maskus, K.E. Skilled immigration and innovation: evidence from enrolment fluctuations in U.S. doctoral programmes. Econ J. 2012; 122(565): 1143–1176.

Siglitz, J. (2002). The subtle truth about Globalisation. http://portal.unesco.org/en/ev.php-URL_ID=6609&URL_DO=DOTOPIC& URL SECT.

Taylor, S. & Henry, M. (2000). Globalisation and educational policymaking: A case study. *Educational Theory*, 50(4), 487-491.www.thes.co.uk

Thomson Reuters InCites, U.S, Washington Post https://www.washingtonpost.com/apps/g/page/local/us-news-global-top-500-universities/1409/

Time, Asia's Great Science Experiment, *content.time.com/time/world/article/0,8599, 2047300,00.htm*

Venter, K., Ashton, D.N. & Sung, J. (2002) Education and Skills in the People's Republic of China: Employers' perceptions, 64. Leicester: ILO/CLMS, University of Leicester.

Vincent-Lancrin, S. (2004) Building capacity through cross-border tertiary education, paper prepared for the UNESCO/OECD Australia Forum on Trade in Educational Services,11-12 October 2004. Accessed at http://www.oecd.org/dataoecd/43/25/33784 331.pdf

World Bank data 2015, http://databank.worldbank.org/data/

SECTION II

Policy Crisis in Indian Higher Education

5.
Higher Education in the Context of Development

M. Kunhaman

Development: What is it? Whose, What Type and for Whom?

There has been no unanimity of views among development thinkers, scholars and policy-makers on the concept, source and measure of development. With the introduction of the Human Development Report by the UNDP since 1990, some degree of clarity has been brought about in the development literature. We say some degree as an over-all high HDI can camouflage deplorably low levels of HDI for specific socio-religious, cultural, racial or ethnic minorities. Also, a high per capita income with high degrees of inequality can unduly influence HDI. Hence, HDI has an inherent tendency to conceal inequities in the distribution of income and wealth. In this sense, the basic questions regarding concept, source and measure of development remain unresolved. None-the-less, the HD approach has the advantage of putting the human being at the centre of the development discourse and practice, both as the source and end of development. A further advance was made by conflating Human Rights and Human Development (vide the chapter by Amartya Sen in the Human Development Report, 2000). Though Sen does not postulate a causation between the two, the desirability of having / ensuring both was clearly established. Subsequent thinking made out a case for human rights to human development.

Development is a tricky, titillating question. Questions such as what is development, what type of development, development for whom, or whose development, etc. are yet to be settled. In the conventional sense, in which development was considered as a panacea for all human problems, and an open sesame to a country's progress and prominence, development was state-led and project-centric. A hegemonic group emerged and arrogated to itself the divine right to think for the people. Scholars thinking for the people, experts formulating programmes for the people, officials implementing programmes/ projects for the people, political parties undertaking people's struggles and lastly, and more dangerously, NGOs working for the people. People, a non-entity and an assumption, had no role in their own development. They were the objects of development. Gradually, they became the object of domination. Development became an instrument to silence and control and the seigniorial state and its footsoldiers and factotums became objects of veneration. People's thinking was appropriated. Their confidence was sapped. A pathological dependency syndrome was created and deeply entrenched in them.

Development is Dead

In the post-Second World War period, ironically, even as development was becoming a desideratum, and more significantly, an ideology, there were also scholars advocating not only alternative development, but also, more emphatically, alternative to development. This was based on the realisation that even if an economy's performance was stratospheric, that did not mean that everything was hunky-dory about society. It goes without saying that the devil is in the details (Stiglitz, 2012; Piketty, 2014). Some, more discerning thinkers and activists wrote the obituary and epitaph of development and started talking about the post-development era. The process was completed in the post-1989 period when the right moved farther to the right and the left moved to the centre of the political spectrum (Joseph A Buttigieg in Peter Mayo, 2015).

Lack of development is a symptom; not a cause. State has failed as a development agency. After all, state means power and development is not about power. People are demanding an agency / non-teleological role. The poor basically need emancipation from various sorts of domination, exploitation and oppression. They need freedom. And this needs liberty, individuality and dignity; and private property is the only means of ensuring these inalienable and parametric qualities. We need to go back to liberalism and classical individualism. The post-dirigiste era demands that the focus be on the individual. The individual must be enabled to achieve progress through the realisation of her / his full potential. The fact is that nobody can develop anybody. Empowerment through entitlement (to property) should be the datum on which to start. The state should undertake a programme of equal distribution of property. Then, it should leave the development field. A laissez faire state, encapsulated in the maxim "minimum state, maximum governance", defending the country and protecting the people is a prerequisite. People should be left free to go for any education they like to acquire entrepreneurial and occupational ability to participate in the competitive world to win success and live with decorum. And, in this, the state should play an enabling, rather than a leading role. In other words, they must get modern education and engage in gainful economic activities and participate in decision-making in every field and at all levels. Rising from subordination to equality with one another is what the poor require. And that calls forth acquiring leadership qualities and initiative. These are essential and possible as liberalisation and opening of the economy create numerous opportunities as never before. Programmes such as financial inclusion, right to education, the novel start-up eco-system and several other back-to-back reform measures visualised and pursued provide unprecedented openings. Aspirational mobility is the renewable energy for vulnerable groups to come out of marginality / exclusion. Missing the new opportunities will be a fatal default. The dialectical conflict between the controlling class and the aspirational class is the taproot of the new historical process. The aspirational class with its unmatched and unprecedented ability to access the social media can be expected to have the indefatigable strength and resilience to vanquish the controlling class zealously fixated with the status quo ante as well as revanchism to herald a new, luminiferous paradigm. The rising aspirational class is the new beacon of hope. And an inclusive meritocracy is the need of the age. Attempts at thwarting the flowering of individualism and putting the public sector on an even keel in the present situation can rebound and backfire.

Looked at in this perspective, basically, it is a question of freedom a la Amartya Sen (Development as Freedom; freedom from poverty, illiteracy, disease, shelterlessness, unfreedom, etc.).Without freedom, nobody can progress. Thus, inescapably, a paradigm shift is the need of the hour; going against the zeitgeist can be sometimes skating on thin ice.

Looking Ahead

In a globalised, i.e., networked, borderless world economy premised on technology, innovation, management and marketing in a legato manner, instrumental value of higher education, in every national economy context, inevitably, takes precedence over intrinsic significance. If it is utilitarianism, so be it. Knowledge economy, with its correlates knowledge society and knowledge workers and operating in an age of flexi-specialisation, requires its skill matrix and its constant upgradation, change and renewal so as to maintain competitiveness (both price and quality) as well as provide employment to an incrementally increasing labour force. Regular innovation is the name of the game.

A cognate issue pertains to the objective of education. Two points are pertinent here.

1. There cannot be a single objective for higher education. Rather, it should be multiple, and should comprise accessibility, affordability, diversity / inclusiveness, equity and quality. Syncretising or concantenating these is easier said than done. However, it bears special mention that an exclusive pursuit of quality / excellence to the neglect of others can be unacceptable and unethical in a diverse and unequal society.
2. Equally, the objective of education depends on the types of education: professional, technical, social sciences, humanities, etc. While the first two types have skill-building as their objective, the latter two should

aim at providing libratory / transformative education (of course, some of the social sciences disciplines also impart skills-analytical skills). Given these, rather than viewing it as a tweedledee-tweedledum situation, skill-building education and transformative / libratory education can move in tandem; a leg-up for one over the other can be counter-productive. Industry's software and university's thought ware should not be considered as mutually exclusive binaries.

Some basic issues besetting the field of higher education in India merits special consideration since it is a fast growing economy with a yawning skill-gap and rising demands for social transformation raised by some of the perpetually deprived social sections, desperate to catch at any straw. Our universities, a metonym for higher education, are still ruled by feudal minds. They lack democratic style of functioning. Democracy means three Ds: discussion, debate and dissent (Sen, 2006, 53). Myopic, narrow minds control the academia with the potential for enervating and eviscerating the larger social system. Student politics is almost dead. Free thought and free speech are anathema. We are increasingly becoming afraid of freedom. In other words, fear of freedom is the hallmark of those ensconsed in power. Parenthetically, it may be mentioned that powerful are fearful; the most powerful are the most fearful. Repoliticising the campus for reinvigorating its innards and for producing innovative and imaginative leaders whose absence can make the system sclerotic, is an absolute necessity. University students are citizens. Rulers have no right to deny freedom to them.

Presently, India is at an inflection point: it has a capitalist / modern basic structure with a feudal super-structure. For removing this paradox, revamping the academia is a prerequisite; using the past to stimulate the present and stoking contrapuntal currents of thought will be counter-productive and backward-looking. The challenge before the nation is to ensure quality higher education and make it accessible, affordable, equitable and inclusive. In a knowledge-capitalist economy, commoditisation of knowledge and the consequent emergence of a market for higher education cannot be decried and deprecated beyond a point. Of course, the field of higher education cannot be left for unbridled and unlimited capital accumulation. Similarly, the central capitalist tendencies, viz., concentration and centralisation of capital, are neither desirable nor permissible. We are simply repeating / echoing Marx when we say that forces of production always expand since such expansion always depends on the application of knowledge to resources and, knowledge has a tendency to perpetually develop. Hence, the role of knowledge in development needs no emphasis. Since higher education is the site of knowledge generation, collation (with value addition) and dissemination, it goes without saying that higher education is and should be the centerpiece of development.

Trends and Tendencies in Higher Education

Seven characteristics of higher education can be considered relevant.

1. Centrality of knowledge: Knowledge economy; knowledge society; knowledge workers.
2. Commodification of knowledge and commercialisation of education.
3. Knowledge explosion: Knowledge production is a systematic activity.
4. Superiorisation and inferiorisation of knowledge types.
5. Relevance of education: Edge of market relevance.
6. Social control through control of knowledge.
7. The alleged corporatisation of the university.

Objectives of higher education should be extrinsically and socially defined and determined. If society and market determine it, no alarm needs to be raised. Educationists' claim to do that is solipsistic and specious, to say the least. While the case for staying clear of party / partisan politics is unexceptionable, depoliticising the campus can be a misadventure and self-destructive. Freedom (of the individual), not the autonomy (of the university satraps) is the lifeblood of the academia.

Continiuing and Institutionalised Inequities

Given the upper castes' long legacy and pedigree in education and scholarship, their advantage in the academic sweepstakes should surprise nobody. They have unquestioned dominance in academic research and strategic decision-making. Dalits and adivasis have only nominal / passive presence in the academia. In faculty positions in higher education, dalits' and adivasis' shares are mere seven per cent and two per cent respectively while they form 16.6 per cent and 8.6 per cent respectively of the population of the country. In the academia, caste discriminations exist in overt and covert forms. Correlatively, in the media, the other site for ideas, there is near-total absence of the dalits and adivasis (excepting the social media). Thus, even in these fast-changing circumstances, the upper castes are able to maintain their lead. In fact, the upper caste front-benchers are not permitting the dalit / Adivasi back-benchers to move forward. Thus, marginalisation has become an inexorable and inviolable reality and a strong instrument for perpetuating upper caste domination in every field of socio-economic life.

The egregious, institutionalised inequities, characteristic of India's higher education system can be discerned from Table 5.1. The low presence of dalits and adivasis, the two stand-out examples in the field of higher education, can be seen in the low enrolment of students belonging to these groups in the higher educational institutions.

Table 5.1: SC/ST Population (2011 Census) and Their Respective Shares in Faculty Positions in Higher Educational Institutions

State	*Dalits*		*Adivasis*	
	Share in Population	*HE Faculty*	*Share in Population*	*HE Faculty*
Tamil Nadu	20.0	8.35	1.1	0.33
Utter Pradesh	20.7	5.7	0.60	0.31
Rajasthan	17.8	5.73	13.5	2.86
Punjab	31.9	3.96	..	0.16
West Bengal	23.5	5.49	5.8	0.77
Maharashtra	11.8	10.57	9.4	1.55
Kerala	9.1	2.7	1.5	0.21
Gujarat	6.7	4.79	14.8	3.62
Bihar	15.9	1.67	1.3	0.32
All India	16.6	6.95	8.6	1.99

Source: S. V. Narayan, All India Survey on Higher Education, Ministry of Human Resource Development, Govt. of India, 2015.

The Table 5.2 shows the gross under-representation of students; with the dalit students forming only 12.2 per cent and Adivasi students 4.4 per cent of total students in the country as a whole. The two Tables also show that India has to travel a long way in ensuring representation and diversity in the field of higher education. In an age when instrumental rationality supersedes intrinsic significance and when educational credentialism overwhelmingly determines one's chances in life, the abysmally low positions of these two groups, despite a plethora of affirmative actions and the policy of reservation pursued all these years, is testimony to the basic and chronic maladies afflicting our system. Besides, casteism and caste prejudices continue to dominate the academia. The impact of this situation is not easily and precisely commensurable; but it is conceivable to be far-reaching and deep-rooted, with the invidious subversion of the collective forward march of the societal order, inciting insidious, fissiparous tendencies. The present system is faulty, myopic and minatory. The higher education system is a patronage-dispensing system. How many selections/ appointments in our higher educational institutions, at present, take place for reasons of merit and competence? The present system of interviews must be abolished and an anonymous selection process must be put in place on the basis of an objectively and scientifically designed process based on attitude, aptitude and passion for academic pursuits. Pending that, a commission should be immediately constituted to study the situation in higher educational institutions with regard to both faculty selections and student enrolments.

Table 5.2: Enrolment of Dalit and Adivasi Students in Higher Education.

State	*Dalit*	*Adivasi*
Tamil Nadu	15.63	0.93
UP	14.91	0.60
Rajasthan	11.90	8.87
Punjab	12.26	0.28
West Bengal	16.08	2.86
Maharashtra	11.25	3.99
Kerala	7.02	1.01
Gujarat	7.23	7.37
Bihar	9.30	1.47
All India	12.28	4.44

Source: All India survey on Higher education 2012-1 3

Higher Education and Equality

It may be mentioned, en passant, that it is not possible to bring about economic equality through education; rather, education reproduces and reinforces the unequal economic structure. Education is not a leveler or equalizer; nor is it a seculariser. Establishing economic equality and secularism is a denouement of a political masterstroke geared to social reconstruction. More often than not, academia can throw spanner in the works. In social reconstruction, academia can, at best, be called to play an adjunct / supportive role. Proclamations made by the well-heeled mandarins of the academia to establish an equal / egalitarian society are a sham and perfidy, for what it means is formal equality (of opportunity, not of outcome). As Pierre Bourdieu rightly asserts, "...formal equality in a situation of real inequality favors' the dominant" (Bourdieu, 2005,225). These facts emphasise the need for state, political and social interventions for treating these deep-rooted maladies on a war footing.

Our universities, particularly state universities which are just plodding along and seldom in the idea loop, need an image makeover. The distillate of education is understanding / thinking. Just acquiring knowledge cannot be the sole or main objective of higher education when one thinks of societal transformation which also an inescapable demand is vociferously made by many an oppressed / depressed group. Knowledge can be a burden and dead-weight unless it leads to understanding and promotes thinking. Transformational education, in its teaching, study, learning and research, is a political activity. This is true even in the case of status quoists. For the oppressed, knowledge is not just for understanding the system, but, crucially, for designing counter-hegemonic strategies for changing it. A true learner's mind is an intellectual workshop. Thinking should be based on foresight and not on reality today. Potential, not the real, should be the guide-post. The dilettantes, really round pegs in square holes, must be shown the door so that we get rid of contretemps.

Rebooting and Repositioning the University

The above discussion points to the imperative for repositioning the fussy and involute university on the temporal continuum geared to producing not sluggards and somnambulists but agile entrepreneurs of various types and persuasions. A university, generally, contributes to knowledge, policy and practice. The shifting objective of education, mentioned above notwithstanding, the university today should be reorganised around certain parametric values such as liberty, equity, and justice. Unfettered freedom, the mainspring of ideas, should be the defining feature of the University. Academic programmes on the campuses should be unrestrained and uncontrolled. The state which is the eponym and the strongest instrument of repression and oppression, and has an insatiable propensity to hold the university in leash, should not meddle in academics (in administrative and financial matters, it must definitely make judicious, well-calibrated interventions). Unconstrained academic freedom calls forth anarchy and chaos. The campus should be, to recall the words of Kenneth Galbraith, "A functioning anarchy". Or, to put it in the words of Paulo Freire, "organized disorder" (Freire 1972, 37) should prevail on campuses so as to prepare a fertile terrain for the germination and surge of free thinking and free-wheeling discourses

The university should aim at producing not efficient administrators, but imaginative leaders. An administrator is today's person; a leader is tomorrow's. For an administrator, it is control; for a leader, it is change. Universities in developing countries, particularly in India, are faced with the double whammy of increasing control and diminishing freedom. Hence, the trade-off between freedom and power. Where one rises, the other falls. This is a serious issue. Any knee-jerk attempt, sans foresight and forethought and based purely on expediency, to reconcile the two or strike an optimum will come to naught and make mincemeat of their vaulted academic programmes.

A related point is the undue emphasis on relevance. Universities should be disabused of their myopic insistence on immediate relevance (of curricula or research), either social or market, in setting academic agenda as well as funding priorities; else, they will be short-selling themselves and ignominiously bowing out of the academic firmament. In many a case, funding agencies, by the power of purse, set the academic agenda, subverting or inverting priorities of the academia, killing, in the process, freedom and creativity of academics. Functioning under duress, and being distracted by red herrings, universities are inexorably subject to atrophy and the resulting dystopia, forces them to throw to the wind whatever vision and mission they might have started with. Being put on the backfoot, they resort to stonewalling on the issues of quality and equity of higher education.

Vanishing Teacher and Rising Career Researcher

Another area of serious concern is the professionalisation of teaching. Mostly, teaching has become slide-reading, rendering reading new books and updating domain knowledge unnecessary. Hence, teaching has become mechanical, stale, insipid and uninspiring. Proud, bold and self respecting teachers are becoming a vanishing species. Position-seeking teachers are replacing them. Devaluing the teacher can lead to stasis and block speciation resulting, invariably, in academic cretinism. Ultra-conservative modernism cannot be permitted to replace time-tested, creative intellectual practices. At the same time, it must be admitted that teaching without research becomes dull and drab. Hence, the new world needs a new breed of academics who can conflate teaching and research praxiologically.

Foreign Collaborations

Universities in developing countries must explore the possibilities of collaboration with Ivy League universities in the West. It goes without saying that those universities maintain high quality, a reason why persons with their degrees get appointed in key academic and plum policy / advisory positions in developing countries. These persons are invariably from the upper crest of society, for the poor, these universities are off-bound. The degrees of front-ranking universities must be made available to less rich persons through franchisee, twinning and such other programmes. Such programmes can benefit both individuals and universities in the receiving countries. Universities should epitomise universality of knowledge; they should not be distinguished as national and foreign. Students and faculty should be footloose, internationally mobile. In a highly (not fully) globalised world, global mobility should be the esprit de corps of rhizomatic, meshworked universities. Rather than functioning in silos, universities should be part of the global academic chain, thus, forming consortia, consortia of consortia and academic corridors. Thinking, ideas and perspectives must flow without respecting national boundaries and local parochialisms which make students strain at the leash. In such a milieu, shunning collaboration to a default and in an ostrich-like manner entails a race to the bottom, rather than a futurity race.

There is nothing wrong in each university developing distinct epistemology, philosophy, ontology, methodology and theory. In fact, such attempts must be the sine qua non of a university, since indigenous / in situ knowledge reserves, rather than being effaced / ignored and scoffed at, can be resuscitated, built up on, theorised and tested using inductive method and finally exteriorised. Rather than theory testing, theory building (through different conceptualisation, problematisation and strategisation), must be attempted with the scaffolding of local / indigenous knowledge system, resulting not only in new modes of intellectual enquiry but also reviving and strengthening of the pride and self confidence of the social groups who's inherited knowledge is so used. Thus, simultaneous interiorisation and exteriorisation of knowledge dynamise a society with multiplier effects and beneficial spin-offs.

Repositioning the university requires a relook at the entire field of education, primarily at the school level. In the pre-reform period, poverty was the all-consuming problem, what was widely distributed through the government and aided institutions was low quality education which did not equip the educated to face the challenges of life. Of course, the well-off got high quality education which was, in fact, reserved for them, which made them eligible, qualified and competent for higher, decisive positions. Realising this ruling class perfidy, today, even low-income parents, whose patience is wearing thin, are withdrawing the children from low-quality government schools and sending them to private English medium schools. This is a promising sign, indicative of the new and forward-looking attitude of parents, who not only aspire for a better future for their children, but, more importantly, also want them to compete in the highly competitive, meshworked (Escobar 2014) world economy which is increasingly unfolding before them, with tantalising opportunities. Declining poverty triggers their thinking about tomorrow. Poverty, after all, deprives people of optimism and expectations, encrusting in them fatalism and desperation. There are tell-tale signs that in contradistinction to this, people with new imageries are envisioning a future that is brighter and more promising than today. The parochialism and localism of entrenched interests now preventing the upward mobility of vulnerable communities must be opposed tooth and nail as these interests want the students belonging to these communities only to shout slogans, paste posters and get beaten up by police while conducting strikes.

These leaders, claiming to be the saviours of the oppressed send their own children to English medium schools and Ivy League universities in the West. Their bluff should be called. The students from oppressed communities must study English, study in English, or not study at all. If they could not get quality education in the pre-liberalisation period, it was their misfortune; if they do not try to get it now, is their mistake. In the new world order, they must redefine themselves. If they think their problem is that they are poor, they must become rich; if they think their problem is that they are labourers, they must become capitalists. How? This is not a capitalist manifesto, but the text of an address at an international seminar on higher education. However, reading the history of capitalism can be rewarding.

Today, children need nutrition and quality schools. The youth want quality higher education, gainful employment and bright career prospects. Thus, there has been an exponential growth of aspirational mobility among them. Education is the fulcrum of aspirations. No wonder we are witnessing an unprecedented demand for education which can be ignored only at our peril. And, consequently, we will be doing great injustice to the present and future generations by not repositioning the university and setting new benchmarks in keeping with the dynamic transformation taking place all around. It is time we tore asunder the antediluvian ideological blinkers of a pre-modern ruling class (belonging to the Right, Centre, and Left) and thwarted the unrelenting attempts pursued through subtle and subterranean means, to turn the university into a crematorium of liberty.

It may also be germane to point out in this context that every mode of production faces two over-riding objectives of education: One, at its progressive and ascending phase, and the other in its regressive and declining phase. An objective geared to fighting archaic and feudal values must be transmogrified into one promoting values, practices and skills of a modern society.

Concluding Observations

This paper emphasised the need for taking a relook at higher education in the development context. Higher education cannot have a unifocal objective; rather, it should envision a package of objectives such as accessibility, affordability, inclusiveness / diversity, quality and equity, pursued not in a staccato but in a syncretic mode. The purpose of higher education depends on the levels and types of tertiary sector education. While technical and professional education must meet the demands of a growing economy, the university sector must provide mainly liberatory and transformative education for, alongside promoting forces of production (through the application of knowledge to resources), questions pertaining to production relations must be addressed with abiding seriousness and unswerving commitment, lest social resistance to unchanging production relations should be the inevitable consequence. Higher education for the dominated is a liberatory instrument, rather than a cosy delectation. It will inescapably lead to run-ins between the dominating and the dominated.

University in India needs repositioning and new bench-marking. It continues to have its feudal moorings with the upper castes dominating faculty and powerful positions and controlling student enrolment. Dalits and adivasis have only a token / feeble presence. Feudal minds control our higher education system and impose their Victorian moralism. Using the academia as a panopticon, they impose, with the repressive state power behind them, archaic views on the campuses, thwarting academic freedom and democratic functioning. Freedom for questioning, the renewable energy of a university, is crushed with demands for obedience and respect. The present system of faculty selection and appointments is defective; it needs to be abolished. Interviews which are often in reality, after selection, should be done away with and an anonymous selection system put in place. The prevailing patronage-dispensing system should yield place to a quality / competence-recognising system. Anarchy should be brought back to campuses to foster free thinking, crystal-gazing and flight of imagination.

Regarding equity, it bears mentioning that, through formalised / instititionalised education, equality cannot be brought about. Higher education reproduces and accentuates the existing unequal structure. Higher education is neither an equaliser nor a seculariser. For attaining equality and secularism, strong political and societal action is called for. Academics should not be asked to bite what they cannot chew. Nor can they be asked to heal ailments with which they themselves are afflicted. Also, knowing far better, they may not be prepared to shoot themselves in the foot by advocating measures for revamping the academia.

The academic should be clearly delineated from the social. The disjuncture of the two is important for policy reasons. The social should not be left to the academic hucksters strongly and deeply moored in medieval muck. As the university is part of society, more often than not, much of the social garbage is thrown on to the campus, or even into the class room. The feudal and ultra upper caste supremacists, who rule the roost in the academia are the trusted handlers of social garbage. To be sure, it is unrealistic to expect to accomplish all these in one fell swoop; but given social determination, it is not impossible.

The paper has also presented a kaleidoscopic view of the evolution of the development discourse. It takes the position that development as state-led and project-centric is passé. Development is dead. The focus should be on the individual with the underpinnings of liberalism and individualism. Development should be innovation-driven, rather than state (i.e., bureaucratically) driven. State is an instrument of oppression irrespective of whether, politically, it is led by right, left, or center. In the field of development, state is a miserably failed, cranky institution. Hence, its place is in the dust bin of history. Minimalist state and maximalist individual must be the new credo.

Decentring the state and recentring the individual brook no delay. Thus, the individual becoming the subject of development, rather than its object, and the architect of her destiny is the crux of the matter. The role of the state is that of an umpire and not of a player. The system should benefit from individual achievements rather than the other way around. With socialism nowhere in sight and nobody promising or committed to bringing it about, this is the only positive sum game one can think of. Back to Adam Smith? We keep our fingers crossed. Finally, as we still need the academia, warts and all, purging it of visceral negativism and diffidence and putting it on a recovery track in step with a fast-growing economy, and, ultimately, making both grow in simpatico with each other are not an option but an urgent necessity.

References

Bourdieu, Pierre (2005). *The Social Structures of Economy.* Polity USA

Escobar, Arturo (2014). "Other Worlds are (Already) Possible. Self–Organization, Complexity and Post Capitalist Cultures" In Savyasaachi and Ravikumar (Eds) *Social Movements. Transformative Shifts and Turning Points.* Routledge.

Freire, Paulo (1970). *Pedagogy of the Oppressed.* Penguin Books.

Narayan, S.V. (2015). "Higher Education is Still a Bar Too High for Muslims, Dalits." The WIRE. http//thewire.in10214/higher – education is – still – a bat-too – for – muslims – dalits/

Piketty, T. (2014).*Capital in the Twenty-First Century.* Harvard University Press.

Rahnema, M. (1997). *The Post Development Reader.* Zed Book.

Sen, Amartya (2006). *Identity and Violence.* Penguin Books.

Sen, Amartya (1999). *Development as Freedom.* Oxford University Press.

Stiglitz, Joseph (2012). *The Price of Inequality. How Today's Divided Society Endangers Our Future.* W.W. Norton and Company.

UNDP (2000). Human Development Report.

6.
Diversity and Institutional Discrimination in Higher Education in India

C. M. Malish and Nidhi S. Sabharwal

According to Trow (2006), higher education system is in its elite stage when Gross Enrolment Ratio (GER) is below 15 per cent, system is massified when GER crosses 15 per cent and universalised when GER crosses 50 per cent. In 2002-2003 with 9.95 million enrolment and GER of 8.97 per cent Indian higher education was in elite stage (Varghese, 2015). In last one decade and so, higher education has experienced massive expansion. In 2014-15, with 32 million enrolment and GER of 23 per cent, India was in its early stage of massification and second largest higher education system in the world (MHRD, 2015). Private sector played crucial role in transition from elite to massification. There are two inter-connected processes that contributed to expansion of the system: 1). Government initiatives to expand the system and to increase GER, 2). Rising aspiration level of population to become college educated. These two processes are intrinsically linked to globalisation and economic liberalisation. As Altbach (2004, p.3) rightly put it, "All of the contemporary pressure on higher education, from the pressure of massification to the growth of private sector, are the result of globalisation."

The higher education sector in India has experienced an unprecedented expansion in the recent decades. The expansion of the sector is a result of increasing social demand and expanding supply conditions. The expansion has been accompanied by diversification of the sector in terms of types of institutions, sources of financing, the nature of programmes of study offered and social composition of students. Higher education institutions have become diverse in terms of socio-economic backgrounds of student population. It implies that more number of non-elite and non-traditional social and income group learners is entering into higher education system. Today students belonging to different religions and lower castes, and poor families, and rural areas, and speaking minority languages co-exist with students from high caste and rich families and urban backgrounds. Non-traditional social groups include historically marginalised groups such as Scheduled Castes (SCs), Scheduled Tribes (STs) and Other Backward Classes (OBCs).

While diversity provides an opportunity to experience richness and variety, it also poses challenges of learning and living in a socially inclusive way (Thorat and Sabharwal, 2013). As students are coming to campus with varying socio-economic and cultural background, competency levels, pre-college credentials and aspiration levels, campuses are now becoming a site of political contestation, assertion and assimilation of identities. As informed by the vast literature, education can serve as source for both social reproduction and social transformation. Social transformation potential of education cannot be achieved unless and until there is concerted effort and approach to education process. The role of state through social policies and programmes is crucial here. Since no education process is 'neutral' (Freire, 1972), how higher education is experienced by diverse student body in a massified era is of pivotal significance. Given the social hierarchy and social division that exist in India, how do diverse student groups experience higher education campuses is an important aspect of equity dimensions in higher education (HE).

Does increasing student diversity make an impact on higher education campuses? Are higher education institutions (HEIs) responding to changing nature of student diversity? This chapter attempts to answer these crucial questions by analysing nature of discrimination in HEIs and how it is addressed institutionally. This chapter is based on large scale national study carried out in 12 higher education institutions located in six states, such as Bihar, Delhi, Karnataka, Kerala, Maharashtra and Uttar Pradesh. Case study states were selected in such a way that they represent different regions of the country and stages of socio-economic and educational development. Case study institutions include different types of HEIs such as university, institute of national importance, institution offering traditional arts and science courses and professional courses and different types of colleges such as Government college, private aided college and constituent college of university.

Following a mixed methodology approach data / information has been gathered from a wide variety of sources. It includes secondary data from administrative records and primary data from students, faculty members, institutional leaders, faculty in-charge of cells / committees dealing with student welfare and student grievances. Over 3200 student questionnaires were administered among the students. Additionally, separate focus group discussions were conducted among the student social groups such as SCs, STs, OBCs, women and minorities. In-depth interviews were carried out among the faculty members, faculty in-charges of cells and committees, institutional leaders such as heads of the departments, deans, wardens of hostels, principals of colleges and vice-chancellors of university.

Approach to Discrimination in Higher Education

Discrimination is a complex notion in education. How the term discrimination is defined and approached is largely dependent on disciplinary canons and traditions one follows. Till mid of the 20th century, discrimination was debated in terms of prejudices (McCrudden, 1982). Discrimination was thus viewed as a manifestation of that prejudices. Here prejudice denotes psychological attribute of an individual. Later, concept of prejudice was found to be inadequate in explicating structural roots of discrimination. Studies on racial relations in USA particularly critical race theory have greatly contributed to radical thinking about discrimination.

In 1960s, UNESCO Convention against Discrimination in Education initiated a global debate on discrimination in education and attempted to define discrimination in educational context. According to convention, 'discrimination' includes any distinction, exclusion, limitation or preference which, being based on race, colour, sex, language, religion, political or other opinion, national or social origin, economic condition or birth, has the purpose or effect of nullifying or impairing equality of treatment in education" (article 1, UNESCO, 1960). Though it is applicable to all levels of education, major consideration was school education as higher education system was then in the early stage of expansion even in the rich countries. International Convention for Elimination of all forms of Racial Discrimination (ICERD) in 1969 and Convention of Elimination on all forms of Discrimination Against Women (CEDAW) in 1979 followed the same approach to define discrimination. Close reading of the definition of discrimination implies that action which is intended to have a negative effect and not intended but has a negative effect on certain groups is considered discriminatory. Similarly, definition explicitly and implicitly challenged then dominant approach to discrimination, i.e., prejudiced discrimination.

As higher education system expanded across the globe, discussion on discrimination was extended to higher education. In higher education, discrimination can take different forms. Two important forms are individual discrimination and institutional discrimination (Pincus, 1996). Individual discrimination is related to behaviour of an individual. Individual discrimination can be overt and covert. While overt forms of discrimination is visible forms of discrimination such as derogatory remarks, covert forms of discrimination are hidden. The notion of micro-aggression that was put forwarded by critical race theorists captures essence of covert discrimination. Daniel Solo´rzano, Miguel Ceja, and Tara Yosso (2001) define micro-aggression as "subtle insults (verbal, nonverbal, and / or visual) directed toward people of color, often automatically or unconsciously" (as cited in Rasmussen and Salhani, 2010, p.501).

Discriminatory attitudes, behaviours, and actions of individuals are examples of direct forms of discrimination. This form of discrimination is comparatively easy to identify. But indirect forms of discrimination are difficult to capture. Let us take the example of labour market discrimination. Thorat and Attewell (2007) based on correspondence methodology showed that in India disadvantaged groups are less likely to get interview call despite they have equal qualification as of their upper caste counterparts. Authors of this study sent job applications to employer with different names with identical qualification. Since employers can make a better guess about social group origin of applicants from names (ex: Muslim) and surnames (i.e. caste names), lower rates of employer response to lower castes and minority is seen as a manifestation of discriminatory recruiting practice. This is a direct form of discrimination. On the other hand, employer's reliance on referral system for recruitment is an indirect form of discrimination (McCrudden, 1982). McCrudden elaborates that when referral system is followed, applicant has to be referred by the employees of the firm in order to be considered for job interview. Since representation of disadvantaged groups is negligible in workforce of corporate and private firms, potential candidates from disadvantaged groups are less likely to get a reference from current employees. Thus, applicants belonging to 'advantaged' groups get undue advantage in recruitment process. Obviously 'disadvantaged' groups are less likely to have social network with employees belonging to advantaged social groups. Here selection process is fair and applicants are not discriminated during interviews. But criterion for reference put a bar on potential applicants from disadvantaged social groups. Therefore, it is an indirect form of discrimination.

Many studies have cited instances of overt form of discrimination and micro-aggression against SCs and STs in Indian campuses (Ovichegan, 2013; Rao, 2013; Sukumar, 2008; Malish, 2013; Malish & Ilavarasan, 2016; Sabharwal & Thorat, 2014; Sabharwal & Malish, 2016b). Some of the examples of discrimination against historically marginalised groups such as SCs and STs are as follows. Students belonging to SCs and STs are referred to by derogatory names such as 'reservation category', 'cata students' and 'SHED'. 'Cata students' and 'SHED' (SHED is an abbreviation of Scheduled Castes and Tribes) is a short form used to call SC and ST students in a demeaning and dehumanising way. Cracking caste based jokes is another form of discriminatory practice that exists in campus. It often gets percolated into class room transactions in the form of being labelled as a reserved category in class and receiving lower academic support in comparison to other students (Sabharwal and Malish, 2016c). In some colleges, caste category is mentioned in student identity cards. As a result, they have to carry their caste tag from admission to till they exit the college. There is a delay in allotting supervisors for Ph.D students belonging to SCs and STs. Similarly, faculty members refuse to guide students from SCs and STs. Unequal grading and distribution of internal marks is another form of discrimination. Caste stereotypes and discriminatory attitude of faculty members such as belief 'that reservation policies has deteriorated the quality and standards in higher education and disadvantaged groups have poor IQ' is another manifestation of discrimination.

Another form of discrimination is that of institutional discrimination. Here focus is on how institutions produce and reproduce social inequalities through their every day practices. Institutional discrimination refers to policies of institutions and behaviour of people who implement policies and control institutions which often appears as neutral but has a negative and harmful effect on certain social groups (Pincus, 1996). Unlike individual discrimination, institutional discrimination is difficult to identify since it is ingrained in the ways in which institution functions. Since it is a part and parcel of institutional culture evolved over a period of time, discriminatory actions are often seen as neutral and normal. These cultural norms are felt when someone tries to break the norm. Unless and until it is not broken, presence of cultural norms is invisible though all are adhered to it. In other words, 'business as usual' approach of institutions often conceals discriminatory institutional practices. Forms of institutional discrimination include insensitivity of institutional leaders towards disadvantaged students and dysfunction of institutional mechanisms to protect students from discrimination. Here not solely the intention but impact determines the prevalence of discrimination. Institutional discrimination is one of the least explored forms of discrimination in HE in India. This chapter attempts to fill that gap by providing nuances of institutional discrimination in HEI in India.

Initial Days' Experience

How diverse student body experiences academic and social life of campus during initial days of admission is an important indicator of how conducive and receptive is institutional culture towards disadvantaged social groups. The correlation coefficients for initial days experience in Table 6.1 indicates that students from the socially excluded groups such as the scheduled castes, and scheduled tribes felt unwelcomed; felt nervous; were unable to form peer group and it was hard for them to adjust.

Table 6.1: Correlation between Initial Days Experience and Social Group belonging

Initial Days Experience	*General*	*OBC*	*ST*	*SC*
I felt welcomed	.089**	-.052**	-0.018	-.040*
I felt nervous and under-confident	-0.022	-0.033	.038*	.055**
I found it difficult to form peer group	-0.019	-0.029	.036*	.047**
I felt I was deliberately ignored	-.041*	0.009	0.026	0.031
It was hard to adjust	-0.006	-.037*	.049**	0.031
This College has a lot of tension around social differences and divisions	0.022	-.060**	.065**	0.014
I was searching for students of my background to avoid feeling of out of place	-0.028	-0.005	.051**	0.014
It was difficult to follow the classroom teaching	-.045*	0	.042*	.038*
Difficulty in dealing with the subjects	-.036*	0	.040*	0.027

Source: Sabharwal and Malish (2016c). P 101
* Significant at 5 per cent level.
** Significant at 10 per cent level

The OBC and general categories, on the other hand, as compared to those of their SC and ST counterparts had a good initial day experience. The other backward classes, although felt unwelcomed but they did not find it hard to adjust (similar general category students) as indicated by the correlation coefficients in Table 6.1. It is to be noted that at aggregate level, OBCs are the single largest social group in campuses. In Bihar, Kerala and Maharashtra, OBC account for more than half of the respondents. It reflects emerging dynamics of higher education in India. Since most of the elite upper caste and general category has withdrawn from arts and science public institutions, OBCs are now enjoying benefit of being numerically dominant status earlier enjoyed by general category.

In terms of academic adjustments, students from the SC / ST social group found it difficult to follow the classroom teaching and dealing with the subjects. These results indicate that these students had difficulty in adjusting with social, cultural and academic life of college. For the students specifically from the scheduled tribe groups, a positive correlation coefficient on searching for students from their own background to avoid feeling of 'out of place' is, perhaps, a coping mechanism to feeling unwelcomed in initial days.

Group discussions with students indicate that low competency in English language, financial problems, poor information about student support system and difficulty to form peer group are the major obstacles SCs and STs face during initial days. A feeling of 'being a fish out of water' aptly captures the initial days experience of SCs and STs. It was found that this feeling was much higher among the SCs and STs in elite engineering college than arts and social science institutions. Drawing from Reay Crozier and Clayton (2009), experience of SCs, STs and sections of OBCs in elite institutions can be better captured by the phrase "strangers in paradise".

Two of the important initiatives that reflect the institutional receptivity and commitment towards the student diversity are that of organisation of orientation programme and welcome party for the newly admitted students. As we can see in Table 6.2, more than one third of the students did not get an invitation for official orientation programme organised by the institutions. One can also see that compared to general category, higher share of SCs, STs and OBCs did not get an invitation for orientation programme.

Table 6. 2: Invitation for Orientation Programme (%)

	Were you invited for an orientation programme during initial days?		
Social Group	***Yes***	***No***	***Total***
SC	59.9	40.1	100.0
ST	56.8	43.2	100.0
OBC	61.5	38.5	100.0
GENERAL	70.5	29.5	100.0
Total	64.6	35.4	100.0

Source: Sabharwal and Malish (2016a)

Similar trend is visible in the case of attending welcome party during initial days (Table 6.3). There are two issues. Firstly, higher share of general category students attended welcome party compared to SCs, STs and OBCs. Secondly, half of the SCs, STs and OBCs did not get an opportunity to attend welcome party. Given the fact SCs and STs have lower levels of social and cultural capital required to sustain in higher education campus, these institutional practices may have adverse affect on these groups.

Table 6.3: Welcome Party at the Time of Joining (%)

	Did you have a welcome party at the time of joining?		
Social Group	***Yes***	***No***	***Total***
SC	48.50	51.50	100.00
ST	49.00	51.00	100.00
OBC	49.10	50.90	100.00
GENERAL	61.90	38.10	100.00
Total	54.10	45.90	100.00

Source: Sabharwal and Malish (2016a)

Awareness about Cells and Committees on Student Welfare and Grievances

There are many mechanisms and structures existing in campuses to deal with welfare of diverse student groups. Some of the mechanisms are mandatory as per UGC norms such as SC-ST cell, equal opportunity cell, anti-sexual harassment cell and anti-ragging cell. These committees and cells consist of a faculty-in charge and other faculty members as members of committee. They are expected to address variety of issues and problems faced by student groups and to evolve policies and practices to facilitate the social inclusion and academic integration and hence higher education success of beneficiary student groups. One can see from Table 6.4 that, awareness about different types of institutional mechanism and its role is poor among the actual beneficiary groups. Awareness about where and whom to contact in case of a complaint is also poor among SCs and STs (Table 6.5). Comparatively lower awareness among the disadvantaged groups who are actual target group of these initiatives indicates alarming situation in HE.

Table 6. 4: Awareness about the Cell/ Committee and its Role (%)

	I know about the cell	*Total*	*Women*	*SC*	*ST*
1	Equal opportunity office	37.2	38.5	35.4	26.6
2	Anti-ragging cell	73.5	73.4	69	42.6
3	Anti-sexual harassment cell / women cell	61.3	62.5	57.9	41.2
4	Discipline committee	61.6	63.1	57.1	36
5	Student welfare cell	62.7	63.6	56.5	35.5
6	Career guidance cell	50.8	52.1	46.2	32.4
7	Placement cell	45.5	46.7	41.7	28.3
8	Student grievance redressal cell	40.6	39.1	38.2	25.5
9	Minority welfare cell	29.0	29.7	27.9	14.5

Source: Sabharwal and Malish (2016c). P 158

Equal opportunity office (EOC) is conceived as an umbrella organisation to deal with specific challenges faced by disadvantaged groups in colleges and universities. It can be seen that majority of the beneficiary groups are unaware about faculty involved with EOC (Table 6.6). Interestingly, comparatively higher share of general category is aware about faculty involved with EOC.

Table 6.5: Awareness about Where and Whom to Contact in Case of Complaint (%)

	I know Table where and whom to contact in case of complaint	***Total***	***Women***	***SC***	***ST***
1	Equal opportunity cell	24.8	22.1	24.2	14.4
2	Anti-ragging cell	57.9	57.9	57.2	32.8
3	Anti-sexual harassment cell / women cell	48.3	47.3	45	31.9
4	Discipline committee	41.1	40.4	37.8	22.7
5	Student welfare cell	46.7	46.8	41.4	23.6
6	Career guidance cell	38.1	37.1	32.7	18.2
7	Placement cell	35.6	33.9	29.7	17.7
8	Student grievance redressal cell	31.3	31.6	27.7	21.2
9	Minority welfare cell	17.8	16.7	13.5	5.5

Source: Sabharwal and Malish (2016c). P 158

Table 6.6: I know the Faculty Involved in the Equal Opportunity Cell (%)

Social Group	***Yes***	***No***	***Total***
SC	18.5	81.3	100
ST	9.7	90.3	100
OBC	15.9	83.7	100
General	22.6	77.4	100
Total	18.4	81.4	100

Source: Sabharwal and Malish (2016c). P 158

Remedial coaching is one among the schemes to facilitate success of disadvantaged students and equip them to stand academically at par with others. It is clear from that Table 6.7 that large share of students is unaware about the remedial and bridge courses available in their institutions. Higher share of SCs and OBCs are unaware about the remedial classes.

Table 6.7: Awareness about Bridge / Remedial Coaching among the Students (%)

Are you aware of Bridge / Remedial / Add-on / Enrichment Courses offered by your college?			
Social Group	***Yes***	***No***	***Total***
SC	38.20	61.80	100.00
ST	43.90	56.10	100.00
OBC	38.50	61.50	100.00
General	40.80	59.20	100.00
Total	39.70	60.30	100.00

Source: Sabharwal and Malish (2016a)

Interviews with institutional leaders clearly show that there is a lack of adequate understanding about the need for special efforts to facilitate academic and social integration of disadvantaged students especially during initial days. Firstly, there is a resistance to fully acknowledge the changing nature of student diversity and evolve new practices to meet the emerging scenario. Secondly, many of the institutional leaders are non-supportive to idea of reservation in higher education. When enquired about policies of inclusion, the head of social science department in one of the selected HEI responded immediately: "I do not have much interest in the policies of inclusion because it is tertiary, it is university and that is enough." It is clearly indicative of dominant attitude of institutional leaders about the educational inclusion of disadvantaged.

On our questions to idea of student diversity and inclusion in elite engineering college, one professor who holds a senior academic position commented: "I have 16 years of experience here. I didn't see any discrimination here. We did not bother about the reservation quota; actually we didn't check what has happened to the reservation quota (students). For us all of them are students, there is no diversity among them. But peoples are there for checking these sorts of things; they are doing research related to this. Lot of papers and social studies are there relating to this. As a Dean I didn't check these sorts of things."

In fact, the selected elite engineering college in the study is one of the most diverse higher education campuses in India. But student diversity is not recognised there as an important feature of campus. According to institutional leaders across the case study institutions, diversity associated discrimination is non-existing in their own institutions. They mostly discard any possibilities of discrimination in their college or their department. However, some of them agree that discrimination exists in 'other states', 'other colleges' and 'other departments' in their college. In a nutshell, according to institutional leaders there are no instances of caste and ethnicity based discrimination in their institution and extremely rare and isolated incident if any, exists does not require any attention. They charge fault with media for making 'exaggeration of small incidents'. However, majority is not denying the possibilities of discrimination in higher education institutions except 'ours'.

Interview with faculty in-charge of cells clearly demonstrated that with few exceptions cells and committees are mostly dysfunctional in colleges and universities. Though it is a committee, most of the cells are running as 'one man show' with inadequate support from their own faculty colleagues and administration. Most of the cells are in redressal mode and it acts as and when there is a complaint. Proactive engagement is largely missing. Only exception is anti-ragging cell. It was also found that there is sheer lack of guidelines to run the cells. Poor understanding of larger significance of these cells and committees further acts as an obstacle. More importantly, there is no institutional level planning, monitoring and evaluation of overall activities of cells and committees. Each cells and activities are functioning as water tight compartments. There is no coordination between various cells which look after related issues.

What We Learn from Initial Days Experience and Institutional response to Diversity?

There is a greater agreement among the scholars that first year is a 'critical year' for student life as it determines major decision making of students to stay and leave campus and student success (Astin, 1993; Tinto, 1988; 2006; Trotter and Roberts, 2006; Pasceralla and Terenzini, 1991; Rayle and Chung, 2007; Yorke and Longden, 2008). It was also empirically verified that first six weeks in college in first semester is most crucial (Daubman, Williams, Johnson and Dan, 1985). However, studies in this direction have not yet begun in India. Our analysis shows that institutions fail to provide opportunities for diverse student groups to socially and academically integrate with institution. The fact that higher proportion of students belonging to SC and STs has poor initial day experience is a convincing example that institutions are less sensitive to marginalised social groups. As a result, disadvantaged students are disproportionally denied the opportunity to integrate with social and academic life of campus. This is a clear evidence of institutional discrimination that exists in HE campuses.

Why institutional mechanisms fail to address the concerns of disadvantaged students? In fact, institutional leaders and teachers are not adequately sensitised to various forms of social and academic challenges faced by diverse students. As a result, institution as a system and its major stakeholders do not feel they need to play a serious role. One can see that ideologies of merit winning over ideologies of social justice is a major driving force of affirmative action policies. Equity is narrowly defined in terms of provision of access or providing admission. As noted by Tawney (1964, pp. 102–03), "equality of opportunity depends not simply on the removal of disabilities but also creation of abilities". Instead of addressing structural roots of educational inequality, institutions find faults with affirmative action and competency levels of students. Social and academic challenges are merely seen as a problem of students and their inability to adjust with new environment. This blaming the victim approach does not get along with perspectives of equity in higher education.

The situation discussed above leads us to look into deeper structure and process of institutions. Therefore, notion of institutional culture found to be effective tool to understand deep-rooted structure of institution. Swidler's (1986) idea that culture is to be seen as a lynchpin that holds ideology and actions in an organisational context is particularly relevant. Since culture is 'historically transmitted meaning embodied in symbols' (Geerts, 1973, p.89) prevailing ideology that stakeholders possess is often invisible. Every day practices which are often discriminatory take place quite naturally for actors. Kuh and Hall (1993, p.2) comprehensively define culture of institutions as "the collective, mutually shaping pattern of institutional history, mission, physical settings, norms, traditions, values, practices, beliefs and assumptions that guide the behaviour of individuals and groups in an institution of higher education which provide a frame of reference for interpreting the meaning of events and actions on and off campus".

Since institutional culture is evolved over a period of time and institutional stakeholders are product of that culture, ideology of equity is not ingrained into the system. Unless and until there is change in attitude, values, assumptions and beliefs of institutional stakeholders particularly institutional leaders, faculty members and administrators, institutional culture continue to exist as it is. This scenario seems to be in conflict with changing nature of student diversity. Overcoming this structural conflict is a big challenge for higher education institutions in a massified era. External factors like legal measures are less likely to have a serious effect on institutional culture, though they are important. Change must begin from within. Therefore purpose of framework of institutional culture, as noted by Tierney (1988), is "to diagnose culture in colleges and universities so that distinct problems can be overcome".

Conclusion

We attempted to elaborate nature of institutional discrimination that exists in higher education institutions in India. The practice of institutional discrimination is a major hurdle for achieving equity in higher education and facilitating success of disadvantaged groups. Unlike individual discrimination, institutional discrimination is difficult to identify. Thus, the notion of institutional culture is found to be an important tool for analysing way in which institution functions.

The findings of the study suggest that assumptions, attitudes and ideology of institutional leaders and those responsible for implementing institutional mechanisms to protect the interests of the students are less sensitive and conducive to disadvantaged social groups. It makes a negative impact on disadvantaged students. The findings indicate that although institutional mechanisms in the form of cells such as equal opportunity, anti-ragging, and women's cell exist, awareness of students from the disadvantaged groups was low on functions of various cells; whom to contact in case of complaint and faculty member responsible of the cells. Furthermore, the idea of equity is not reflected in actions and practices of institutions. Institutions that are supposed to provide additional learning inputs and support system for disadvantaged fails to perform their role. Moreover, there is no institutional level planning, monitoring and evaluation of student support programme targeting disadvantaged groups to make it more effective. Lack of proactive engagement from cells and committees also poses challenges to ensure support to students.

The findings call for explicit institutional mission that value diversity and design strategies to achieve diversity as a value of inclusion. Developing evidence-based strategies by taking into account experiences of students in their social and academic life on campus will strengthen the institutional level planning process. Further, a wider dissemination of entitlements and opportunities available to the students from disadvantaged groups is required. Importantly, sensitising institutional leaders, faculty members and administrative staff about the idea of student diversity and inclusion is essential. A lack of perspective towards diversity and insensitivity of the institutional leaders can create a vacuum in the discourse on diversity and equity in higher education. Hence, developing a positive perspective towards diversity, wherein student diversity is valued is an important step. Therefore, there is a need for further studies on institutional culture in the specific context of massification. Nuanced understanding about institutional culture will eventually lead to evolve new policies and practices at institution level to foster equity in higher education and creating discrimination free campuses.

References

Astin, A. W. (1993). *What matters in college? Four critical years revisited.* San Francisco: Jossey-Bass.

Daubman, K. A., Williams, V. G., Johnson, D. H., & Crump, D. (1985). Time of withdrawal and academic performance: Implications for withdrawal policies. *Journal of College Student Personnel.*

Freire, P. (1972). *Pedagogy of the Oppressed.* London: Penguin Books.

Geertz, G. (1973). *The Interpretation of Cultures.* New York: Basic Books.

Kuh, G. D., & Hall, J.E. (1993). Using cultural perspectives in student affairs. In G. D. Kuh (Ed.), *Cultural perspectives in student affairs work* (pp. 1-20). Lanham: American College Personnel Association.

McCrudden, C. (1982). Institutional discrimination. *Oxford Journal of Legal Studies, 2*(3), 303-367.

Malish, C. M., & Ilavarasan, P. V. (2016). Higher education, reservation and scheduled castes: exploring institutional habitus of professional engineering colleges in Kerala. *Higher Education, 72(*5), 603-617.

Malish, C.M. (2013*). Negotiating Cultural Capital in the Knowledge Economy of India: An Empirical Study of Scheduled Caste Engineering Students in Kerala.* Unpublished Ph.D Thesis. New Delhi: Indian Institute of Technology, Delhi.

Ministry of Human Resource Development (MHRD) (2015). *All India Survey of Higher Education: 2014-2015*. New Delhi: Government of India.

Ovichegan, S. (2013). Social Exclusion, Social Inclusion and Passing: The Experience of Dalit Students at one Elite Indian University, *International Journal of Inclusive Education, 18*(4), 359-78.

Pascarella, E. & Terenzini, P. (1991). *How college affects students.* San Francisco: Jossey Bass.

Philip G. Altbach (2004). Globalisation and the university: Myths and realities in an unequal world, *Tertiary Education and Management, 10(1),* 3-25.

Pincus, F.L. (1996). Discrimination comes in many forms: Individual, institutional, and structural. *The American Behavioural Scientist, 40(2),* 186-194.

Rao, S.S. (2013). Structural Exclusion in Everyday Institutional Life: Labelling of Stigmatised Groups in an IIT, in Geetha Nambissan & S. Srinivas Rao (Eds.). *Sociology of Education in India: Changing Contours and Emerging Concerns* (pp. 199-223). Delhi: Oxford University Press.

Rasmussen, B. & Salhani, D. (2010). Contemporary Kleinian Contribution to Understanding Racism. *Social Service Review, 84*(3), 491-513.

Rayle, A. D. & Chung, K. Y. (2007). Revisiting first-year college students mattering: Social support, academic stress, and the mattering experience. *Journal of College Student Retention: Research, Theory & Practice, 9*(1), 21-37.

Reay, D., Crozier, G., & Clayton, J. (2009). 'Strangers in paradise'? Working-class students in elite universities. *Sociology, 43(6),* 1103-1121.

Sabharwal, N.S., & Malish, C M (2016a): Diversity and Discrimination in Higher Education. Research Project. New Delhi: CPRHE/NUEPA and ICSSR Research Project.

Sabharwal, N.S., & Malish, C.M. (2016b). *Student Diversity and Civic Learning in Higher Education in India.* CPRHE Research Papers 1. New Delhi: Centre for Policy Research in Higher Education, National University of Educational Planning and Administration.

Sabharwal N.S. & Malish, C.M. (2016c). *Diversity and Discrimination in Higher Education: A Study of Institutions in Selected States of India.* Research Report. New Delhi: Centre for Policy Research in Higher Education, National University of Educational Planning and Administration.

Sabharwal, N.S. & Thorat, Sukhadeo (2014). *Diversity, Academic Performance, and Discrimination: A Case Study of a Higher Educational Institution.* Working Paper, 8 (4). New Delhi: Indian Institute of Dalit Studies.

Sukumar, N. (2008). Living a Concept: Semiotics of Everyday Exclusion, *Economic and Political Weekly*, 15, 14–17.

Swidler, A. (1986). Culture in action: Symbols and strategies. *American Sociological Review*, 51, 273-286.

Tawney, R.H. (1964): *Equality*. London: Unwin Books.

Thorat, Sukhadeo, & Attewell, P. (2007). The legacy of social exclusion: A correspondence study of job discrimination in India, *Economic and Political Weekly, 42*(41), 4141-4145.

Thorat, Sukhadeo & Sabharwal, N. (2013). *Need for Policy Reforms in Higher Education: Education for Civic Learning, Democratic Engagement and Social Change*. Policy Brief, No. 14. Indian Institute of Dalit Studies, New Delhi.

Tierney, W G (1988). Organisational Culture in Higher Education: Defining essentials. *The Journal of Higher Education, 59*(1), 2-21.

Tinto, V. (1988). Stages of student departure: Reflections on the longitudinal character of student leaving. *The Journal of Higher Education*, 438-455.

Tinto, V. (2006). Research and practice of student retention: what next?, *Journal of College Student Retention: Research, Theory & Practice, 8*(1), 1-19.

Trotter, Eileen, & Roberts, C.A. (2006) Enhancing the early student experience. *Higher Education Research & Development 25*(4), 371-386.

Trow, Martin (2006): Reflections on the transition from elite to mass to universal access: Forms and phases of higher education in modern societies since WWII, In James J.F. Forest and Philip G. Altbach (Eds.). *International Handbook of Higher Education*. Springer: Dordrecht.

UNESCO: (1960). *Convention against Discrimination in Education*. Paris: UNESCO.

Varghese, N.V. (2015). *Challenges of Massification of Higher Education in India*. CPRHE Research Papers 1. New Delhi: National University of Educational Planning and Administration.

Yorke, M., & Longden, B. (2008). *The first-year experience of higher education in the UK*. York: Higher Education Academy.

7.

Autonomy and Accountability of Universities in India

A Critical Look at Policy since Independence

Aishna Sharma

Accountability has been sought from the universities and faculty since the very conception of higher education policy. There has been a growing emphasis on accountability in the recent times, particularly post 1990s, in the quest to improve the quality of work performed by the faculty. It needs to be noted that accountability is gaining significance in the policy discourse particularly because of suggestions to making universities autonomous, that is free from the direct control of the state. To avoid any misuse of that autonomy, accountability is being sought with great fervour in the policy texts in terms of quality assurance cells, quantifying the performance of faculty through performance based assessment system (PBAS), subjecting universities to NAAC ranking and more recently National Institutional Ranking framework.

This is not to say that the discussion of accountability did not find place before 1990s. The nature of accountability and its location have altered due to change in the meaning of university autonomy. As a result, what does it mean to be quality work is getting altered. However, the location of accountability has altered over time, with a change in the paradigm in policy. This shift in the nature of regulation has implications on the kind of behaviour expected from the faculty; it is expected that the faculty would be rational and subject themselves to the race of competition. However, the policy fails to take note of the possibility of unethical practices which may also be rational.

The objective of the paper against this backdrop is to unravel the shift in the meaning of autonomy and hence accountability and quality in the higher education policy. This would be undertaken using the method of critical discourse analysis. It would also be seen if the subjects of neo-liberal discourse are indeed autonomous. The second objective is to understand how the possibility of moral hazard problem percolates under the present neo-liberal discourse, where a game theoretic model would be used.

Policy Analysis — Autonomy and Accountability as Policy Technologies

A brief look at policy since Independence

The Radhakrishnan Commission (GOI, 1949) clearly spelt out that the central government should be responsible for finance, coordination of facilities, liaison between universities and research laboratories. Universities were suggested to be teaching institutions. It conjectured that students be socially consciousness and that no individual freedom can be without social responsibility. It accorded freedom to the teachers to speak even on controversial issues. Before that, in the mid-1960s, the Kothari Commission (GOI, 1971) had shown a preference for State funding of universities and that accountability should be towards the society at large. It was argued that independent thinking can develop only in an institution which is free from regimentation of ideas and short-term needs, which is required for the development of society. It discussed about academic autonomy of teachers; that the teachers should be free to pursue truth and write and participate in debates on significant national and international issues. Gnanam Committee (GOI, 1990) had advocated for autonomy of universities, as a freedom from external interference but not an unbridled freedom as it also iterated that universities be accountable to the society. However, it suggested an annual review of universities based on quantifiable outputs like number of teaching days devoted, number of research studies and so on.

The 1990s ushered in suggestions for gradual withdrawal of the State from funding universities. For instance, Punnayya Committee (GOI, 1993) and Ambani Birla Report (GOI, 2000) vouched for autonomy of universities by diversifying the funding base through student vouchers (GOI, 1993:88). To make universities accountable to produce output, the National Accreditation Assessment Council (NAAC) was set up in 1994 which would assess the performance of universities. In a somewhat similar light, the CABE Committee (GOI, 2005) argued that in order to enhance efficiency, the universities become financially autonomous by exploring other sources of funding like introducing self-financing courses, generating internal resources through student fees and undertaking consultancy and sponsored research projects, establish linkages for academic and research collaboration with their counterpart academic and research organisations, industry and professional organisations in India and abroad. At the same time, the universities were recommended to set up internal quality assessment cell (i.e. academic audit of teachers and universities) to make their output performance public and ensure quality in education. Raising tuition fees and creating salary differentials between performers and non-performers was suggested in the National Knowledge Commission (NKC) (GOI, 2009), and also universities must be made accountable to the students. Similarly, Yashpal Committee (GOI, 2009) proposed connecting universities with industry to promote innovations. A strong resentment towards the direct role of the State in the Indian higher education was further clearly presented by the Narayana

Murthy Committee in 2012. It had expressed concerns over limited public funds allocated to the higher education and as a solution to this problem suggested bringing in corporate sector for funding, determining curricula, outcomes, collaborating in research, etc. Also it was posited that corporate sector is a direct beneficiary of the higher education. Recently, there have been suggestions of setting up Higher Education Funding Agency which would provide loans to the universities.

In addition to change in the mode of funding suggested, the principles of the New Public Management have been sought to percolate as a governance mechanism in the public funded universities. Under the NPM, the principles of private sector are installed in public sector institutions. In public funded universities, it seeks to apply the techniques of competitive markets like written contracts, audits and accountability, contracts, output monitoring, performance pay (Marshall & Peters, 1999; Marginson, 2008). To make faculty accountable in 2010 Performance Based Assessment Scheme (PBAS) was introduced, whereby the faculty has been made accountable to produce output in terms of: a) research, b) teaching, and c) co-curricular activities. This is to justify the salaries that they get from the State. The State made accreditation of all universities mandatory in 2013 (GOI, 2013), making the funds flow to universities contingent upon their performance. The performance based funding for the state universities has been mooted in the *Rashtriya Uchchatar Shiksha Abhiyan* (RUSA, GOI, 2013), making them accountable for the funds they would receive from the State.

More recently, the preliminary suggestions to the New Education Policy clearly mention about the paradigm shift from regulation to facilitation, that should come about to promote autonomy of institutions. With respect to funding it says that public funding is inappropriate to deal with expanding higher education and therefore funding base should be diversified including students as a potential source of funding. Further, universities should engage with industry to provide skills to the students, which would make them employable. Recently the State has put forth a framework for ranking the universities and colleges through the National Institutional Ranking Framework (NIRF) in order to improve their ranking in the global space. Understanding a policy is not just looking at the recommendations but going deeper into the effects it seeks to create to legitimise the present discourse.

Policy Analysis

To analyse the policy means to analyse the content of the policy and its effects that it would generate (Codd, 1988). The present paper uses Foucauldian framework of critical discourse analysis to understand the contents of any policy documents and governmentality to look at the policy effects that can be generated. Foucault (1972) understands discourse as a general domain of all statements or as a regulated practice that accounts for a certain number of statements. In other words, the discourse analysis of texts involves asking the following question: What rules / practices were behind the existence of a statement *A*? The intention is never to understand the hidden meaning of a statement (*ibid.*). Thus, discourse can be defined as a set of ideas, concepts and beliefs that have become established as knowledge (Doherty, 2007; Powers, 2007). Foucault (1980) further clarifies that these rules that govern a statement are nothing but "power" or disciplinary power. This notion of power is quite different from a repressive power or coercion. This power is creative as it creates certain relations in the various elements of the society and legitimise its own exercise. Disciplinary power is concerned with production of willing and able bodies that support the status quo of power relations (Powers, 2007). The power does not exist at some central point but gets imbedded in individuals and institutions and the relationship between them. These individuals and institutions become the subjects of power.

Studying the notion of power entails a discussion on *Governmentality*; which is the political rationality underpinning policy. Foucault defines government as "the conduct of conduct" and thus a term which ranges from governing the self to governing others. The practice of government leads to a multitude of techniques, schemes and ideas deliberately mobilising in attempting to direct or influence the conduct of others (Doherty, 2007). In the present context, autonomy and accountability are two such tools of the government which seek to create amenable subjects which further the present discourse. The following paragraphs would look at how the discourse in policy texts legitimise itself by seeking to create certain subjects or relationships.

The way autonomy has been conceptualised signals a change in the role of the state. There exists a positive role of the State even now, but to facilitate market like conditions. This has called for greater accountability to mitigate abuse of autonomy. The present notion of accountability seeks to create individuals who control their own behaviour by rationally subjecting themselves to the standardised performance assessment. Thus, the notion of accountability as discussed in the policy is that of creating a self-regulating and self-interested individual, who aims at maximising their own utility. It fosters individualism. This is not to say that the policy does not talk about accountability and the autonomy is uncontrolled freedom. The accountability remains but to the market needs than the societal interests. This is expected given that markets have been looked at as a potential source of funding than the State, in the name of autonomy.

It is extremely difficult to conceptualise quality. As per the given framework of assessment, the quality is reduced to only certain performance indicators, which must be measured and recorded. The educational institutions as a result are shifting from process to the outputs (Codd, 2005; Tam, 2001). Secondly, due to the presence of different stakeholders, what quality means differs according to their different purposes. For instance, for a student it may mean the kind of education that can provide employability. Under the performance assessment exercise, if a faculty member teaches for a minimum number of hours, or devotes a certain minimum number of hours, it is understood as tantamount to producing quality output.

To argue that the above notion of autonomy and accountability are the technologies that the government uses to create subjectivisation and mould the relationship between different constituents of higher education, we need to understand the effects they create to perpetuate the neo-liberal discourse. The important level of analysis for power relations is at the level of micro practices, the everyday activities of life, the terminal points of the web of relations (Powers, 2007) and how these practices shape the ways that individuals and institutions can think, speak and conduct themselves (Hodges, Kupers & Reeves, 2008). The political rationality of neo-liberalism is exercised by the rational actions taken up by individuals and institutions.

Given the above framework, the paper seeks to answer the following questions: a) How the present discourse is subjectivising different micro-level individuals or institutions?, b) How the relationship is being altered amongst various constituents of higher education, as follows.

a) The process of subjectivisation is happening at the level of the State, higher education institutions and the individuals (faculty, students, etc.).

Till the 1990s, the role of the state was found crucial in funding the higher education and was not regarded as hampering the autonomy of universities. The role of the State is altered, with it creating more space for market like conditions. This kind of regulation is not a reduction in the role of the State but a positive conception of the State, where it provides conditions for markets in higher education to flourish. It is not a trade-off between regulation and competition, but a third best option which is stimulating competition as a function of regulation (Jongbloed, 2004). Under this model, control cannot take place anymore through increasing interventions and regulations by government but through designing "clever frameworks for interaction between individual clients and individual providers". The neo-liberalism changed the role of the State as only a steerer from a distance, which acts more as a facilitator of privatisation, by cutting the public expenditure, encouraging private mode of funding and collaboration of universities with industry to produce knowledge. The presence of State is construed more as interference. This has particularly been the tone of policy post-2000.

The present state of policy seeks to create self-regulating, individualistic, self-interested subjects, who are freed from the direct control of the State. A subject of neo-liberal discourse would be the faculty, who are moulded into self-regulating individuals. They are required to register output under PBAS, salaries differentials has been suggested between those who work and those who do not, ushering in competition, performance based pay is understood as a motivating factor, etc. Thus, they are created as competitive subjects, who would maximise their scores. They become subject to numbers and become numbered subjects (Ball, 2015). Similarly, the students are subjectivised by providing them autonomy to evaluate the faculty, under PBAS. They are required to be self-regulating by paying the fees or securing the loans to fund their education and be responsible for their education.

The universities have been rendered freedom from the State and are suggested to look for alternative sources of funding by collaborating with industry, corporate sector, raising student fees, etc. This makes them competitive vis-a-vis other universities. Also, the universities have become self-regulating by registering outputs under NIRF and to secure performance based funding through accreditation. The universities would be required to act competitively, focusing more on industry collaboration, student satisfaction, quantifying the non-quantifiable like teaching-learning, etc.

b) The relationship has been altered as a result between various constituents of higher education which is required for the sustenance of the neo-liberal discourse. These relationships require rational behaviour from various individuals in order to perpetuate the discourse. Before 1990s, addressing the needs of society was rendered rationality. Under the neo-liberal discourse, it is expected of rational actors to meet the needs of funders or other stakeholders. For instance, the teachers have been made accountable to not only the State by registering outputs under PBAS but also students who are amongst evaluators of faculty and a potential source of funding. Universities would look forward to students as potential source of revenue and therefore would focus on providing labour market oriented, skill-based courses which would not be all-encompassing in nature. Universities are also now suggested to compete among themselves through the ranking framework. It would entail greater collaboration between academia and industry. The nature of knowledge as a result with research output being applied in nature and would be patented to serve as source of return to investment made by the industry. Thus, as neo-liberal subjects, individuals and institutions are incited to invest in themselves, and to improve ourselves, to confirm to the 'truth', the truth of neo-liberalism (Ball, 2015). If they fail to do so they would be forced to not to enjoy the rewards of the system and would be left out.

However, the actions, whatsoever, taken by a faculty member still fall under the purview of rationality. Becker (1993) argued in his lecture on '*The Economic way of looking at Behaviour*' that even the crime performed by an individual can be touted as rational because the action is undertaken after weighing the costs and benefits. Rationality implies that crime is simply conducted because of the financial and other rewards from crime compared to the punishment, legal work or conviction. Similarly, a dishonest faculty member might resort to unethical practices in order to get scores under PBAS. Thus, their rationality must not be confused with ethics. Rationality can have a conflict with ethics. And that is why certain 'rational individuals' (but ethical) would not commit crimes despite knowing the benefits of defecting or the profits from taking short cuts (Becker, 1993).

Not only this, the culture of performativity may lead the faculty or universities as a whole to resort to unethical means to deliver output; they may produce more at the cost of quality. The next section would throw light on this conflict between rationality and ethical practices.

Possibility of Moral Hazard and Free Riding — A Game Theoretic Exposition

The state may suffer from information asymmetry regarding the type of the faculty and thus the quality of actions taken by the faculty to produce output (The actions may not always produce quality work). Despite contracting, it needs to be noted that the performance assessment of faculty members is grounded majorly only on quantification of their work and then the interview. The university administration or the State can never have complete information on the quality of the faculty members' work because they lack information on their objectives in their career paths which depends on their types, like quality of their interaction inside and outside the classroom with their students, the quality of their research work, or the quality time spent in administrative activities. This is because capability cannot be gauged since it is directly related to quality. In addition to this, as also argued by Stiglitz (2002, p. 463), a worker who is at the bottom of ability distribution has incentive to conceal such information and convince his potential employer of his ability being higher than his actual ability. Those at the bottom of ability distribution, in the context of PBAS, can hide their ability by producing outputs in numbers and maximize their individual gains. The faculty members who are aware of their low quality output tend to hide their incapability by projecting large numbers.

The output registered by faculty members in quantitative terms is the 'signal' or it acts as a 'screening device' for their productivity. Only after a certain period of time is their productivity or capability in qualitative terms revealed to the administration. In the recruitment process, some labourers of low productivity also get hired. The problem arises due to possibility of manipulating the signals (Spence, 1973). A signal here means the credentials of potential candidate in the present context. Credentials may or may not be of quality. Ideally, as under the signalling theory of Michael Spence, the cost of acquiring signals is assumed to be negatively correlated with one's productivity; more productive a person is lesser the time required by them to acquire that signal. But, in case of registering signals by faculty members under performance assessment regime, the cost of acquiring those signals in terms of time may not be negatively correlated with one's productivity. An honest, creative and productive faculty member would invest more time in their activities vis-à-vis dishonest or less productive faculty member, *ceteris paribus*. Creativity requires time; be it the process of teaching or research. A dishonest faculty member might save on time by taking short cuts through unethical practices, investing less time and producing poor quality but greater number of outputs. The dishonest would therefore appear to be more productive according to the assumption of signalling theory.

This problem of information asymmetry gives rise to moral hazard under hidden information, also called post-contractual adverse selection, as explained by Akerlof (1970) using the example of automobile market. There exist both good cars and bad cars in the market, the difference between which is known only to the sellers. Both kinds of cars sell at the same price because the buyer lacks information on their quality. It is only after having bought the car, can the buyer judge the quality of the car. However, both the bad quality cars and the good quality cars sell at the same price, which is the average price of both. Most often, sellers dealing with good quality cars would not sell the cars because the market price of these cars is less than their reservation price. At the same time, the sellers dealing with bad quality cars would sell their cars because they are able to make a profit given the higher market price of the cars compared to their reservation price. As a result, bad quality cars have a greater likelihood to be traded. This is the problem of adverse selection.

The possibility of poor quality work proliferating can be further understood using an adverse selection game.

Moral Hazard or Post-contractual Adverse Selection Game

Using the analogy above, suppose there are two types of faculty: honest faculty, T_1 or those who are high ability and know that they have high ability and focus on quality work only; and those who have adjusted themselves at lower level in ability distribution or those who are dishonest faculty, T_2 .

Both types have two strategies, either of cheating or knowingly producing poor / moderate quality output, or playing fair and good quality output. The state has to choose amongst these types for promotion / recruitment based on their PBAS scores. The T_2 type of faculty would have an objective of maximising output in numbers, often at the cost of quality work. The type T_1 faculty would emphasise on quality of output and hence on creativity. Since creativity takes time, more often than not, the output produced by such faculty would be less in number as compared to what is produced by the T_2 type faculty. The state, however, does not know for certain which faculty is honest and which is not. Let the probability assigned by the State be 'p' that the faculty is honest and (1-p) that the faculty is dishonest. The state has two strategies, given at the nodes, overlook (O) or inspect (I). The faculty can either play fair or cheat. The following figure represents the game tree (Fig. 7.1).

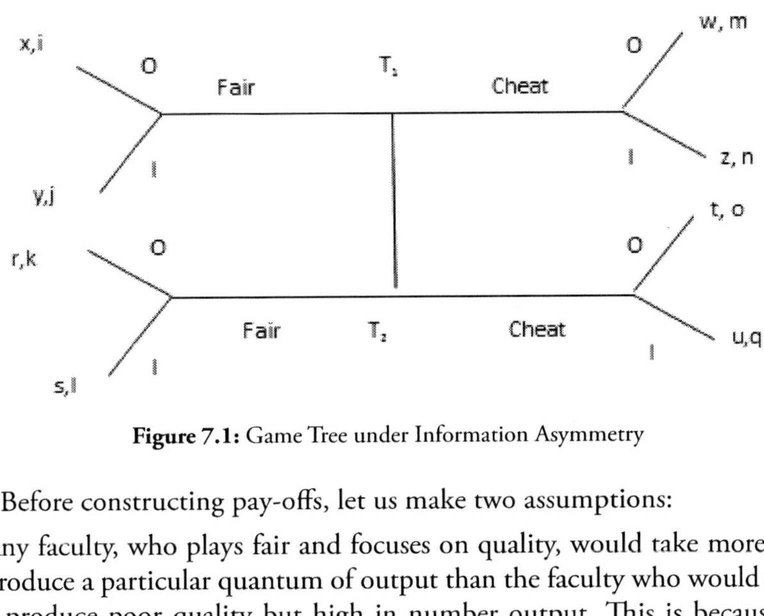

Figure 7.1: Game Tree under Information Asymmetry

Before constructing pay-offs, let us make two assumptions:

1. Any faculty, who plays fair and focuses on quality, would take more time to produce a particular quantum of output than the faculty who would cheat and produce poor quality but high in number output. This is because the former would undertake creative tasks and creativity needs time to come to fruition. The reason for this lies in the way performance assessment incentives are constructed, valuing quantum more than the quality.[1] This implies

1 There is an exception in certain universities which value quality. However, even in such universities, after a certain bad quality work gets excluded from assessment exercise, it is the quantity which is considered for measuring the performance of faculty, be it for recruitment or promotion.

$w>x$ .... (1)
$z>y$ .... (2)
$t>r$ .... (3)
$u>s$ .... (4)

2. The strategy of cheating under performance assessment would mean producing only in terms of numbers, or reporting number of hours devoted to teaching when actually it did not happen, compromising on quality. The dishonest / bad faculty would perform this strategy better than the honest ones, on an average[2]. Therefore,

$t>w$ .... (5)
$u>z$ .... (6)

3. The State has undertaken the performance assessment exercise of faculty to enhance the quality of their work; that is the objective function of the State is to maximise quality. Therefore, a good quality / fair work by the faculty would render the State a higher pay-off.

Let us look at the pay-offs of the honest or high ability faculty. When the honest faculty is playing fair, then their pay-off from the State overlooking would be greater than that under inspection. This is because inspection can signal a lack of trust reposed in the faculty by the State which would reduce their motivation to perform. At the same time overlooking would render them with academic freedom, which would motivate them to work better. Suppose if the honest faculty cheats. An honest faculty may sometimes resort to cheat if due to performance assessment measures their objective function changes from maximising the quality output to maximising scores, even at the cost of quality. This might be particularly true in case of younger faculty who want to move up the ladder or in case the university culture is such which forces the faculty to alter their objective function. If the state overlooks, then their pay-off from cheating would exceed from inspection; if they are caught while cheating (which may not be possible because the performance assessment is focused only on quantity of output than quality, except if the university culture is such which values quality work more than the quantity), the punishment would be imposed in terms of less chances of promotion / less score etc. Therefore, for honest faculty following conditions hold true:

$x>y$ .... (7)
$w>z$ .... (8)

2 Though by definition an honest faculty would never cheat but if the pressure of producing quantity than quality exists if the university culture is such or the peer competition is such, they may change their objective function slightly.

Suppose a dishonest faculty or those who have adjusted their abilities at lower level, plays fair. In rare cases, this might be possible due to peer pressure where the cost from social shame would be much higher to the faculty than benefit from private benefit from maximising scores by cheating. If the state overlooks, it motivates them to produce quality work, than if state was to inspect. Inspecting when a faculty is playing fair would lead to some lack of motivation, causing a fall in the faculty pay-off. However, what is to be noted is the overall quality, which may not be as good as an honest, good quality faculty, but these pay-offs would be less than the respective pay-offs of an honest / good quality faculty. Similarly, when dishonest ones are cheating (the chance of which is high), their pay-offs from the State overlooking would exceed from the State inspecting because there would be no punishment in case of former and, therefore, they can easily maximise their scores.

When an honest / good quality faculty plays fair, then the pay-off to the State from overlooking would be greater than the pay-off from cheating because the latter strategy would make the state incur unnecessary cost of inspection when the faculty is already doing what the State wants them to do. Let us assume the pay-off to the State, from overlooking to be i and from inspecting to be j. Similarly, when the same faculty change their objective to maximising scores and cheat, the State gets higher pay-off from monitoring their activities than overlooking because the latter would lead to proliferation of poor quality outputs, thwarting the very purpose for which the performance assessment exercise is undertaken.

Therefore,

$i>j$ .... (9)

$n>m$ .... (10)

In case of a dishonest / bad quality faculty, the pay-off to the State would be more from inspecting than overlooking when the faculty is cheating, because it would ward off any potential fall in the quality. If the same faculty now plays fair, then the relative pay-off that the state would get would be higher than what they would have gotten when if the faculty was cheating because the quality of work by faculty would be relatively better in this case. But due to additional costs incurred in monitoring, the pay off from inspection would be less than overlooking when faculty is playing fair.

Therefore,

$k>l$ .... (11)

$q>o$ .... (12)

Given the above pay-off, it can be seen that the pay-offs to both the faculty types would be higher when a faculty cheated or focused on producing more output in terms of quantity. This is because taking the honest way or producing quality work entails creative endeavours which are time consuming. Thus, given the same time availability to the honest faculty and the dishonest faculty, the latter would produce more output per unit of time. And because the incentives or scores are related to output in terms of numbers, cheating would render faculty greater pay-offs. This means that a rational faculty would cheat. Now given that cheating is a dominant strategy, the State would choose inspect always because $n>m$ and $q>o$. Thus, for any value of p, the pay-off from inspecting exceeds that from overlooking. Ironically, the faculty would cheat with the State inspecting. This is possible because the faculty is assessed in terms of only the numbers or quantifiable. The State cannot assess always that the quality has been compromised upon. This causes a fall in the quality of output produced by the faculty.

Collective Action Game: The Problem of Free Riding

Sometimes, the output is assessed at the aggregate level, i.e. at the university or departmental level. The problem associated with it is that any dishonest or lax individual faculty may choose to not put in the requisite efforts and free-ride on the benefits that the university or the department as a whole would gain after the output has been produced, by the other diligent faculty.

Suppose there is no binding contract amongst the faculty to cooperate with each other, which makes the game non-cooperative. Suppose the cost of their total contribution is given by A units, which represents the time, energy, effort and opportunity cost of labour (forgone leisure) that they devote to their work. For simplicity, let us assume that there are two faculty only, faculty 1 and faculty 2. The cost should ideally be, therefore, divided equally between the two. The benefit, B units, of producing the output accrues to the entire department or the university. The faculty have two choices, either to contribute to producing output (given by C) or to refrain from contributing (given by D). This scenario can be represented in the matrix form as (Fig 7.2).

		Faculty 2	
		C	D
Faculty 1	C	B- (A/2), B-(A/2)	B-A, B
	D	B, B-A	0, 0

Figure 7.2: Collective Action Game: the Problem of Free-riding

If one faculty contributes, he pays the entire cost. If no one pays then both get 0 as pay-off. Suppose faculty 1 chooses to contribute, the best strategy for faculty 2 would be not to contribute, that is not to cooperate rendering him B as they pay-off, which is higher than if he was to contribute, i.e. B- (A/2). Similarly, if faculty 2 contributes, faculty 1 would not cooperate and get a higher pay-off. The game has therefore two equilibria (C,D) and (D,C) (if, B-A>0). If the benefit that each faculty receives is worth less than the cost incurred by only of the faculty, then that faculty would rather choose not to put in any effort. That is if B-A<0, then the equilibrium outcome of the above game would be (0,0). This outcome is, however, not optimal as the faculty get less pay-off then that what they would have gotten if they both would have contributed, i.e. (B-(A/2), B-(A/2)). Thus, there has to be a mechanism which should make shirking at the hands of each faculty costly and less lucrative than cooperation. One such solution is to instil a culture of collegiality amongst faculty. The social humiliation and shame from not contributing can induce the faculty to contribute towards producing quality work.

Concluding Remarks

Over time the policy has emphasised autonomy from the State funding and accountability as policy technologies. Accountability has shifted from the State to the immediate funders or other stakeholders, particularly with the advent of neo-liberalism post 1990s. This is legitimated through seeking to create rational individuals and institutions. It is through these rational actions and relationships that they legitimise the present policy discourse. But often the rational behaviour may be unethical or producing moderate quality work as per the ability they impute on themselves. Thus, the present conception of accountability, where quality is quantifiable and the quality of actions of individuals is not observable may run inimical to quality, the very purpose for which it is instituted in the first place.

References

Akerlof, G.A. (1970). The market for lemons: Quality uncertainty and the market mechanism. *The quarterly journal of economics, 84 (3),* 488-500.

Ball, S. (2015). Education, governance and tyranny of numbers. *Journal of Education Policy, 30 (3),* 299-301.

Becker, G. S. (1993). Nobel lecture: The economic way of looking at behaviour. *Journal of Political Economy, 101 (3),* 385-409.

Codd, J.A. (1988). The Construction and deconstruction of Education Policy Documents. *Journal of Education Policy, 3(3),* 235-47.

Codd, J. A. (2005). Teachers as managed professionals in the global education industry: the New Zealand experience. *Educational Review, 57(2),* 193-206.

Doherty, R. (2007). Critically framing education policy: Foucault, discourse and governmentality. In Michael A. Peters and Tine Besley (eds.). *Why Foucault? New Directions in Educational Research.* New York: Peter Lang Publishing Inc.

Engebresten, E., Heggen, K. & Eilertsen, H. A. (2012). Accreditation and Power: A discourse analysis of a new regime of governance in higher education. *Scandinavian Journal of Educational Research, 56 (4),* 401-417.

Fimyar, O. (2008). Using governmentality as a conceptual tool in education policy research. *Educate-Special Issue,* 3-18.

Foucault, M. (1972). *The Archeology of Knowledge.* London: Routledge.

Foucault, M. (1980). Two lectures. in *Power/Knowledge. Selected interviews and other writings. 1972-77,* edited by Colin Gordon. Great Britain: Harvester Press Limited, 78-108.

Government of India. (1971). *Education and National Development. Report of the Education Commission 1964-66.* National Council of Educational Research and Training.

Government of India. (1993). *UGC Funding of Higher Education. Report of Justice Punnayya Committee-1992-93.* Delhi: UGC.

Government of India. (2000). *Report on a policy framework for reforms in education. Prime Minister's council on trade and industry government of India.* New Delhi.

Government of India. (2005). *Report of the Central Advisory Board of Education (CABE) committee on Autonomy of Higher Education.* New Delhi: Ministry of Human Resource Development.

Government of India. (2009). *National Knowledge Commission. Report to the Nation 2006-09.* National Knowledge Commission. Delhi: Ministry of Human Resource Development.

Government of India. (2009). *Report of the Committee to Advise on Renovation and Rejuvenation of Higher Education.* Delhi: UGC.

Government of India. (2010). *UGC Regulations on Minimum Qualifications for Appointment of teachers and other academic staff in universities and colleges and measures for maintenance of standards in higher education.* The Gazette of India. September 18. Delhi.

Government of India. (2012).*Committee on corporate participation in higher education. Report of NR Narayana Murthy Committee.* New Delhi: Planning Commission.

Government of India. (2013).*UGC Regulations for mandatory accreditation.* The Gazette of India. January. Delhi.

Government of India. (2013). *Rashtriya Uchattar Shiksha Abhiyan.* New Delhi: Ministry of Human Resource Development.

Hodges, B.D., A. Kuper & S. Reeves (2008). Qualitative Research: Discourse Analysis. *British Medical Journal 337 (7660),* 570-572.

Hook, Derek. (2001). Discourse, knowledge, materiality, history: Foucault and Discourse Analysis.*Theory and psychology, 11(4),* 521-547.

Huisman, Joroen & Jan Currie (2004). Accountability in higher education: Bridge over troubled waters?. *Higher education, 49,* 529-551.

Lemke, T. (2000). Foucault, Governmentality and Critique. Paper presented at the Rethinking Marxism Conference. Univcrsity of Amherst (MA), September.

Marginson, S. (2008). Academic creativity under new public management: Foundations for an investigation. *Educational Theory, 58(3)*, 269-287.

Marshall, J., D. and Michael. A. Peters. (1999). Introduction, in *Education Policy*, edited by James D. Marshall and Michael. A. Peters, UK: Edward Elgar, 1999

Peters, Michael A. (2004). Educational Research: 'games of truth' and the ethics of subjectivity. *Journal of Educational Enquiry, 5(2)*, 50-63.

Powers, P. (2007). The philosophical foundations of Foucautian Discourse Analysis. *Critical Approaches to Discourse Analysis across disciplines, 1(2)*, 18-34.

Townley, B. (1993). Foucault, Power/Knowledge, and its relevance for Human Resource Management. *The Academy of Management Review, 18(3)*, 518-545.

Spence, M. (1973). Job Market Signalling. *The Quarterly Journal of Economics, 87 (3)*, 355-374.

Stiglitz, J.E. (2002). Information and change in the paradigm in economics. *The American Economic Review, 92(3)*, 460-501

SECTION III

Restructuring of Higher Education in India

8.

Mode of Funding Higher Education and University Governance

A Critical Assessment of the Possibilities

Saumen Chattopadhyay

The higher education sector is undergoing transformation all over the world and India is no exception. It is evidently clear from the series of policy initiatives being mooted and implemented that the government is concerned about addressing the socio-economic needs at the local as well as the national levels, while at the same time, the university system has to embrace the global higher education system. The ongoing massification of higher education is reflective of the growing demand for higher studies in the wake of increasing importance of knowledge in spurring economic growth coupled with an increasing demand to treat higher education as an instrument for social mobility. The gross enrolment rate (GER) in higher education has witnessed a steady rise to around 26 per cent mainly being driven by the growth of the private sector participation which has been pretty high in the last decade. This paper looks at the question of mode of funding and how in certain cases it is envisaged to improve the governance standard in the Indian context.

We begin with a brief discussion of a very contentious issue whether higher education is a public good which helps us setting the stage for the debate on the issue of subsidisation. We present a schema to deal with the issue of mode of funding and what implications it would have for governance and the missions of the university. We begin with input based funding, which is generally the case for the majority of the government funded universities. We follow it up with our discussions on possibility of developing a credit market and a voucher system. We end our discussion with the possible implications of HEFA which has been recently launched bythe government to fund the universities.

Mode of Funding and Governance

An important question for us to address is what type of good/service higher education is before we embark on our analysis of mode of funding higher education. If we go strictly by the definition of public good (Samuelson, 1954) which is defined in terms of two characteristics of non-excludability and non-rivalry in consumption, higher education is not a public good. It is best argued as a quasi-public good (Marginson, 2007; Chattopadhyay 2012). Admission to an institute of higher education is exclusive as the number of seats is given and the expenses on higher education is considered as investment on acquisition of skill as manifest in terms of embodiment of human capital which is supposed to ensure future stream of income to the students. But it also generates positive externalities in terms of inculcation of citizenship which is essential for the functioning of the democratic institutions, arguably reduction in corruption and instilling moral and ethical values among the students and many other traits so essential for maintenance of social order and a vibrant democracy in addition to the imperatives of equalising access to higher education for all those who are capable and willing to study irrespective of their socio-economic backgrounds. Therefore, there is a need for subsidisation of education because of the concern for the people in the margin as well as positive externalities that education, broadly speaking, generates.

Given that the public support is essential for higher education, the two major problems that the government seems to be grappling with are the financial constraints and the issue of low quality of education and research keeping in mind the large size of the Indian higher education system. The three major objectives envisaged at the beginning of the Eleventh Five Year Plan (FYP), expansion, inclusion and excellence have remained equally relevant today and would remain so for the years to come. The fourth one which is often added to the stated three is the issue of employability. In view of the labour market mismatches and increasing concern for poor quality of education, poor employability has emerged to be a concern for the policy makers, the industry and the graduates.[1] Poor employability can be legitimately held responsible for hindering the realisation of demographic dividends, as the incidence of graduate unemployment and underemployment soars. It is needless to mention that without excellence, both expansion and inclusiveness signify very little or virtually nothing.

The policy makers since the initiation of the new economic policy (NEP) in the early 1990s, have been advocating the implementation of structural adjustment policies (SAP) which entails construction of a regulated market for the different sectors with increased private participation to achieve efficiency through competition. Further, the stabilisation policy, as advocated by the IMF, imposes restrictions on fiscal deficit in terms of GDP which necessitates curtailing of expenditure on infrastructure development, physical and social. In the context of a developing country, both the arms of NEP have adverse implications for the social sector as privatisation hampers accessibility to education and health which is compounded by the decline in budgetary support for the social sector.

But despite privatisation the quality of higher education, as pointed out by several studies and reports, has not really witnessed any improvement. The government time and again has looked into the matter as to how to improve the quality of higher education in the country. In terms of employability as well as featuring of the Indian universities in the world ranking, there is enough ground to argue that qualitywise we are lagging far behind the world-renowned universities. This argument is often linked with the issue of resource constraint that the government is faced with. More importantly, it is now being realised that it is not solely an issue of resource constraint always, but it is mode of funding which can be so designed so as to energise the system, to bring about an improvement in the governance structure, in the delivery of education and research. The issues of funding and the governance problem are, therefore, no longer disassociated from each other.

There are basically three questions. One, how to negotiate the overall resource constraint; two, how to encourage the universities to generate more revenues and explore alternative channels; and three, how to design mode of funding to effect changes in the governance pattern. The last is what the government is keen to explore because it deals with both the problem of resource deficiency and poor quality of public higher education in general.

Funding Policies for Public Higher Education Institutions

Policies to reform the government funded institutions would constitute two major areas, reform measures related to funding and functioning or what may be called governance. While the rationale for government support for education in general is derived from the generation of externalities and concern for equity, two main questions which need to be addressed in determining the funding mechanism: what is funded and how is it funded (Jongbloed, 2007). In the traditional models of funding, the policy approach was to arrive at the quantum of funding based on negotiations with budgetary items, such as salaries, maintenance, students' enrolment, etc. This is what is called input-based funding. The major drawback with this kind of funding mechanism arguably is that it fosters inefficiency as the process and outcome are not considered under this type of funding. As a result, there would be very little incentive for the employees of the public sector to economise on the use of resources as gains in efficiency would not be the guiding principle for the employees and the institutions both, because the concept of efficiency in education is rather nebulous and not understandable by the stakeholders and non-profit institutions do not have a profit maximising objective. However, this is not necessarily true for the private sector as discussed earlier. Inefficiency in the use of resources gets in-built over the years in the functioning of the institutions and perpetuation continues. The issue is how to change the mode of funding so as to overcome the inherent inefficiency in the functioning of the HEIs. Therefore, to ensure accountability to the society and incentivise the actors to deliver, the tendency has been to shift towards performance-based budgeting whereby the release of funding would be made contingent upon performances of the stakeholders as reflected in the outcome of the institutions. Q1 is the base scenario where the University Grants Commission (UGC) pays for the inputs directly to the universities independent of the academic performance. In Q2, the UGC also partly pays for the performances of the universities through various schemes like award of additional grants based on the performance both at the departmental level (like DRS, DSA, CAS) as well as at the university level like award under the scheme of University for potential for excellence. The reality is more towards Q1 and a bit towards Q2.

With regard to the second question, one can envisage two types of funding mechanism. One is based on centralised agency where the funds are sanctioned by the topmost agency. In the other extreme case, the funding is through the students as it happens in a typical market where the source of revenue is the demand generated by the customers. The strong advocates of market model would naturally press for moving towards student based funding through the voucher scheme. To generate competition in the market, it is argued that students are to be financially empowered and in the process, the HEIs would have very little scope to rest on their laurels and instead, would have to compete with one another for a larger share in the market as a typical firm would do. In Q3 and Q4, the resources required for university financing in terms of what is it that funded, inputs or output will be determined by the market in a decentralised system. In Q3, the possibility is that the university will offer online courses like MOOCs and self-financed courses where the inputs will be funded by demand it generates for these courses. In Q4, the most notable example is the voucher system.

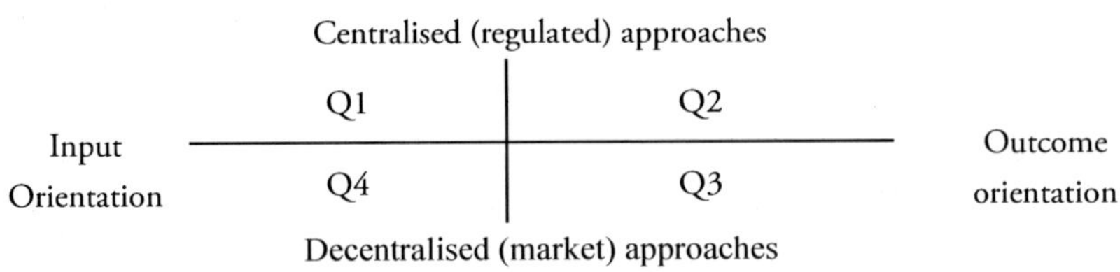

Figure 8.1 Funding Systems in Academic Institutions

Source: Jongbloed (2007).

In Figure 8.1, the horizontal axis shows the degree to which the governments are paying for the various combinations of inputs and the outcomes instead of the inputs alone and the vertical axis depicts the extent of decentralisation. All the four quadrants (Q1, Q2, Q3 and Q4) show how differently funding arrangements can be conceptualised.

The schema presented by Jongbloed (2007) needs to be elaborated by bringing the imperative of distinguishing between student based funding and research based funding as students and research outputs are the two main indicators of research performance of a university. The relative composition between the two, however, would vary depending on the university mandate. Since a public funded university is not supposed to be making profit, offering of the online courses or market oriented courses would be to recover the cost of inputs. In Q4, the funding will be directed towards a university based on the performance of the university. Both students based on reputation and university ranking would make informed choices and research funding will be directed towards a university based on research output.

Though in Q3 and Q4, the market continues to fund, the idea is that the funding is routed through the market. In Q3, the government would help the students to defray higher tuition fees by institutionalising and developing a credit market and provision of scholarship for the meritorious and the needy. In Q4, the students are helped with financial endowments in the form of vouchers.

Case 1 (Q1): Input based funding

Base scenario: Q1 provides us the base scenario. The problem is one of inefficiency as the inputs may suffer from lack of accountability in the system as mentioned above. This provides the rationale for moving towards market based funding which would give more importance to the output or the performance of the universities in determining the quantum of funding.

Case 2 (Q2): Market based funding of inputs

The university seeks to recover the cost of inputs from the market. This would require the universities to respond to the market by offering courses which are in high demand and applying for projects the funding agency is keen to fund essentially to finance basic research. While the market demand is backed up by the purchasing power, the government would like to support the market demand by making provisions for student loans at concessional rates.

a. ***Offering of self-financing and online courses***: Let us now work out the implications of raising fees in a government funded institution. We can conceive of two cases. One, a fall in the budgetary support and therefore in the extent of subsidisation may result in a rise in p. This would require the government to develop a credit market to help those who would otherwise opt out because of higher fees. Two, the government does not reduce the budgetary support but changes the mode of funding as fees are hiked with no commensurate fall in the government financial support. This entails that the mode of funding changes as the students are directly funded and not the institutions.

Implications for raising tuition fees for the economy: Merit and margin

Since there does not exist arguably any relationship between affordability, i.e., capacity to pay fees and talent required for getting admitted to a course in a HEI as proxied by the marks at the higher secondary level, raising fees would lead to a compromise with search of talent unless there exists a credit market to lend money to the talented but financially not so privileged. The imperfect credit market or a market for educational loans, however, has got its own limitations. In general, high fees would lead to a fall in the expenditure on education by all the students due to unaffordability and greater concern if the talented ones reduce their expenditure perforce as Becker (1975) showed in his formulation of the DD-SS model. If those who deserve to pursue higher studies are left out, the quantum and quality of human capital formation for the nation would suffer.

Similarly, a rise in fees leading to a cut in investment expenditure by those who are in the periphery of the society is also a matter of concern which would manifest in terms of their dropping out of the system and agreeing to settle for a low level of education perforce, hindering not only their social mobility, but also of their future generations.

Relationship between fees and cost matter even for quality

This nature of the relationship, the extent of equivalence and causality between fees and cost is interesting and important. Advocacy for subsidisation based on the argument of externalities and fostering of social mobility does not take into account that the level of motivation of the students as well as of the teachers which would depend on the amount of fees that they pay. If the fees are high and pinching, the students would be eager to get the best out of the system through voice and dedication as they internalise the true cost of education. This is evident from the behaviour of the students in a professional institution where the fees are high and the students are paying for their fees out of education loans. It can as well happen and it does happen, that higher fees can make the students so professional that they behave more like consumers and are keen to be awarded with the certificates rather than going through the rigorous process of teaching and learning. This is what Adam Smith (1776/2003) prescribed in his analysis of university failure. He argued if the students pay for the teachers' salaries, teachers would be compelled to deliver and inevitable result would be improvement in the quality of education. However, the formation of human capital in the classroom is a joint process or it is co-produced. Students and teachers motivate each other to attain higher levels of teaching and learning and students are not, therefore strictly speaking consumers.

Students in some universities hardly pay anything in the form of tuition fees but are highly motivated. This academic ambience is a culture which has to be nurtured and developed which can play an important role in the determination of quality after controlling for the quality of human capital present and quantum of funding.

b. ***Developing a credit market as fees become cost recovery:*** The university offers courses which are not all market oriented. In that case, fees are raised with support for taking loans and provision of more scholarships. It is argued that since expenditure on education is akin to investment, why do not we develop a credit market where the students can borrow and fund their education? In fact as we all know, nearly 75-80 per cent of professional education in India is already being catered to by the private sector. The tuition fees are often exorbitantly high particularly in the medical education[2].

There would be students who would not access the loans market as they can afford to pay even the higher fees. There would be students who need not approach the banks as for them it is no longer a worthwhile profitable proposition as given marginal rate of return, marginal cost of financing goes up as loans are extended at a certain rate of interest (based on Becker, 1975).

Besides these, there are inherent imperfections with the credit market for education loans[3]. There are uncertainties in the job market. Studies show there could be discrimination in the name of gender, class and region. The possibility that one has to take loans to study courses distort the choices of the individuals at much earlier stages of education. We all know how expensive coaching industry is for the parents who want their wards to study engineering and medical. Since, choices made in education are irreversible, the underprivileged who can ill afford to pay high fees would suffer the most as they choose courses which are affordable and these courses lack prospects for employment in general. In order to overcome the uncertainty faced by the students in terms of getting a job and even the expected salary to be adequate enough to pay back the loans, policy makers now argue in favour of income contingent loans (ICL).

In general, high fees make the students demanding, willing to learn to enhance their employability so as to repay the loans back. Since the quality of education is co-produced, the accountability to the students would have an impact on the governance as the system gears up to serve the students.

Case 3 (Q2): Performance based funding

The University Grants Commission has some provisions for performance based funding which pertains more to the research based funding. Students' performance in the Indian context is rarely considered for the purpose of funding. Some of the schemes that the UGC has are UPOE and other departmental awards like DRS, DSA and CAS.

Case 4 (Q3): Voucher system, a solution for all the ills albeit impractical

The voucher system was originally proposed by Milton Friedman (1962) who thought it has the great potential to alleviate the problem of poor governance of the institutions as they now face the market competition, the students who acquire the role of consumers. The market creation should lead to efficiency in the use of resources and excellence in the quality of education[4]. Though theoretically this sounds good as both the problems of allocational efficiency and technical efficiency are negotiated with, for all practical purposes and in view of what education is for the self and the society, there are scopes for compromises[5].

We can envisage a system where fees are raised but subsidies are not curtailed. Instead of funding the institutions, students are funded to enable them to choose courses and institutions freely and foster competition[6]. Those who argue for vouchers, donot deny the essential role education plays in character building and nation building as subsidies can be continued with, but with a change in the mode funding of education to tackle the problem of government failure in the delivery of quality education. It is argued that government failure is no less a problem compared to the market failure argument (West, 1995). It is argued that input based funding does not make the institution necessarily accountable to the students and hence they fail to ensure delivery of poor quality as Smith (1776) argued long ago.

How tenable and desirable the development of market for education is?

For application of economic principles to education is rather problematic as the concepts of market, efficiency and competition as conceptualised in economic theory are not readily applicable (Teixeira, 2004; Chattopadhyay 2009; 2012).

Inherently imperfect

Because of the highly differentiated nature of the services due to the uniqueness of the human capital embodied which are not reproducible, the market is inherently imperfect and is best described as a quasi-market. Though it is the sovereignty bestowed on the producers and the students which is required for the construction of the education market, it is neither always feasible nor always desirable (Chattopadhyay, 2012). Further, one important problem is that the students are not the consumers who can buy the degrees but they are required to earn the degrees by dint of hard effort. Apart from the argument that market cannot ensure equal accessibility, the argument that market construction is necessary for quality becomes rather weak.

Efficiency makes little sense for education

Both the concepts of allocative efficiency and technical efficiency are problematic in case of education. While the quasi-market seeks to achieve allocational efficiency, it is technical efficiency which is crucial for good governance. However, the absence of a well-defined technical relationship between the inputs and the output renders the concept of efficiency rather fuzzy and weak. Moreover, efficiency in the use of resources may not lead to quality and good quality need good quality inputs. While efficiency is desirable for ensuring wastage of resources, it is not sufficient as higher the costs better the quality and therefore cost minimisation may lead to a compromise with the quality. Further, competition is always selection based efficiency and not exchange based efficiency which means that good universities would always attract the best of the minds. Fostering competition to achieve quality has, therefore, its own limitations as best of the minds are not replicable like that of the inputs in the industry, say electronic industry.

In absence of technology, quality depends on only motivation and moral values

The conversion of inputs to outputs requires active and motivated participation of the students and the teachers. That is why mere provisioning of infrastructure and availability of the teachers and students do not guarantee quality teaching-learning and knowledge generation. It all depends on the culture or academic ambience that would be motivating for the teachers and the students. Not all government funded institutions are examples of government failure. Some top institutions deliver because of the motivation of the human resources and their self-esteem and pride in being associated with the prestige of the institutions.

Case 5: Higher education funding agency (HEFA)

In order to overcome the problem of funding being faced by the universities and for the setting up of the high quality infrastructure in premier educational institutions, the Union Cabinet recently approved the establishment of a Higher Education Financing Agency (HEFA). "The HEFA would be jointly promoted by the identified promoter and the Ministry of Human Resource Development (MHRD) with an authorised capital of rupees 2,000 crore.

The Government equity would be rupees1,000 crore" according to an official statement made, after the meeting of the Union Cabinet, chaired by the Prime Minister, Mr Modi.

The HEFA is to be formed as a special purpose vehicle (SPV) within a PSU Bank or Government-owned-NBFC (Promoter). "It would leverage the equity to raise up to rupees 20,000 crore for funding projects for infrastructure and development of world class labs in IITs/ IIMs/ NITs and such other institutions," the statement added. The HEFA is authorised to mobilise CSR funds from PSUs or corporates, which would in turn be made available for promoting research and innovation in these institutions on grant basis.

The HEFA would extend a 10-year loan to finance the civil and lab infrastructure projects. The principal portion of the loan has to be repaid through the 'internal accruals' (earned through the fee receipts, research earnings, etc.) of the institutions. The government would pitch in with the offer to service the interest portion through the regular Plan assistance. This scheme is applicable for all the centrally funded higher educational institutions who can become eligible members of the HEFA. What is important is that for joining as members, the institution should agree to escrow a specific amount from their internal accruals to HEFA for a period of 10 years.

Implications of HEFA for quality and governance

Linking capital funding with raising the fees is an innovative step no doubt in the Indian context. Linking it with the internal accruals is a major policy initiative by the government. Raising the fees has been found to be very difficult by the government mainly because of the students' resistance and in absence of a sound basis to determine the fees across the universities. Though the universities would not remain constrained by the want of resources for possible expansion but the university has to ensure resources are generated. This would entail the universities to become strategic, to become visionary and competitive. In this emerging competitive situation, the universities being endowed with research capacity, research culture and the faculty strength and the students' ability and willingness to pay, not all universities will be able to compete. The logic of competition in the market for education does not work. Better endowed with do better and those who are not, will lag behind because of the inherent differences in quality of human capital embodied. In addition, raising the fees will make the system highly differentiated and hierarchical. Higher the fees, better the university in terms of future plan and growth and, therefore, higher the brand values. This will distort the choice for the students who are meritorious but feel handicapped by high tuition fees. Eventually two categories of institutions will emerge and an accentuation in the differentiation will lead to expansion with excellence but not inclusive.

Case 6: Public Private Partnership

The advocacy for PPP is also argued to be dealing with both the problems that the government is faced with: inadequacy of budgetary allocations and governance problem which is symptomatic of government failure. In the partnership between the public and private sector, depending on the various models of forging the partnership, both the investment and running costs will be shared by the public and the private sector. Involvement of the private sector in the running of the HEIs will improve governance and ensure efficiency in the use of resources. While the private sector will most likely embrace neo-liberal type of governance structure, it is not clear as to why the neo-liberal type of governance will improve quality of higher education.

New public management (NPM) is located within the neo-liberal approach to education reform. As Ball and Youdell (2007: 14) put it very succinctly, "NPM has been the primary means through which the structure and culture of public services are recast in order to introduce and entrench the mechanisms of the market form and forms of privatisation. In doing so it affects how and where social policy choices are made and systematically sidelines and disempowers educational practitioners. It also increasingly subjects them to new forms of control through performance management techniques".

Universities adopt a business-like approach and orient practices similar to what corporate entities practise. The key elements of NPM with focus on installation of accounting and audit culture are extensive use of written contracts and performance agreements, economic rewards and sanctions to effect improvement in public service delivery, institutional separation between different categories of functions: advisory, delivery and regulatory functions, contracting out of services, mainly non-core services and emphasis on contestable provision, a larger space created in favour of commercial enterprises, deregulation of market and privatisation, etcetera.

In terms of quantity, of course, there will be an increase in the publications and better compliance with the requirements the UGC demands (Das and Chattopadhyay 2014). The features of NPM will be incorporated in the governance model which will circumscribe academic freedom of the faculty, put them under surveillance, and make them strategic and entrepreneurial to achieve the targets set by the UGC. In the process, both collegiality and creativity will suffer in the wake of the mad rush for maximisation of points subject to ability and time constraint. Though profit maximisation will not become the objective of private sector operation, the effort to indulge in cost cutting remains which is inimical to quality education (Chattopadhyay, 2012).

Different Models of PPP

There could be various ways in which the public-private participation in education can be envisaged. As shown in Table, government can think of in connection with the delivery of education, as: (i) the investor in land and building to begin the operation, (ii) as an employer of the teachers, the main input in this service sector, (iii) producer and the deliverer of services and having control over its delivery in terms of curriculum and pedagogy and finally, (iv) the buyer of services, i.e., education. In case of (ii) and (iii), the private sector will be involved in the governance and most likely it will be designed in line with the NPM.

Concluding Remarks

While inadequacy of budgetary resources for public higher education is identified to be one major reason for the poor quality of education and research, government failure or absence of good governance is the other crucial factor. The issue is, therefore, how to address the funding problem while at the same time, the governance problem is also effectively negotiated with. Given the role higher education plays in the socio-economic development of a nation, how to design the mode of public funding to usher in changes in the governance mechanism. The question is how we can reform the mode of funding higher education which would not only deal with the resource constraint of the government but at the same time can help overcome the poor governance of the universities. This paper looks at the issue of mode of funding from two perspectives, what is it that funded and how is it funded. While the first issue pertains to the funding of university inputs *vis a vis* university outputs, the second issue looks at the how the funding is released to the universities, directly or through the market mechanism where the students assume the centre-stage in the funding mechanism. This paper takes forward the scheme presented by Jongbloed (2007) in a framework of 2 by 2 classification by bringing in the two distinct university outputs, teaching-learning and research and two sources of funding in the context of the market: the students to fund their academic programme and the research funding agencies to fund generation of knowledge. Any deviation from the input based funding with no strings attached leads to some compromise with the university mission and academic freedom, but at the same time, it deals with the problem of abuse of academic freedom and low level of motivation resulting in poor governance. The paper discusses various such interactions between the state and the market by giving examples of the self-financing courses and the online courses, the development of the credit market, the voucher system, performance based funding and the PPP in addition to the recently announced policy initiative by the government, the higher education funding agency (HEFA).

Notes

1. According to the National Employability Report 2013, employability was less than 25 per cent across the majority of the job functions with graduates from science, commerce, arts, etc.
2. Outstandingloans have grown at a CAGR of almost 30 percent since 2005 while education loan accounts have grown from 0.25 mn to 3 mn at a CAGR of 32 per cent during the same period. Education loan accounts for 11 per cent of total enrolment which was only 2 per cent in 2002-03 (Re-imagining Higher Education in India, Yes Institute, 2016).
3. Loans are required to be paid back in the form of interest and capital repayments if the income earned exceeds a certain limit.
4. The link between efficiency and excellence is some what nebulous and tenuous.
5. The neo-liberal approach to policy making emphasises on these two types of efficiencies.
6. There arises an issue of prioritisation of choice of courses *vis-à-vis* choice of institutions. Because of the eligibility criteria for seeking admission into the HEIs, the choice making would neither be free nor should it be so (Chattopadhyay, 2012).

References

Ball, Stephen J. and Deborah Youdell. (2007), *Hidden Privatisation in Public Education,* Preliminary Report, prepared by Institute of Education, University of London presented at Education International , 5th World Congress, July.

Becker, G.S. (1975). *Human Capital: A Theoretical and Empirical Analysis with special reference to Education.* Chicago: University of Chicago Press. Originally published in 1964.

Bhushan, S. (2010).*Public Financing and Deregulated Fees in Indian Higher Education,* New Delhi: Bookwell.

Chattopadhyay, Saumen (2009).'The Market in Higher Education: Concern for Equity and Quality', *The Economic and Political Weekly,* July 18, pp. 53-61.

Chattopadhyay, Saumen (2012). *Education and Economics: Disciplinary Evolution and Policy Discourse.* New Delhi: Oxford University Press.

Das, Dipendra N. and Saumen Chattopadhyay, 2014. Academic Performance Indicator (API): straight jacketing Higher Education Reform, *Economic and Political Weekly,* December 13.

Enders J. and B. Jongbloed (eds.) (2007), *Public-Private Dynamics in Higher Education: Expectations, Developments and Outcomes,* New Brunswick, USA:

Transcript, Transaction Publishers.

Friedman, Milton (1962). *Capitalism and Freedom*, Chicago: Chicago University Press.

Jongbloed, Ben (2007), Creating Public-Private Dynamics in Higher Education Funding: A Discussion of Three Options, in Enders J. and B. Jongbloed (eds.) (2007), *Public-Private Dynamics in Higher Education: Expectations, Developments and Outcomes*, New Brunswick, USA: Transcript, Transaction Publishers.

Marginson, Simon (2007). 'Five Somersaults in Enschede: Rethinking Public/Private in Higher Education for the Global Era' in J. Enders and B. Jongbloed (ed.), *Public-Private Dynamics in Higher Education: Expectations, Developments and Outcomes*, New Brunswick, USA: Transcript, Transaction Publishers.

Samuelson, Paul (1954). 'The Pure Theory of Public Expenditure', *Review of Economics and Statistics*, 36, 4, 387-389.

Smith, Adam (1776/2003).*An Inquiry into the Nature and Causes of the Wealth of Nations*, (New York: Bantam Books) (originally published in 1776).

Teixeira Pedro, Ben Jongbloed, David Dill and Alberto Amaral (eds.) (2004).*Markets in Higher Education: Rhetoric or Reality?* Dordrecht/Boston/London: Kluwer Academic Publishers.

West, Edward G. (1995). The Economics of Higher Education, in Sommer, John W. (ed.) *The Academy in Crisis: The Political Economy of Higher Education*, New Brunswick (USA): Transaction Publishers.

Winston, Gordon C. (1999): 'Subsidies, Hierarchy and Peers: The Awkward Economics of Higher Education', *The Journal of Economic Perspectives*, Vol. 13, No 1 (Winter) 13-36.

Select References

Chattopadhyay, Saumen (2012). *Education and Economics: Disciplinary Evolution and Policy Discourse*. New Delhi: Oxford University Press.

Jongbloed, Ben (2007), Creating Public-Private Dynamics in Higher Education Funding: A Discussion of Three Options, in Enders J. and B. Jongbloed (eds.) (2007), *Public-Private Dynamics in Higher Education: Expectations, Developments and Outcomes*, New Brunswick, USA: Transcript, Transaction Publishers.

9.
Are our Universities Financially Sustainable?
Case of Four South Indian Universities

C. Krishnan

Global forces are combining to fabricate rapid and profound changes on a here to fore unknown scale, that too, in fathomless velocity, leaving none of our systems unscathed, including the global system of higher education. Higher education system, globally, is being placed in an entirely different setting, with the pervading of market, offering a competing paradigm and restructuring the interplay between the Market, the State and the Universities at the advent of globalisation (Kwiek, 2002). It witnesses a series of irreversible changes, upcoming in the form of several paradigmatic shifts from 'local' and 'national' to 'global', 'state controlled' to 'open market driven' and 'teacher centered' to 'student centered' as well as 'life-long education'. It has landed up in a terminological innovation, delivering a few newly coined terms like 'Borderless Education', 'Cross border Education', '*Transnational* and *Transborder* Education'. Weiler (2002) has described this process as a shift from 'input controls' to 'output controls' and a combination of greater autonomy and greater accountability. The rolling back of State to its traditional corners, coupled with 'internationalisation' and 'commoditisation'[1] of education, have triggered off new problems as well as added fresh and complicated dimensions to the current problems. This has witnessed the crumbling of the social democratic ideals of a widely developed Welfare State with State supported higher education. Higher Education ceases to be 'common good' and is being swiftly transformed to be an internationally traded commodity.[2]

Perhaps education will be the one and only sector, standing out, for the high velocity and intensity with which the transitions at the advent of liberalisation, have ensued. The reforms in Higher Education have generated several vibrant trends recently, and the most significant one among them is the search for far diversified income streams towards a self sustenance. Globally, it can be seen that, universities are on their efforts to shift themselves towards a self sustaining mode from the grant accepting mode, and Indian Universities are not an exception to this general phenomenon. This paper examines this aspect with the empirical evidence from four affiliating universities in Kerala, a South Indian state.

Research Questions, Methodology and Data

Kerala has four major affiliating universities, one each of Central University, Science and Technology University, Agricultural University, Health University, Veterinary University, Fisheries University, Sanskrit University and Malayalam University. The one and only Deemed University is the Kerala Kala Mandalam, exclusively in the area of classical performing Arts. In order to understand the efforts of the universities in making themselves sustainable, the study covers the four affiliating universities namely, University of Kerala, University of Calicut, Mahatma Gandhi University and Kannur University (mentioned in the order of their emergence). The study is based on the secondary data published in the Annual Accounts and Budget Estimates of these Universities.

The study addresses a few research questions like: how far are these universities self sustaining? What are the sources they have tapped for generating resources?; and are there any innovative practices adopted by them, which can be replicated elsewhere?

Background

In this age of Sustainable Universities, globally universities are on their way to be sustainable in every sense of the word. Universities are in a big way moving from the status of grant dependent institutions to self-sustaining universities by identifying their own resources and reducing their dependence on public funding and support. It is a widely accepted fact that education, the most critical engine of growth, is getting more costly and the public exchequer can hardly afford to finance the requirements of the community. In addition, the demographic dividend as experienced in several developing countries cast more demand for education at all levels. This has pushed up the cost of providing education which the state alone cannot address. As rightly pointed out by Tilak (1988) that the resources that are being poured into the university system have been increasing at a fast rate, faster than the general economic indicators, but the requirements of the universities have been increasing at a much faster rate, widening the gap between the two continuously. This situation of 'increased cost and diminished income', leading to a crisis or a near-crisis has been a basic characteristic of Indian universities.

Globally, several attempts are being tried for solving the problem of cost escalation in higher education finance. Perhaps the most popular and most sought after technique is the switching over to the financially Sustainable Universities. The European Universities Association (EUA), has taken up this issue very seriously in early 2005 and has commenced a project to examine the European universities' progress towards identifying the real cost of their activities and the relationship between this progress and individual universities' autonomy and accountability, with the support from Directorate-General for Education and Culture of the European Commission. Since 2005, EUA had been examining the issues of funding, autonomy and accountability through engaging its members, some 800 European universities in 46 countries and 35 national rectors' conferences, in launching an evidence-based debate on improving and updating funding structures. Conferences, workshops and projects assessed the status of system changes for funding and analysed various European funding and costing models. The objectives of this study are to provide information and empirical data for the debate on financial sustainability from an institutional perspective, analyse the status quo of the development of full costing and the relationship between autonomy and accountability and financial sustainability. The report addresses several parties and includes policy recommendations as well as practical advice for universities.

In the case of India, this move has become more visible during the late 1980s and became intense during the 1990s. This has been triggered off with the National Policy on Education (NPE, 1986) which has categorically stated that education is the major contributor towards the development of the nation and education needs to be emphasised on consolidation and expansion of facilities in the existing institutions. The additional resources, as expected, will be mobilised by resorting to donations, enhancing fee, introducing more user charges and reducing the burden of state apparatus and will create a sense of autonomy and responsibility within the educational sector. Government at the national level took several measures and appointed several committees for the purpose of consolidation and expansion of resources and institutions in such a way that it relieves the burden on the State apparatus and shifts a larger portion to the institutions and users.

Theoretical basis of withdrawal of the State apparatus is that there is a gradual realisation that education has turned to be a non-merit good which needs to be financed by the users themselves. Subsidies are applicable and effective only if there is a positive difference between the social and private benefit of the good consumed. When there is a positive difference and the social benefit is much greater, in such cases there is the justification for subsidy of the product of public provision of it. The burden to the state exchequer is compensated by the social benefit the product generates. As it has been stated in the Discussion Paper by Ministry of Finance that education is no more a public or merit good, as the sum of private benefits and the public benefits are mostly same in all cases, and this has been highlighted as the rationale for shifting the burden to the students. A report was presented by the Prime

Minister's Task Force on Education in April 2000 that recommended, among other measures, full cost recovery in higher education asserting that students and parents can bear the costs of higher education and that the central and state governments should only fund those disciplines that have no market orientation. As a part of withdrawal of state funds, it has been decided by the Ministry of HRD in May 2000 that the universities and colleges should raise seven per cent of their requirements of the recurring expenditure by their own resources and should raise it by one per cent every year to reach the target of 25 per cent.

Faced with severe budgetary constraints, including the compulsions of reducing budgetary and fiscal deficit on the one hand, and on the other, increasing demand for higher education, in addition to realising the need for increasing the supply of higher educated manpower in a globalised system, the Government of India constituted a committee to examine the issue of mobilisation of resources for technical education (under the chairmanship of Dr. D. Swaminadhan) (AICTE, 1994) and also another committee for central universities (under the chairmanship of Justice K Punnayya) (UGC, 1993). The two committees were also required to specifically look into the needed fee reforms. The two committees had emphasised the need for making special efforts by higher education institutions to raise their own resources. Quality, Efficiency and Innovativeness must be rewarded and institutions failing to improve financial and academic discipline should be discouraged and provided with disincentives.

Affiliating Universities: Towards Self Sustaining Universities

As already stated there are four Affiliating Universities in Kerala, and all of them have been included in the present study. In general, the Universities have four major sources of finance, categorised as follows:

1. Grants: This category includes grants from Central and State Governments, UGC and specific grants from other financing institutions on specific projects.
2. Own Resources: This category includes income from fees and other type of revenue generated by the universities.
3. Earmarked and NSS funds: This source deals with the receipts against funds earmarked for specific purposes and activities of NSS.
4. Debts and deposits: This item comprises transaction in respect of which the university incurs a liability to repay the money received or requires a claim over the amount paid together with the repayments of the former and recoveries of the latter.

The summary of the financial position of the universities (excluding earmarked funds) under study during the last five years is clear from Table 9.1. Except the Mahatma Gandhi University, all the three universities depend on the state treasury for the upkeep of the system on a large scale. The internal resources constitute only 28 per cent each in Kerala and Kannur, while it is 36.39 in Calicut and 52.93 in M.G.University. However, the government direction that each university should generate resources to the tune of 25 per cent has been followed and achieved by these universities. It may be interesting and worthy to look into the internal composition and trends in the resource generation process of these universities individually. Necessarily, the analysis of process of resource generation and structure of it must be preceded by a brief note on these individual universities. This section is devoted for that purpose.

Table 9.1: Sources of Finance of Universities in Kerala during 2007-08 to 2011-12 (%)

Particulars	*Kerala*	*Calicut*	*M.G.*	*Kannur*
Grants	50.56	50.21	31.85	63.18
Own Resources	28.28	36.39	52.93	28.01
Debts & Deposits	21.16	13.39	15.23	8.81

Note: Average of each parameter for the five years ending in 2011-12

Source: Annual Accounts and Budget Estimates of respective universities

University of Kerala

University of Kerala, the oldest university in the State, was established as University of Travancore in 1931 by the Government of Travancore. After the formation of the State of Kerala, it was renamed as University of Kerala with state-wide jurisdiction in 1957. Subsequent to the formation of University of Calicut and Mahatma Gandhi Universities, the command area of the university has been limited to Thiruvananthapuram, Kollam and Alappuzha districts and some parts of Pathanamthitta district. Known as the 'Mother University' of the State, University of Kerala has been engaging in teaching, research and extension activities in disciplines like science, technology, humanities and social sciences. The university has 236 affiliated colleges coming under the categories of government, private aided and private unaided. The university has 42 teaching and research departments offering post-graduate, M.Phil and Ph.D programmes. The financial position of the university is summarised in the Table 9.2. The share of grants have been steadily decreasing over the period of study, while the share of own resources has been on the increase. Kerala University has been able to generate 28.28 per cent of the total resources from the internal resources. The increasing ratio for the debts and deposits indicate the burden of pension payment in the universities.

Table 9.2: Resource Generation in Kerala University 2005-06 to 2011-12 (%).

Particulars	*2005-06*	*2006-07*	*2007-08*	*2008-09*	*2009-10*	*2010-11*	*2011-12*	*Averages*
Grants	54.17	57.62	53.32	49.60	50.72	49.81	38.65	50.56
Own Resources	27.98	28.70	29.53	27.23	29.46	27.68	27.39	28.28
Debts and Deposits	17.85	13.68	17.15	23.17	19.82	22.51	33.96	21.16
Total	100.00	100.00	100.00	100.00	100.00	100.00	100.00	100.00

Source : Annual Accounts and Budget Estimates of Kerala University 2005-06 to 2011-12

It may be interesting to look into the components of internal resource generated by the University of Kerala (Table 9.3). The major components of internal resources are General Administration and Examination Fees. Unlike the University of Calicut, Distance Education and Self Financing Courses have not formed the major contributors towards internal resources in the Kerala University. Distance Education has been contributing only 7.93 per cent of the internal resources. This may be due to the specific demographical and historical circumstances of the population in the jurisdiction of Kerala University. The geographical area under the University had achieved much progress in education in the early years of the formation of the State of Kerala, as the region was under the direct rule of the Rajas of Travancore, who had been promoting education in a big way. Perhaps this aspect has limited the market and scope for distance education in the areas under Kerala University.

Table 9.3: Components of Internal Resources in Kerala University 2005-06 to 2011-12 (%)

Particulars	*2005-06*	*2006-07*	*2007-08*	*2008-09*	*2009-10*	*2010-11*	*2011-12*	*Average*
General Administration	25.96	19.70	18.17	18.72	17.20	15.37	11.92	18.15
Examination Fees	29.08	31.67	30.17	31.30	34.63	41.87	41.64	34.34
Academic Depts.	3.97	4.42	5.84	4.62	7.02	8.13	5.97	5.71
Non Academic Depts.	3.93	4.17	3.69	3.59	2.49	2.93	1.04	3.10
Distance Education	8.80	8.33	8.79	8.31	7.72	7.27	6.26	7.93
University Centers	15.34	18.53	23.89	23.22	17.97	9.64	9.18	16.83
Miscellaneous	12.92	13.18	9.47	10.24	12.96	14.79	23.99	13.94
Total	100.00	100.00	100.00	100.00	100.00	100.00	100.00	100.00

Source: Annual Accounts and Estimates of Budget, Kerala University, 2005-2012

University of Calicut

University of Calicut, established in 1968, the second oldest and the largest university in Kerala, catering to the educational needs of the population of Thrissur, Palakkad, Malappuram and Kozhikode districts and some parts of Wayanad district, with a student population of around four lakhs, is one of the prominent education institutions in Kerala. It is a residential and affiliating University with 30 P.G. Departments and 373 affiliating colleges with an annual intake of 1,00,000 students, a strength of 1,565 Non Teaching Staff Members and 200 Teaching Faculty Members on its pay rolls. While going through the annual accounts and reports one can clearly see that it has been generating its own resources continuously for many years. Table 9.4 clearly illustrates this fact.

Table 9.4: Resource Generation in Calicut University 2005-06 to 2011-12 (%)

Year	*2005-06*	*2006-07*	*2007-08*	*2008-09*	*2009-10*	*2010-11*	*2011-12*
Grants	50.08	51.09	50.58	48.74	48.92	52.10	49.98
Own Resources	35.77	34.13	36.29	37.55	39.42	35.49	36.1
Debts and Deposits	14.15	14.78	13.13	13.71	11.66	12.41	13.91
Total	100.00	100.00	100.00	100.00	100.00	100.00	100.00

Source: Annual Accounts and Budget Estimates of Calicut University 2005-06 to 2011-12

It is clear from the Table 9.4 that there has been concerted efforts for the generation of own resources by the University of Calicut during the period of study. However, grants continue to be a major source of revenue for the Calicut University too. The resources generated from own sources constitutes 36 per cent on the average for the last five years ending on 2011-12, while the grant component has been on the decrease, though the magnitude is so small. All this shows that there has been concerted efforts on the part of the University towards the generation of internal resources during the recent years.

It may be interesting to go into the composition of the internal resources during these years. Major components of the internal resources are Examinations Fees, Self Financing Institutions and Distance Education. (*See* Table 9.5) On the average, these three major components have been contributing around 83 per cent of the resources generated by Calicut University. Examination fee contributes 38 per cent of the total own resources and it is the largest component. The second largest component is Self Financing Courses, which contribute around 33 per cent of the internal revenue. These two components, taken together, constitute around 71 per cent of the internal resources in Calicut University. The third component is Distance Education which contributes around 13 per cent of the total internal revenue. In this context, it may be interesting to look what Muraleedharan (2004) has stated from one of his studies in the area of revenue generation by the universities in Kerala. He has looked into the process of revenue generation through Distance Education Institutes attached with the Universities in Kerala.

Table 9.5: Components of Internal Resources in Calicut University 2005-06 to 2011-12 (%)

Particulars	*2005-06*	*2006-07*	*2007-08*	*2008-09*	*2009-10*	*2010-11*	*2011-12*	*Average*
General Administration	6.39	8.28	9.54	12.83	12.26	10.72	7.02	9.58
Non- Academic Depts.	5.72	4.87	3.15	3.19	3.16	3.77	2.80	3.81
Academic Depts.	1.00	0.56	0.60	0.44	0.64	0.82	0.93	0.71
Examination Fees	35.11	37.03	36.70	38.37	42.02	40.68	34.30	37.75
Distance Education	9.75	10.73	11.44	13.93	11.57	13.72	21.33	13.21
Self Financing Institutions	41.01	37.16	35.57	28.31	28.23	28.56	29.91	32.68
Capital Account Works	0.50	0.56	1.02	0.56	0.47	0.47	0.55	0.59
Miscellaneous	0.52	0.81	1.98	2.37	1.65	1.26	3.16	1.67

Source: Annual Accounts and Budget Estimates of respective years, Calicut University

Mahatma Gandhi University was established in 1983 and has a jurisdiction over the revenue districts of Kottayam, Ernakulam, Idukki and parts of Pathanamthitta and Alappuzha, and meets the educational needs of the people of central Kerala. It is a University that conducts a range of programmes at the undergraduate, postgraduate, M.Phil. and Doctoral levels through its 18 University Departments, one International Inter-University Centre, six Inter-University Centres, seven Inter-School Centres, 36 Self-Financing Departments, 82 Aided Affiliated Colleges (of which eight are Colleges with Potential for Excellence), 230 Unaided Affiliated Colleges and 273 Recognised Research Institutes. The University has also made its educational presence felt outside the territorial jurisdiction through a chain of Off-campus Centres under the School of Distance Education. Of the 76 off-campus centres, 62 centres are within Kerala, seven centres are outside Kerala and seven centres are working abroad. Out of its 245 affiliated colleges, 163 are in the self financing stream.

Mahatma Gandhi University

Unlike the other two affiliating universities discussed above, M.G.University exhibits a different pattern of financing with the internal own resource component outstripping the grant component during the analysis period. Table 9.6 explains this phenomenon.

Table 9.6: Internal Resource Generation in M.G. University 2005-06 to 2011-12 (%)

Particulars	*2005-06*	*2006-07*	*2007-08*	*2008-09*	*2009-10*	*2010-11*	*2011-12*	*Average*
Grants	44.4	42.5	41.04	23.49	28.49	36.8	29.41	35.16
Own Resources	35.2	36.2	37.40	62.99	58.24	49.29	56.71	48.01
Debts and Deposits	20.4	21.3	21.56	13.52	13.27	13.93	13.88	16.83
Total	100.00	100.00	100.00	100.00	100.00	100.00	100.00	100.00

Source: Annual Accounts and Budget Estimates of M.G. University 2005-06 to 2011-12

As it is clear from the Table 9.6, the University has been able to generate 48 per cent of the resources they require on the average internally. Besides, the own resources component has contributed around 62.99 per cent in 2008-09. It may be interesting to examine the composition of the internal resources during the period of study. Table 9.7 illustrates this case.

Table 9.7: Components of Internal Resources in M.G. University 2007-08 to 2011-12 (%)

Particulars	*2007-08*	*2008-09*	*2009-10*	*2010-11*	*2011-12*	*Average*
General Administration	11.45	9.38	15.51	15.23	12.99	12.99
Exam Fees	20.83	22.10	29.68	28.91	24.45	24.44
Academic Depts.	8.73	0.23	0.12	0.20	0.16	0.16
Non-Academic Depts.	1.75	0.70	1.43	1.67	1.18	1.18
Distance Education	8.99	8.78	11.53	12.18	10.17	10.17
Self Financing Institutions	54.95	58.81	41.73	41.81	51.05	51.06
Total	100.00	100.00	100.00	100.00	100.00	100.00

Source: Annual Accounts and Estimates of Budget, M.G. University, 2005-2012

As it is clear from Table 9.7, the major component of internal resource in M.G. University is Self Financing Institutions. The contribution of this component was as high as 58 per cent in 2008-09. The next component in the size of proportion is the Examination Fees, followed by Distance Education.

Kannur University

Kannur University was established in 1996 to cater to the educational needs of the Kasargode and Kannur districts and Manathwady Taluk of Wayanad district. The University has seven campuses spread across three districts. There are 27 Government and aided private colleges under the University. In 2011-12, the University had 396 employees, consisting of 50 teaching and 346 non-teaching staff members. A casual glance at the resources of Kannur

University makes it clear that the resource generation position is so pathetic and they were able to generate only 28 per cent of the resources by their own and they were depending on the grants to the tune of 63 per cent on the average during the period of study. Table 9.8 explains this aspect.

Table 9.8: Resource Generation in Kannur University 2005-06 to 2011-12 (%)

Particulars	*2005-06*	*2006-07*	*2007-08*	*2008-09*	*2009-10*	*2010-11*	*Average*
Grants	67.28	58.47	57.08	63.94	69.14	63.18	67.28
Own Resources	24.26	32.31	31.65	27.64	24.17	28.01	24.26
Debts and Deposits	8.46	9.22	11.27	8.42	6.69	8.81	8.46
Total	100.00	100.00	100.00	100.00	100.00	100.00	100.00

Source: Annual Accounts and Budget Estimates of Kannur University 2005-06 to 2011-12

The general picture of Kannur University is that it has been largely depending on the grants from either agency for running the day to day business. However, the composition of the resources generated by the university is of much interest. Table 10.9 explains this aspect in detail. It is clear that Examination Fees and Revenue from Distance Education have been the two major sources of internal revenue in the case of Kannur University.

Table 9. 9: Components of Internal Resources in Kannur University 2005-06 to 2010-11 (%)

Particulars	*2005-06*	*2007-08*	*2008-09*	*2009-10*	*2010-11*	*Average*
General Administration	20.57	13.74	24.59	17.82	14.48	18.24
Exam Fees	28.40	23.74	25.17	25.95	33.83	27.42
Other Receipts Exam	4.86	10.42	2.36	3.47	3.89	5.00
Academic Depts.	13.02	12.40	11.24	9.68	9.77	11.22
Engineering Unit	7.43	0.64	0.39	0.26	0.43	1.83
Dept of Physical Education	2.88	1.87	1.96	1.85	1.95	2.10
Dept of Students Welfare	2.06	0.96	0.95	1.16	1.40	1.31
Distance Education	0.00	19.22	20.03	21.83	17.86	15.79
University Centers and Courses	19.34	15.50	11.68	11.72	11.66	13.98
Miscellaneous	1.44	1.51	1.63	6.26	4.73	3.11

Source: Annual Accounts and Budget Estimates of Kannur University 2005-06 to 2011-12

Concluding Remarks

The aforesaid discussion on the internal resource generation in selected universities in Kerala brings forth several interesting facts. While the universities across the world are moving towards sustaining universities, the case studies carried out in Kerala have given a quite opposite picture. Still the day-to-day functioning of almost all the universities of our country is conditioned by the grants of State or Central government. Even, though these universities are active in their efforts to generate their own resources and moving towards self sustenance, their dependence on the grants given by the State and Central governments is glaring.

As Tilak and Geetha Rani (2003) pointed out, given a deficit situation in the budgets of the universities and near maximum levels of hike in fees, the need to mobilise the resources through internal sources of income and other sources is being increasingly felt. Strengthening internal sources of income as well as other sources of the universities would be more desirable than further increasing the share of fee income. Income from internal sources can be mobilised through increased levels of consultancy and research activities, sale of university publications, etc. Other source of income will have to be boosted up by strengthening and establishing the industry-university linkages, encouraging private donations and endowments, strengthening community participation, etc. It is quite clear that with limited public funds, some institutes need to acquire other funding sources from productive activities for their effective functioning. However, the practice of acquiring resources from other sources differs from country to country. For instance, in the United States, the funds generated from sales and services alone accounted for 22.2 per cent (NCES, 1997). In China, the total self-generated funds were from university enterprises, commissioned training for enterprises, educational services, research and consultancy, logistic services, donations, student tuition fees, and other funded activities (World Bank, 1997).

However, it is quite disheartening to note that there has been hardly any attempt for innovative practices identified for resource generation in the selected universities under study. Most of these universities have stuck to the worn out method of shifting of the cost burden by the introduction of self financing courses which are run on the basis of cost based fee structure, by collecting the entire cost from the students. In the case of Kerala University, the major component of own resources is the Examination fee. Self Financing Sector has not formed the most significant component in the case of Kerala University. The picture is entirely different in the case of Calicut University, where the revenue from the Self Financing Sector forms a major share of 33 per cent against 38 per cent from the Examination Fees. The M.G. University presents a glaring example of resource generation to the tune of 48 per cent, of which 50 per cent of the internal resources is from the Self Financing Sector. The M.G. University has advanced much in the area of self sustenance, as they have taken the replicable efforts in the area of generation of resources and move towards self-sustenance. Kannur University, the younger university in Kerala, has not made much effort in this direction, as they still depend on the grants to the tune of 67 per cent on the average. Besides, it is the examination fee and Distance Education that has formed the major components of internal resources.

Thus, the self sustenance of universities, as envisaged by the European or American counterparts, still continues to be a mirage as far as the Indian Universities are concerned. The Indian Universities, in spite of the strong directions of the UGC and the Central Government, continue to depend on the grant component, with no or less efforts for identifying the fresh sources of resource generation. The examination fee and the cost sharing devices of self financing still form the major component of resources. They have not resorted to any type of innovative techniques for generating resources such as consultancy projects or knowledge generating devices that can contribute towards their sustenance in future. It is high time that the Universities in India should resort to identify and tap innovative streams of resources that can contribute towards the future sustenance of them, which will rescue them from the excessive dependence on grants.

Notes

(This paper is based on the results of the major research project on 'Internal Resource Generation and Utilization in Indian Universities: A Study in South Indian States' sponsored by the Indian Council of Social Science Research, New Delhi. I greatly acknowledge the support extended by the ICSSR).

1. For a detailed account of commoditisation and internationalisation of higher education, *see* Gillan, et al. (2003) and Noble, F. (2002).
2. Higher education meets many of the conditions, as observed by Barr (1993) as characteristic of a private good, amenable to the forces of the market. First, higher education cannot be treated as a purely public good, as it exhibits conditions of rivalry (limited supply), excludability (often available for a price), and, rejection (not demanded by all) all of which do not meet the characteristics of a purely public good, but reflect at least some important conditions of a private good. Second, the consumers of higher education are reasonably well informed and the providers are often ill informed — conditions which are ideal for market forces to operate. This market orientation has lead to elements of the reform agenda such as tuition, which shifts some of the higher education cost burden from taxpayers to parents and students, who are the ultimate beneficiaries of higher education, more nearly full cost fees for institutionally-provided room and board, and more nearly market rates of interest on student loans, all of which rely upon market choices to signal worth and true trade-offs.

References

All India Council for Technical Education (1994), *Report of the High Power Committee for Mobilization of Additional Resources for Technical Education*, New Delhi.

Barr, Nicholas (1993), *The economics of the welfare state*. Second Edition. Weidenfeld and Nicholson. London. pp. 106, 345.

EUA (2008), *Financially Sustainable Universities: Towards Full Cost Pricing in European Universities*, European University Association.

Kwick, M. (2002*), Marketing the Education or Educating the Market? Perspectives on a global education marketplace.* Institute of Philosophy, Adam Mickiewicz University, Poznan, Poland.

Michael, Gillan, Bill Damachis, John, McGuire (2003), 'Australia in India: Commodification and Internationalisation of Higher Education' *Economic and Political Weekly.*

Muraleedharan, K. (2004), "Internal Resource Generation and Utilization in Conventional Distance Education Institutes: The Case of Three Universities in Kerala" *JEPA,* Volume XVIII, No: 2, Pp 199-215

Noble, David. F. (2002), 'Technology and the Commodification of Higher Education', *Monthly Review*, Vol. 53, No.10, March.

NCES (1997), *National center for education statistics: Finance FY97 survey, integrated Post secondary education data system.* U.S. Department of Education.

Tilak, J.B.G. (2000), *University Finance in India: A Profile*, National Institute of Educational Planning and Administration (India), NIEPA

Tilak, J.B.G. and Geetha Rani (2003), "Changing Pattern of University Finance in India", *Journal of Services Research*, Volume 2, Number 2 (October '02-March)

Tilak, J.B.G. and Geetha Rani (1988), University Finance in India: A Review of Problems and Prospects, *Higher Education*, 17(6), 603-635

UGC (1993), *UGC Funding of Institutions of Higher Education, Report of Justice Dr. K. Punnayya Committee*, 1992-92, University Grants Commission, New Delhi.

Weiler, Hans, N. (2001), *"States and Markets: Competing Paradigms for the Reform of Higher Education in Europe".* National Center for the Study of Privatisation of Education. Occasional Paper No.16.

World Bank (1997), *China higher education reform*, The World Bank, Washington, D.C.

10.
Government Withdrawal and Privatisation of Higher Education in Kerala

Rajan Varughese

Ever since education came to be imparted in a well-organised fashion, schools and colleges were being established in India both under public and private initiatives. Their relative share has varied from state to state. In Kerala, private sector has been playing a dominant role in all layers of education in the state. This has been mostly in the form of a public-private partnership (E.T. Mathew, 1996). The policy makers and the academic community in state confine the debate on the problems of higher education to the professional education sector in the context of the government and court verdicts related to admission and fee. The arts and science colleges including the government and aided-colleges built on public assets which played a crucial role in the growth and development of higher education in the state, have been left out in discussion. But of late, the higher education sector especially the private aided sector is undergoing a transformation in its structure, ownership and management, which can adversely impact equity and excellence in higher education. Here, an attempt is made to trace the process of privatisation of public assets in higher education in the context of the recent transformation of private aided colleges in the state of Kerala.

Expansion of Higher Education

There has been considerable increase in the number of higher educational institutions and enrolment of students. Kerala had pursued a liberal higher education policy from 1956 through to the mid-eighties in terms of quantitative expansion and access to higher education. At present, there are 14 universities functioning in the state, excluding NAULS and central university, constituting less than one per cent of the 611 degree awarding institutions in India (UGC, 2011). There are 210 Arts and Science Colleges in the State comprising of 152 Private Aided Colleges and 58 Government Colleges. Total number of students enrolled in various Arts and Science colleges (excluding unaided colleges) under the four general universities in Kerala during 2014-15 is 2.27 lakh. There are 164 engineering colleges in the State with a sanctioned intake of 58237 students in 2015. Out of these engineering colleges 152 (92.68%) are self-financing colleges (unaided), nine (5.49%) are government colleges and three (1.83%) are private aided colleges (*Economic Review, 2015*).

There is a general impression that higher education in Kerala is already over expanded (JBG Tilak, 2001). The number of students enrolled in the universities and colleges has increased. Of the total enrolment of 3.78 lakhs students, 49010 students (12.96%) are enrolled in the university departments and 329068 (87.04%) are in affiliated colleges which interestingly is in line with the all India average (UGC Annual Report 2009-10). The percentage of population in higher education in the relevant age group (18-22) is higher at 24 per cent as compared with the national average (12.4%). On the other hand, Kerala's higher education system has not expanded as much as it should have in a state where elementary education is nearly universal and secondary education has expanded reasonably well.

College Education Scenario

The college education (arts and science colleges) scenario in Kerala is characterised by four important features:

1. The role of the government in college education is limited as government colleges, are small in number, only 58 out of 210 in 2015, which forms only 27.6 per cent of the total.
2. A dominance of the private sector with more than 72.3 per cent of the colleges being run by private managements which are financed by the state, they being aided private colleges – 152 of 210 (in 2015)
3. Growth of self-financing or private unaided colleges. There are 370 such arts and science colleges as in 2015
4. The emergence of unaided courses and off-campus / study centres of other universities in aided colleges.

Evolution of College Finances

Several experiments have gone into the financing of colleges in Kerala. However, the full details of such experiments are not easily available, as the published accounts of private managements are scanty (E.T. Mathew, 1991). The finance required for starting and maintaining a college can be studied under the following headings.

Initial Capital Expenditure

The initial capital expenditure is the cost of land and building for the college. Three different ways of securing land for a college were experimented in the initial phase of establishing a college in Kerala: (1) Gift from the state government; (2) Gift from private individuals; and (3) purchase of land by the management (financed by donations raised from the public and / or members of the particular community under whose auspices the college was to be started).

As far back as 1813, the land for the Old Seminary (Syrian College), Kottayam and about quarter of a century later, for the CMS College, Kottayam, and in recent times for the Mahatma Gandhi College, Thiruvananthapuram and the Sree Narayana College, Kollam, were donated by the government. The Old Seminary at Kottayam was established entirely at the cost of the Travancore Government. Later Rani Lakshmi Bai of Travancore made a grant of 16 acres of land on the banks of the Meenachil River free of tax and a sum of rupees 20,000 to the Seminary which led to the establishment of the C.M.S. College, Kottayam. Nearly 200 acres of land (Montro Island at Kollam district) was given to C.M.S. church management for meeting the recurring expenditure of the college. In more recent times, there have been several instances in which the state government donated the required land for the establishment of colleges. To mention only a few prominent cases, the Union Christian College, Alwaye, (1921) was started in an old Cutchery (the first court building in the Travancore state) building which stood on an 18 acre plot of land, donated by the Maharaja of Travancore, on the banks of the Periyer river. Forty-six acres of land at Thiruvananthapuram were given in 1948 to the Nair Service Society for the establishment of the Mahatma Gandhi College. In the same year a 30-acre plot at the Cantonment Maidan at Kollam was granted to the S.N.D.P. Yogam for starting the Sree Narayana College. A decade and a half later in 1964, the state government made a grant of 26 acres of land for starting the Devaswom Board College at Sasthamcota in Kollam district. Land for the establishment of colleges used to come in several instances also from donations by individual or organisations. For instance, the offer by V.S. Sivarama Krishna lyer of an amount of rupees 50,000 enabled the Payannur Educational Society in Kannur district to purchase 157 acres of hilly land for starting the Payannur College in 1965. The entire land for the NSS College at Manjeri in Malapuram district was donated by P.M. Thirumulpad. The establishment of the S.N. College, Chelannur, in Kozhikode district was made possible by a gift of 67 acres of land by the Sree Narayana Educational Society of Chelannur.

By and large the land required for the establishment of colleges in the private sector were acquired with funds raised from the public, mostly from the members of the community which sponsored the colleges and to a limited extend from members of other communities. Confronted with major obstacles in raising funds, the NSS invented a new technique of financing, known as "Ulpanna Pirivu" (produce collection), according to which each household was to donate in cash a certain percentage of whatever agricultural produce it raised. This remarkable ingenious technique fetched about rupees 6.5 lakh in the 1940s.

For colleges started by other organisations, particularly the Christian churches, the problem of raising funds varied from management to management. While relatively rich (mostly Catholic) dioceses like those of Thrissur, Palai and Changanachery, found it possible to finance the founding of colleges largely out of their own resources, the task was not so smooth in respect of colleges started by other dioceses, especially the non-Catholic churches. In the case of colleges run by individual parishes of the Christian churches, the problem was of a different order and magnitude. Since most such parishes derived stable and substantial incomes through the offering received in the church especially during the annual "perunal" (religious festival), they were in a position to raise adequate funds from own resources. The St. Aloysius College run by the St. George Church, Edathuva, and the St. Mary's College owned by St. George Church, Aruvithura are typical examples of such colleges. There is a close parallel between these colleges and the Guruvayurappan College, Calicut, which in 1952 received a handsome grant of rupees five lakh from the surplus funds of the Guruvayurappan temple at Guruvayur.

Among items of recurring expenditure, the most important is salaries of the teaching and non-teaching staff. With the "Direct Payment Agreement" of 1972 between the state government and the managements of private colleges, payment of salaries has become the responsibility of the government. In return, the colleges are bound to remit the tuition fee collected into the government treasury. Under this agreement, other recurring expenditures, such as maintenance of buildings, are also met by the government. The direct payment agreement was the culmination of a series of attempts made to regulate and standardise the financial management of colleges about which there had existed long drawn criticism from teachers, educationalists and the general public. Colleges in Kerala have gone through, in relation to their finances, mainly three periods, namely (1) the period prior to 1962, (2) the period from 1962 to 1972, and (3) the period since 1972.

Period Prior to 1962: The period prior to 1962 began with the establishment of the first college in Kerala in the early nineteenth century. It represents a period of almost complete financial autonomy for private colleges. The only control was the academic control exercised by the university in matters such as course and syllabi, norms of admission of students to different courses and qualifications for appointment of lecturers and professors. The government almost entirely kept aloof from the functioning of private colleges. The fees collected from students were retained by the colleges concerned and were used for payment of salaries of teachers and other staff and for meeting other expenses. There were only 36 private arts and science colleges in the entire state of Kerala prior to 1962.

Period 1962-1972: According to the Grant-in-aid Code implemented with effect from 1 April 1962, a sum of money was annually set apart by the state government "with the object of maintaining, improving and extending higher secular education". Under the new dispensation, colleges were entitled to three different types of grant-in-aid; (1) teaching grant (for salaries of teachers), (2) building grant (for the purchase, acquisition, erection or enlargement of buildings for the colleges and the hostels attached to them), and (3) equipment grant (for the purchase of books for libraries, apparatus for laboratories and furniture).

Period Since 1972: The Grant-in-aid Code did not, however, resolve the long standing conflict between the management and the teachers. The latter accused the former of several malpractices. The teachers demanded unification of fees in private colleges as well as between the private and the government colleges. At the end of an agitation which lasted three months from June to August 1972, the "Direct Payment Agreement" was reached between the state government and the managements. With the introduction of direct payment, the state government assumed responsibility for the payment of: (1) salaries of the teaching and non-teaching staff, (2) library and laboratory grant, (3) maintenance grant, and (4) contingency grant of private colleges in the state. These items together form a major part of the recurring expenditure of a college. Thus, the state government is now playing an undoubtedly predominant role in the financing of colleges in the private sector. The other institutional sources of finance, though far less important, consist of the management (the educational agency), the university to which the colleges are affiliated, and the University Grants Commission.

Non-Institutional Sources

The non-institutional sources of financing consist mainly of: (1) fees other than tuition fees, (2) donations, and (3) miscellaneous receipts such as income from property, interest on bank deposits, and borrowing. Here, donations received by the colleges may be classified into: (a) donations from staff, (b) donations from students and / or parents, (c) donations from the general public. Donations are playing an important role in the financing of colleges today. Since the college accounts are subject to government audit, it is very likely that normally the major share of the donation is received by the management and shown as such in its accounts. So college accounts show only a small portion of the total funds raised by the management by way of donations.

So, it is the institutional and non-institutional sources of funds that together contributed to the growth and development of private aided colleges in the state. In reality, both these sources are sources of public funding. The aided higher education sector managed by the private managements in Kerala owes its existence to public assets created or mobilised over a period of time from varied public or social sources.

Privatisation of Public Assets: Disinvestment Route in Higher Education

The consequences of the growth of unaided sector as a separate entity in higher education are widely debated in terms of its impact on equity and excellence. But very little attention is focused on the emerging trends of privatisation of public assets in higher education in Kerala, especially in the private aided college sector in the state.

The White Paper (2001) of Kerala Government

The White Paper (June 2001) of the government of Kerala portrays investment in higher education as a drain on the exchequer and contains suggestions to curtail it in a phased manner. The major suggestions pertaining to college sector include:

1. Raising the tuition fee,
2. No aided / government colleges in the future,
3. Starting of new courses in the self-financing stream only,
4. Starting of unaided colleges, and
5. Autonomous status to colleges with sound financial background.

There are several factors that contributed to the initiation of disinvestment process of social sector in Kerala. Among them the most important one is the policy of the state government as spelled out in the White Paper. The de-linking of pre-degree courses from the colleges (from 1997 onwards) created large idle infrastructure in the private aided colleges. The attempt to start new aided courses in these colleges was defeated by the government and universities when permission was given to private managements to decide on the nature of these courses. So in the first instance, it is the acceptance of the philosophy of privatisation by the state government that encouraged private aided managements to explore various methods which steadily paved the way for disinvestment in higher education in Kerala.

Self-financing Courses in Aided Colleges

It may appear paradoxical, but it is true that aided colleges in Kerala are today centres of self-financing courses. Some of these courses are affiliated to other universities in the state and even outside the state or abroad. Except in recent years, aided colleges have not subscribed to the idea that the education given should be retailed with a price tag keyed to profit. A cursory examination of the sources from which funding came, and the manner in which expenses were made and the Spartan frugality that characterised the early years, will show that the aided colleges never reveled in the prospect of profit. The so-called self-financing mode (a misnomer which should be understood as 'student financed') in its spirit and praxis is alien to the professed commitment of the aided colleges to value-based education. To launch courses reserved for the affluent is absolutely hostile to the principle of equity and benevolence. A stray case of concession, scholarship or reward cannot be accepted as the justification for crude commercial models in higher education.

Off-campus Courses in Aided Colleges

The off-campus parallel courses in the aided affiliated colleges signify crass commercialisation as its worst. It is demoralising to accept and believe that 19 aided colleges in Mahatma Gandhi University have preferred to join hands with profiteers that have sold their souls to rank commerce, while 43 colleges in the same university have had the integrity to resist the temptation of easy money. The infrastructure facilities of the colleges established with the funding of UGC and built on public assets from various sources mentioned above are denied to the students in the regular stream. These unregulated off-campus programmes, held on their campuses are bad caricatures of higher education. The authorities at different levels have always shied away from any discussion of the academic credentials of this misadventure. The state universities were reeling under financial difficulties thanks to state government policy on expenditure reduction, which in turn encouraged forces within the university system to experiment with these new revenue models in higher education. The recent UGC directives and court orders have placed some restrictions on the activities of these off campus centres in the state.

Commercialisation of Courses and Marginalisation of the Aided Stream

The reputation of aided colleges in Kerala vis-à-vis higher education is mainly a function of the aided UG and PG courses (with research facilities leading to Ph.D) in affiliated colleges run on well-established and socially relevant norms, laid down by the government and universities. It is important to recognise the principle of social control, which the aided stream embodies. But the aided courses are neglected, marginalised and even abolished in the context of the undue privileging of self-financing stream within the aided colleges. Just as the space that became available after the delinking of pre degree course went to the self-financing stream, the space generated by the closure of aided courses is likely to be earmarked for commercial objectives. The unauthorised fund collection during the time of admission in open merit quota under the cover of PTA/Lab funds is rampant in aided colleges in the state. For management quota, compulsory donations have become the norm. This is often justified through comparison with other colleges that charge higher amounts in the state and outside. The aided colleges have been volunteering to conduct an astounding number of university examinations for private and off-campus students. Regular classes are being cancelled with regularity for this purpose and teachers in the aided stream assigned for invigilation. The burden falls exclusively on the students of the aided stream. The self-financing stream enjoys the privilege of not being disturbed or dislocated by such mundane events. In some colleges there were weekly value education sessions for the aided stream. It was not felt necessary that a major segment of the self-financing stream should have these sessions. The self-financing stream in aided colleges is a form of dissaving of social capital for private enrichment as it curtails the educational opportunities of weaker sections of society.

Commercialisation of University System

The university authorities in the state sensing the intention of the state government came forward to protect the vested interest. The violation of university statutes by private agencies in the state was conveniently overlooked by the authorities. The aided affiliating system faced onslaughts from within and outside. The universities which are duty bound to protect and strengthen the aided affiliating system, sided with the forces of disintegration. They competed among themselves in extending the boundaries of off-campus courses, even violating UGC guidelines in this regard, in India and abroad. The universities in the state directly conduct a large number of self-financing courses thereby forfeiting the moral and sometimes statutory authority in controlling the private agencies engaged in crass commercialisation. In some cases, the universities share the profits with the private agencies. All these sins are committed in the name of decreasing financial support to the universities by the state government. To facilitate this, elected syndicates of the universities are replaced nominated 'experts' in the state universities. The market friendly forces have been reining the university system in Kerala and they are well entrenched with strong financial and political clout in the realm of higher education.

Influence of Assessment and Accreditation Agencies in the State

The accreditation of colleges by various quality assessment agencies has reached crescendo in the state. In Kerala four universities, and 135 colleges are accredited by the National Assessment and Accreditation Council (NAAC) as on November 2015. The universities and colleges in the state are trying all known techniques of securing the highest grade. The managements of private colleges have incurred some expenditure to showcase their institutions before the peer teams from these quality assurance agencies. But the operation of these agencies has created a false sense of excellence among the higher educational institutions in Kerala as all the colleges that go for assessment are accredited with grade. Additional resource mobilisation by the colleges was a pet theme for the peer terms that visited aided colleges in Kerala. The resistance of the academic community in Kerala towards commercialisation of higher education was blunted by the operation of these quality assurance agencies. The private managements in the state consider the quality certificate from these agencies as a prerequisite for securing the Centre of Excellence / Autonomous status for their institutions which in turn will strengthen their claim for more public funds in future.

Hence quality seal of the NAAC is used for further privatisation of higher education in the state than for improving the quality and equity aspects of it.

Build, Operate and Transfer (BOT) in the Reverse Gear

Disinvestment of PSUs earns some income for the government, but privatisation of public assets in higher education offers no income to the government or society. It is in a sense BOT (Build, Operate and Transfer) in the reverse gear. Aided colleges are created and maintained with public fund or resources from several sources. They are public funded institutions by the government, charitable institutions and educational agencies like the Church, Nair Service Society (NSS), Sree Narayana Dharma Paripalanasanghom (SNDP) and Muslim Educational Society (MES). During a certain period of history, these educational institutions functioned within the parameters of social control outlined by the State Government rules and University Acts / Statues. But with the freedom given by the government and the universities in the matter of running the colleges and starting of courses, all these public funded institutions built on social assets are now freely operated by private managements in the state. The new move of the government of Kerala to replace the existing land leases with title deeds to private managements in education will further accentuate the process of disinvestment in higher education in the state. This is a form of social sector disinvestment silently taking place in the higher education sector in Kerala. The private aided colleges are really public wealth. The real owners of these institutions are the public or the society at large. Greater social control and growth of these public funded centres of higher learning are needed, at least, to sustain the achievements of Kerala in the field of higher education.

Autonomous Colleges in Kerala

The government order (2013) permitting autonomous colleges in Kerala for the first time shows that the aided college authorities, in addition to the academic freedom, have the financial freedom to start courses of their choice in the unaided stream. This move will further accentuate the process of privatisation of higher education in the state. Kerala government decision to allow autonomous colleges in state is throwing a fresh challenge to public funded system of higher education in the state of Kerala. The aided college managements in the state controlled by sectarian interests without any democratic arrangements of governance and transparent mechanism of appointments of teachers in their institutions are likely to use in this opportunity for private gain than for public good.

Proposal for Private Universities in the State

The decision of the KSHEC (2014) to recommend the establishment of Private Universities in the state will pave the way for complete commercialisation of higher education in Kerala. The performance of private universities in the country is dismal except in a handful of cases. The champions of the new system has declared that private university status will not be given to government / aided institutions. So the intention is to elevate self-financing institutions with sound financial basis and infrastructural facilities in the state to the level of universities.

Need for Alternative Policies

(a) Scheme of Cluster of Colleges

The concept of cluster of colleges needs to be examined seriously in the context of the opportunities the system provides for collaborative learning. Different models of clusters have emerged across the world. Clusters have been set up around administrative structures, which would co-ordinate the functioning of the units. Individual institutions have also grouped together on their own to share the benefits of mutual cooperation. There are also clusters with one dominant member supporting smaller units. Clusters have been formed for specific purposes, like sharing Information Communication Technologies (ICT) in teaching-learning, civic engagement by institutions of higher education, etc. Apart from sharing resources, the Clusters have provided opportunities for teachers to develop and offer new courses. Students have gained by exposure to experts in different institutions. The possibilities of opening up new areas of knowledge have emerged in the process. Obviously clusters have developed in response to the infrastructure and academic needs. The College Clusters that may be set up in affiliating universities in the State may draw upon the above concepts and practices. The report prepared by the KSHEC (2010) can be taken as a starting point in this regard. An attempt was also made in 2011 to start college clusters in Thiruvananthapuram, Ernakulam and Kozhikode. The non-cooperation of the private managements was a big problem at that time.

(b) College Cluster Multi Campus Universities (CCMCU)

The Kerala State Higher Education Council again (2012) recommended college cluster multiple campus Universities (CCMCU), which is considered as an alternative to affiliation system. In this system colleges are not affiliated but form a part of the university, but as autonomous campuses. This is in tune with the XII plan proposal of UGC and substantial central funding is expected for establishment of such college cluster. While clustering the colleges, two models are considered. One, clustering them based on the categories like Aided, Self-financing and Government colleges and the second making a mixed cluster. Each cluster may have colleges ranging between 10 to 30.

(c) *Scheme of College Cluster Universities under RUSA*

The XII Plan proposed a holistic plan for the development of higher education in the country by ensuring access, equity and quality. The Plan which recommended strategic utilisation of central funds to ensure comprehensive planning at the State level recommended a new centrally sponsored scheme (CSS), Rashtriya Uchchatar Shiksha Abhiyan (RUSA). The second component of the scheme refers to the creation of universities by conversion of the colleges in a cluster. Cluster universities, with an average allocation of rupees 35 crore per university, aim essentially at addressing the critical gaps in the spatial distribution of higher educational institutions across the States. In this scheme existing affiliated government and government-aided colleges constitute the cluster. In the funding pattern envisaged in the scheme, states are free to mobilise up to 50 per cent of their share through private grants and donations, Corporate Social Responsibility (CSR) contributions, Public Private Partnership (PPP), etc.

(d) Reform of the Structure and Governance of Higher Education

There is an urgent need for reforming the structure and governance of higher education in the state to protect and strengthen the public funded system of higher education. This, among other things, calls for a thorough reform of the laws governing the same in the state. The Kerala State Higher Education Council under the Chairmanship of Dr M. Ananthakrishnan, constituted a committee to review the Acts of Universities in Kerala in 2009.

The committee made significant recommendations in regard to the synergic relationship between the principles of autonomy and accountability and between the key players in the system such as the government, universities and affiliated colleges. The U.R. Anathamurthy Committee Report (2010) on state policy on higher education provides similar inputs for strengthening the public funded system of education in Kerala.

A progressive perspective on higher education in Kerala today should address the concerns of expansion, excellence and equity, in the overall context of the country as a whole and the specific context of the State in particular.

References

Economic Review (various issues): Kerala State Planning Board.

Gurukkal, Rajan & Varughese, Rajan (2012): *Encounters: A University on Trail* Published by the National Book Stall (NBS), SPCS, Kottayam.

Inclusive and Qualitative Expansion of Higher Education — 12th FYP 2012-2017 (UGC2011)

Mathew, E.T. (1991): Financing Higher Education – Sources and Uses of Funds of Private Colleges.

Reports of the Kerala State Higher Education Council (2009-2015).

Tilak, JBG. (2001): Higher Education and Development in Kerala, CSES, WP No.5 Feb 2001.

Varughese, Rajan & Narayaran, Aju (edited) (2015): Autonomous Colleges — Myth and Reality (In Malayalam), National Book Stall, SPCS, Kottayam.

Varughese, Rajan — Privatization of Public Assets in Higher Education: Emerging Trends in Private Aided Colleges in Kerala, *Journal of Educational Planning and Administration* Vol. XX. No.3, July, 2006. Pp. 313-320.

11.
Access and Equity
A Study on the Impact of Self-financing Colleges in Kerala

S. R. Sheeja

Education has a key role in the socio-economic progress of any nation. It creates the human resource base of nations. It is through higher education that people acquire wide range of skills required for enhancing productivity. In today's global knowledge economy, skill based activities have a crucial role and, therefore, skills developed through quality education are the major determinants of employability. Higher education equips younger generation with skills required for the labour market and provides them the opportunity for social mobility. Hence, the best solution to enhance economic opportunities and thereby reduce inequality is to improve the educational qualification and skill sets of common people.

It is the advancement in higher education that determines a country's relative position in today's competitive global environment. Lack of higher education facilities makes the nation less competitive, less capable, and ill-equipped to assert itself among other countries. Hence, all nations attach great priority to the expansion of higher education facilities. In the light of the huge demographic dividend enjoyed by India, development of higher education assumes greater significance. To maximise the utilisation of India's human resource potential, expanding higher education facilities to the common people is very critical. Along with the question of access, equity in higher education is also very important in a populous developing country like India as education is the most potent change maker and the most effective mode of redistribution of resources. In this context, an attempt has been made in this paper to examine the issues of access and equity in higher education in India. It also examines the important policy measures adopted by the government to make the higher education system more inclusive. The study is descriptive in nature and is based on a survey of literature available in this area as well as secondary data published by the Department of Higher Education, Government of India.

An Overview of Higher Education Sector in India

Indian higher education system expanded steadily in the post-independence period and, at present, it is one among the largest education systems in the world in terms of enrolment and number of institutions. There were only 27 universities and 578 colleges in India in 1950-51. Table 11.1 shows the latest available number of different categories of education institutions all over India. Definitely, it gives an idea about the expansion of Indian education system in terms of numbers.

Table 11.1. Number of Higher Education Institutions in India, 2014-15

Type of Institutions	*2014-15*
Universities	757
Affiliated Colleges	38056
Stand Alone Institutions	11922
Total	38813

Source: Department of Higher Education, 2015

At present, the higher education sector in India is vast and is of great variety comprising of 38813 institutions, made up of 757 universities and 38056 colleges. Out of the 757 universities, there are 43 central universities, 316 state public universities, 37 deemed universities, 267 private universities. In addition, there are 14 open universities and 69 institutions of national importance. Seventy six per cent of the colleges are privately managed institutions. Total enrolment in higher education (Department of Higher Education, 2015) has been estimated to be 33.3 million with 17.9 million male students and 15.4 million female students. Nearly 46 per cent of students enrolled are females.

According to TSR Subrahmanian (2016), the Chairperson of the Committee for Evolution of New Education Policy 2016, nearly one fourth of the population in India is directly involved in teaching learning process. There are at least 200 fields of specialisation and expertise in the scope of the operations of higher education sector. Private sector, which accounts for 63 per cent of the total number of institutions and 52 per cent of the total enrolments, is the major player in Indian higher education sector. Majority of the private institutions offer professional or vocational programmes almost exclusively.

The fact that we have been able to build up such a modern system of higher education virtually from scratch since independence is a major achievement. This was possible only through the initiatives of successive governments which have been focussing heavily on education. Despite all these efforts, our education system is fraught with a large number of problems. One of the most serious drawbacks of Indian education system is related to the reach and inclusiveness of higher education. We are far behind the international community on the basis of several dimensions of access and equity.

Access to Higher Education: Present Scenario

Gross Enrolment Ratio (GER) is an important indicator of access to higher education. GER is widely used to show the general level of participation in higher education and the capacity of higher education. GER expresses total enrolment in higher education as a percentage of the eligible population of 18-23 years of age group in a given year. There has been an unprecedented improvement in GER in India in the last two decades. Currently GER in Indian higher education is 23.6. According to Martin Trow's (1973) classification of higher education system on the basis of enrolment, when GER is less than 15 per cent, there is elite higher education system whereas there is mass higher education system when enrolment is between 15-50 per cent and there is universal state when GER is more than 50 per cent. It was during the Eleventh Plan (here it is important to remember that inclusive growth strategy was also formulated during this plan) that India's GER crossed 15 per cent, taking the country's higher education from an "elite" to a "mass" higher education system. It is quite noteworthy that there has been a steep increase in GER in the last decade and this is quite appreciable considering the ever increasing population in India. However, it reveals that only 23.6 per cent of university-eligible age group children get enrolled in the colleges despite our continuous efforts to expand our education system. Higher education is not accessible to more than 76 per cent of people in India.

In order to understand the relative position of India among other countries across the globe, an international comparison is shown in Table 11. 2.

Table 11.2. International Comparison of GER, 2013

Country	*GER*
China	30
Russia	78
UK	57
USA	89
India	23.6
Brazil	46
World average	32.9

Source: World Bank, 2013

The international comparison shows that though we have witnessed unprecedented improvement in the reach of higher education, India still lags behind the world average as well as GER in most of the countries. While the world average is 32.9, GER in advanced countries like the USA and Russia is 89 and 78 respectively. Comparatively India's GER is much less than that of other member countries in BRICS like Brazil and China.

Despite the fact that we have one of the largest education systems in the world, more than 76 per cent of the university-eligible age group students are not getting enrolled in the colleges. This appears to be a great paradox. Ultimate outcome of this is the abundant supply of unqualified and unskilled workforce. This proves detrimental to the overall growth and development of the country. Further, people belonging to elite social groups and categories have better access to quality higher education. Expanding access to higher education is a very important challenge to the Indian higher education system. Infrastructure development, adequate trained and qualified faculty, use of Internet and communication technology, financial assistance to weaker sections, changing the curriculum to match industrial requirements, etc. are some of the prerequisites of increasing access to the Indian higher education system.

Equity in Indian Higher Education

Equity refers to equal opportunity for all sections to participate in higher education. All modern democratic societies try to ensure equality of opportunity to citizens. Extending educational facilities to the deprived people enables them to come to the mainstream. In populous developing countries like India, education is the key to equity as it has been considered as the most potent changemaker and the only viable mode of redistributing the means for social mobility (Despande, 2016). However, a fundamental weakness of Indian higher education system is related to the issue of inclusiveness. Students from the economically backward and socially disadvantaged groups of the society do not get enough opportunities in India's higher education system. Even though several programmes have been developed by the government to enhance access to higher education and to make it inclusive, there still exists discrimination based on gender, caste / community, location, etc. Many studies (Dubey, 2008; Tilak, 2015) have shown that there are a large number of barriers in Indian higher education relating to gender, social group, religious group, etc. Often, the people belonging to the under privileged sections like women, people in the lower rungs of caste hierarchy like SC, ST and OBCs, etc., the poor, physically disabled, religious minorities, people from remote / rural areas and migrants find it difficult to access higher education.

In the following pages an attempt has been made to assess the inclusiveness of Indian higher education system on the basis of some important dimensions like gender, caste / community, geography, etc. Here also GER is used as an important indicator to assess whether the expansion of higher education in India was inclusive or not. Apart from GER for different categories, Gender parity index is also used to examine gender disparity in higher education.

Gender Inequality

First, an attempt has been made to examine the gender-wise GER in higher education in India. While GER for males in India is 24.5, the corresponding figure for females is only 22.7. This indicates that in India, in comparison with their male counterparts, lower number of females come to higher education institutions. Within different communities also there exist gender disparities. Among the Scheduled Castes while GER for male population is 19.3, its value is 17.6 for SC females. In the case of Scheduled Tribes GER is 14.6 for males while it is 12 for females.

Gender Parity Index (GPI) is another indicator of gender disparity in higher education. Gender Parity Index (GPI) is obtained by dividing the female GER by the male GER. If GPI is equal to 1, there is parity between sexes, if it is between zero and 1 there is disparity in favour of males, and if GPI is greater than 1, there is disparity in favour of females. GPI for the country is around 0.89. GPI among SCs is 0.89 and GPI among STs is 0.79. Both GER and GPI figures indicate the prevalence of unequal opportunities for men and women in Indian higher education.

Caste/ Community Based Disparities

Let us have a look at the extent of community / caste-wise inequalities in higher education. The GERs for SCs, STs have always been very low as compared to other communities in the India. GER for Scheduled Castes students is 18.5 and for Scheduled Tribes students GER is 13.3 as compared to the national GER of 23.6 (Department of Higher Education, 2015). To enhance the participation of the disadvantaged groups of the society, various policy measures such as reservation system, provision of scholarships, special hostels, meals, loans, etc. have been implemented by the central as well as state governments.

Geographical Inequalities

The skewed regional distribution of universities and colleges in India creates a huge challenge for inclusion. Majority of higher education institutions cluster around metropolitan and urban centres while there are a few institutions in remote areas. Spatial distribution of university level institutions is highly uneven across states also. Nearly one third of colleges (33%) are in the southern region and the lowest numbers of colleges are in the North-East.

While five small states have only one university each, five other states have more than 20 university level institutions. As many as 16 states do not have a single central university. The number of colleges per lakh population in the age-group of 18-23 years (college density) varies from seven in Bihar to 58 in Puducherry while the all India average is 27 (Department of Higher Education, 2015). Such glaring imbalances act as a barrier to the balanced regional development of the country.

Enhancing Access and Equity: Initiatives of the Government

In the following pages an attempt has been made to examine the important initiatives undertaken by the government to increase the reach and equity of higher education in India as well as some recent developments in the field of education which have much implications to access and equity of higher education.

Most of the five year plans have made significant provisions for improving the reach of higher education across the country and to reduce inequalities prevailing in the field of higher education. This is particularly true regarding the 11th and 12th plans. During the 11th Plan public spending in education was raised to 6 per cent of GDP and many efforts were made to make higher education more inclusive. During this plan period (2007-2012), India witnessed the increase in GER from 12.3 per cent to 17.9 per cent. Major policies initiated during the 12th Plan include increased funding for disadvantaged groups and measures to correct regional and social imbalances. The government aims to achieve enrolment of 35.9 million students in higher education institutions, targeting a GER of 25.2 towards the end of the plan period. It also aims to reach the target of 30 per cent GER by 2020-21.

Several schemes and programmes were implemented by the government to address the concerns of access and equity. As part of efforts to promote equality in opportunity nations rely on affirmative action. Affirmative action refers to policy measures designed with objective of reducing marginalisation of groups that have historically suffered from discrimination, exclusion and that are under-represented in a society's desirable positions (Weisskopf, 2012). Affirmative action includes non formal measures of supports like encouragement, recruitment, etc. and formal devices like quotas or reservation. As children belonging to these stigmatised groups often live in surroundings which are not conducive to maximum development of their potential, affirmative action in the field of higher education has a crucial role in identifying and nurturing their potential. Successive governments in India took various initiatives to help the deprived people to overcome their socio-economic backwardness. Among these, reservation in higher education institutions is central to the policy of inclusive growth and distributive justice. The basic objective of the reservation system in India is to increase the opportunities available to the underprivileged communities for improving the social and educational status and, thereby, bring them to the mainstream.

Apart from the policy of reservation, a number of initiatives have been implemented by the government to enhance the educational opportunities of students from the weaker sections of the society. Among them a few interventions at higher education level are given below:

1. Setting up of National commission for Minority Educational Institutions
2. Setting up of National Monitoring Committee for Education of SCs, STs and persons with disabilities and earmarking funds for the welfare of SCs and STs.
3. Student Support Initiatives such as National Merit-cum-Means Scholarship Scheme (NMMSS)
4. Special Scholarship Scheme for Jammu & Kashmir, and Scheme of Interest Subsidy on Educational Loans
5. Indira Gandhi Scholarship for Single Girl Child for Pursuing Higher and Technical Education
6. Construction of Women's Hostels for Colleges
7. Development of Women's Studies in Universities and Colleges
8. Post-Doctoral Fellowships for Women
9. Special Scheme of construction of hostels for women in colleges located in the North East
10. Special concessions in the regulations of setting up women technical institutions
11. Establishment of Equal Opportunity Cell in colleges and universities for the effective implementation of programmes for disadvantaged groups and to provide guidance and counselling
12. Establishment of the Model Degree Colleges in educationally backward districts including minority concentration areas.

The National Education Policies also gave due attention to the issues of access and equity. The National Education Policy of 1986 emphasised the importance to removal of disparities and equalisation of educational opportunities particularly to women, SCs and STs. To achieve this many new initiatives like new scholarship programmes, recruitment of more teachers from the deprived sections, development of new institutions which provided housing facilities, etc. were introduced. Rashtriya Uchhatar Shiksha Abhiyan

(RUSA), the centrally sponsored programme introduced in 2013 also aims to correct regional imbalances in access to higher education by creating opportunities for students from rural areas to get access to better quality institutions and setting up institutions in un-served and under-served areas. It also aims to provide adequate higher education opportunities for SCs, STs, OBCs, women, minorities and differently abled persons.

In order to expand the institutional base of the higher education successive governments have been establishing new institutions and creating additional capacity in existing institutions. As conventional mode of education has the capacity to meet the requirements of only a meagre proportion of educational aspirants, Open and Distance Learning (ODL) has become an alternative approach to reach out to the masses particularly the disadvantaged. Nearly 11.7 per cent of the total enrolment in higher education is through the distance mode and 46 per cent of the learners are female students (Department of Higher Education, 2015). ODL can effectively play a positive and interventionist role in bridging the social and gender gaps. Recent developments: ICT has enabled the academic institutions to provide real learning experience without much compromise on quality through distance mode.

Massive Open Online Courses (MOOCs), the relatively recent online learning model, is yet another innovative development which offers freedom of access to higher education. The evolution of MOOCs is based on the principle that the urge to learn should not be limited by economic, demographic and geographical constraints. Creative use of technologies adds to the potential of MOOCs as an innovation towards greater openness in higher education.

Challenges

Despite all these efforts, still there exist some barriers to entry into the field of higher education. Moreover, some of the recent trends in the field of higher education raise a host of issues related to access, equity and quality.

At present, private sector now accounts for more than 64 per cent of total higher education institutions in the country and over 53 per cent of total enrolment is also through the private sector. Active involvement of the private sector was expected to increase the reach and quality of the Indian higher education system. Concentration of private investment particularly in professional and technical education has restructured the entire higher education system in the country which has thrown up policy debates on their implications. Financially weaker and other disadvantaged segments of the society find it difficult to afford the cost of education offered by these private institutions and as a result they are being excluded from these institutions. Only rich and elite sections of the society can afford the cost of education offered by the private sector. Thus, vast majority of people belonging to the marginalised sections are deprived of educational opportunities.

Most often, higher education gets lower priority in budget allocation also. In India we spend less than 1 per cent of GDP on higher education. For the effective functioning of public institutions, financial support from the government is very critical. Gradual withdrawal of the state from the higher education sector is the major push factor behind the rise of private funding which in turn leads to the commercialisation of education. This is particularly true in the post-reform period resulting in the exclusion of people from the lower rungs of social strata from the field of higher education.

Some unprecedented changes are taking place in the field of higher education in India in the last two decades. Indian higher education witnessed a silent transformation with the entry of more women and first generation learners from the deprived sections of the society who did not have access to higher education previously (Despande, 2016). Lot of frictions and tensions accompanied this transformative process and higher education sometimes becomes a sight of conflict.

The proposed Policy on National Education, 2016 focuses more on quality and 'employable skills' tailored for the global market. If the government pursues this policy without any compromise, people belonging to the deprived sections of the society including women and minorities will have to face much greater exclusion. Too much emphasis on quality and employability is expected to undermine the country's efforts toward expansion of the reach and inclusiveness of higher education.

Conclusions

Nations cannot sustain their growth momentum and maintain competitiveness unless problems in higher education are settled. Despite our continuous efforts, the issue of increasing access and reach of higher education with greater equity remains as a major problem in higher education. Setting up higher education institutions all over the country surely enhances the intake capacity of the system. However, this does not necessarily make higher education system more accessible and inclusive. As inclusion is complex and multidimensional in nature, innovative and appropriate strategies are essential to achieve it. Careful planning and policy frame work are essential to eliminate different types of barriers prevailing in higher education and to revamp and upgrade this sector to meet the future challenges.

References

Agarwal, P. (2009). *Indian Higher Education: Envisioning the Future.* New Delhi: Sage Publications India Private Ltd.

Department of Higher Education. (2013). '*Annual Report 2012-13*'. Ministry of Human Resource Development, Government of India. New Delhi. Retrieved form http://mhrd.gov.in

Department of Higher Education. (2015). '*All India Survey on Higher Education 2014-15*'. Ministry of Human Resource Development, Government of India. New Delhi. Retrieved form http://mhrd.gov.in

Despande, S. (2016). Higher Education: An Uncertain Policy Process, *Economic and Political Weekly*, 51(35), 37-40.

Dubey, A. (2008). '*Determinants of Post- Higher Secondary Enrolment in India*'. Higher Education in India: Issues Related to Expansion, Inclusiveness, Quality and Finance, New Delhi: University Grants Commission.

Musthafa, M.N., Nasimudheen, T. (2014). Marching Towards Access and Equity in Higher Education – An Exploration of Infinite Possibilities of *MOOC, Issues and Ideas in Education, 2(2), 203-216.*

Thilak, J.B.G. (2015). How Inclusive is Higher Education in India, *Social Change*, 45(2), 185-223.

Trow, M. (1973). *Problems in the Transition from Elite to Mass Higher Education.* California: Mc Graw-Hill.

Subrahmanian, T.S.R. (2016). Education in Disarray: Need for Quality Upgradation and Inclusivity, *Economic and Political Weekly*, 51(35), 37-40.

Weisskopf, T.E. (2012). Rethinking Affirmative Action in Admissions to Higher Educational Institutions. In Hasan and Nussbaum (ed.) *Equalising Access: Affirmative action in Higher education in Higher education in India, United States, and South Africa.* New Delhi: Oxford University Press.

12.

Gender Participation in Science, Technology, Engineering and Mathematics (STEM) Education

Emerging Challenges to Innovation in India

Christabell P J and Rajeev B

All the economies in the world are shifting into a new phase of development based on the production, communication and consumption of knowledge. This is popularly known as "the knowledge-based economy" (KBE) which in turn describes greater dependence on knowledge, information and high skill levels, and the increasing need for ready access to all of these by the business and public sectors (OECD, 2005). In other words, it can be defined as KBE is an economy in which the production, distribution and use of knowledge are the main drivers of growth, wealth creation and employment across all industries (OECD, 1996). In a KBE, a significant part of a nation's or company's value consists of intangible assets, such as the value of its citizens' or workers' knowledge (intellectual capital). The knowledge-based economy is one in which the generation and exploitation of knowledge has come to play the predominant part in the creation of wealth. It is not simply about pushing back the frontiers of knowledge; it is also about the most effective use and exploitation of all types of knowledge in all manner of economic activity (DTI Competitiveness White Paper, 1998). Obviously, the idea of the knowledge driven economy is not just a description of high tech industries, but it describes a set of new sources of competitive advantage which can apply to all sectors, all companies and all regions, from agriculture and retailing to software and biotechnology (Leadbeater, 1999). The success of KBE is increasingly based upon the effective utilisation of intangible assets such as knowledge, skills and innovative potential as the key resource for competitive advantage. The knowledge society is a larger concept that is just an increased commitment to R&D. It covers every aspect of the contemporary economy where knowledge is at the heart of value added – from high tech manufacturing and ICTs through knowledge intensive services to the overtly creative industries such as media and architecture (KoK, 2004). At the heart of the development of the knowledge economy is continuing innovation. Innovation will result in a successful economy, increased wealth, employment generation and social equality. Knowledge – and hence the knowledge society – transcends national boundaries and represents a global phenomenon (Castells, 1996).

The emergence of the knowledge economy, partly attributed to globalisation and technological advances, has ushered in a wide ranging debate on the demand for higher levels of competencies. While there is a growing agreement on the importance of skills per se as a key engine for economic growth (OECD, 2000) and the spread of the knowledge economy, there is far less agreement on which competencies and skills make the difference. Within and outside of the education sector, the discourse often refers to higher educational attainment in general, focused on the development of broadly-based competencies that can support further lifelong learning. Therefore, in a knowledge-based economic system STEM (an acronym for science, technology, engineering and mathematics) education has a pivotal role to play. STEM had its origins in the 1990s at the National Science Foundation (NSF), USA and has been used as a generic label for any event, policy, programme, or practice that involves one or several of the STEM disciplines. The Economics and Statistics Administration (ESA) defines STEM jobs to include professional and technical support occupations in the fields of computer science and mathematics, engineering, and life and physical sciences (Beede et al. 2001). In many countries, attention is being given to the participation of students in tertiary Science, Technology, Engineering and Mathematics (STEM) education. Industry, government, and academic leaders cite increasing STEM workforce as a top concern. This is a result of internationally competing economic ambitions, coupled with acute shortages on the STEM labour market, a declining interest among students for STEM education and a long-lasting under-representation of women. However, despite similarities concerning policy attitudes and identified problems, countries differ considerably from one another concerning the percentages of students who choose STEM education and the proportion of female students included here (van Langen and Hetty, 2005).

STEM is essential for producing a highly skilled workforce capable of competing in the twenty first century and hence producing a sufficient pool of qualified graduates in STEM has long been a challenge for Indian Universities and Colleges. India holds the world's largest young population, but she must also be a possessor of the largest young work force with the highest level of knowledge skills in the world. As per the latest ADB Report (2014), given leveraging its strengths in human capital, India can become a major global KBE in the years to come. For that, she needs to increase education attainment levels as well as the proportion of scientists and engineers in the population and in order to achieve the same, higher education and high level skills at the tertiary level are necessary. India upholds to be the abode of one of the largest higher educational systems on the earth with about 17 million students studying in hundreds of universities and colleges all over the country. A total of 2,00,000 full time researchers are found to be working in Indian universities, the comparable figure for US universities being 12,00,000. In India, just four out of 1000 young students opt for science and technology or research as their calling. The comparable figure was 110 for Japan, 76 for Germany and Israel, and 46 for South Korea. India has been far behind in STEM investment, expending just 0.88 per cent of its GDP in science research compared to 7-8 per cent for the US and 3-4 per cent for South Korea. Of that, nearly a quarter is spent on basic research that has little to do with innovation or economic growth while China spends five per cent (Chhapial, 2014). As a result, India is one of the countries with the most acute talent crisis globally. Hence, the nation needs to increase the number of experts in STEM fields to drive innovation and to keep the country competitive in the global economy.

The gender inequality in STEM education has long been a concern to educators and policymakers all over the world. In India, there has been a phenomenal growth in the number of women students enrolled in higher education since independence. The women enrolment which was less than 10 per cent of the total enrolment on the eve of Independence rose to 44.40 per cent in the academic year 2013-2014. The women enrolment has been the highest in the faculty of Arts (44.91%), followed by Science (18.11%) and Commerce (16.42%), constituting 79.44 per cent in the three faculties, leaving the remaining 20.56 per cent in all the professional faculties. The maximum percentage of women enrolment in professional faculties had been in the faculty of Engineering / Technology (9.41%) (UGC 2014). The above cited evidences showing that there exists a gender gap in higher education particularly in STEM education in the nation.

The paper examines how the gender gap in STEM participation poses a challenge to the future of knowledge-based economy and the resultant innovations in India as well as in the state of Kerala. It is based on empirical evidences collected from different universities of Kerala on female participation in STEM education and the effects of the same in innovation and scientific research in India.

Objectives

1. To assess the STEM participation by gender in India and to determine the gaps existing in various fields of study.
2. To find the STEM participation by gender in Kerala and to determine whether the gaps existing are as glaring as that of India.
3. To understand the participation of females in various fields of STEM research education in universities of Kerala.

4. To evaluate the various activities which enhance the innovation and creativity in STEM research education by scholars in universities of Kerala.
5. To look into the differences in perceptions on employment opportunities and job preferences of females *vis-a-vis* males towards STEM jobs.
6. To bring out the challenges faced by females in STEM research education and the possible ways to improve the same.

Methodology

The study used both secondary and primary data. Secondary data were collected from various sources ranging from different educational departmental bodies to ministerial data, published works, journals, newspapers and government reports. Primary data needed for the study generated through primary survey in five major Universities in Kerala – Kerala, Mahatma Gandhi, CUSAT, Calicut and Kannur. Using a pre-prepared questionnaire, information was gathered from 220 research scholars who undergo full time Ph.D in STEM fields. The major thrust of the study was regarding the nature and level of higher education among females in STEM education, academic opportunities and challenges, participation in STEM communication activity and their aspirations and suggestions for the improvement of quality of education system.

Findings

STEM Participation by Gender in India

In the international regime of KBE, higher education quintessentially plays a major role. Indian higher education is characterised by a large variety of educational institutions with a total of 712 in number (Table 12.1). The universities set up under state legislative act occupy the largest share in the picture with a total of 310. It is followed by 143 state private universities, 127 deemed universities, 68 institutions of national importance and 42 central universities.

The enrolment pattern of undergraduate level in higher education gives a vivid picture on participation of students in different disciplines in the universities. The enrolment rate is 41 per cent for Arts/ Humanities/ Social Sciences. The combined entry to STEM field in higher education especially at under graduate level is found to be 33.05 per cent. The rest of the fields constitute 26.26 per cent. The data clearly show that only less than 40 per cent of undergraduate students chose science as their calling (Table 12. 2).

Table 12.1 Number of Institutions by Type 2013-14 (Provisional)

Sl. No.	*Universities*	*Numbers*
1	Central Universities	42
2	State Public Universities	310
3	Deemed Universities	127
4	State Private Universities	143
5	Central Open university	1
6	State Open University	13
7	Institutions of National Importance	68
8	Institutions under State Legislature Act	5
9	Others	3
Total		712

Source : GoI (2015) All India Survey on Higher Education, MHRD

Table 12. 2: Enrolment in Different Disciplines / Subjects at Under Graduate Level in Higher Education 2012-13 (Provisional)

Discipline	*% Enrolment*
Arts / Humanities / Social Sciences	40.69
Engineering and Technology	16.34
Commerce	14.53
Science	12.60
IT and Computer	4.11
Medical Science	2.87
Management	2.19
Law	0.95
Education	3.10
Oriental Learning	0.46
Agriculture	0.55
Others	1.60

Source: GoI (2015) All India Survey on Higher Education, MHRD

The gender gap in literacy rates in India is showing a narrowing trend over the decades, i.e., according to 1991 census it was 24.8, but it was 16.3 in 2011. The corresponding decline in the gender gap is also noticeable, where it was 13.1 per cent between 1991 and 2001, it was 24.7 per cent in the decade between 2001 and 2011 (Table 12.3).

Table 12.3: Gap in the Literacy rates of Males and Females over decades

States	*Gender Gap*			*% decline in gender gap*	
	1991	*2001*	*2011*	*1991-2001*	*2001-2011*
Kerala	7.5	6.3	4.0	15.3	36.3
India	24.8	21.6	16.3	13.1	24.7

Source: Census of India, Office of Registrar General, India, 2011

The gross enrolment ratio (GER) of students in India shows a mixed picture. While the girls outnumber the boys in the primary, upper primary, secondary and senior secondary level, the marked difference could be seen in higher education (Table 12. 4). The overall participation of boys in higher education is 22.3, while that of girls is 19.8.

Table 12.4: Gross Enrolment Ratio (GER)

Level	*All*		
	Boys	*Girls*	*Total*
Primary (I-V)	98.1	100.6	99.3
Upper Primary (VI-VIII)	84.9	90.3	87.4
Elementary (I-VIII)	93.3	96.9	95.0
Secondary (IX-X)	73.5	73.7	73.6
I-X	89.4	92.4	90.8
Senior Secondary (XI-XII)	49.1	49.1	49.1
I-XII	83.3	85.9	84.6
Higher education	22.3	19.8	21.1

Source:For School Education: U-DISE-2013-14 (Provisional) For Higher Education: AISHE-2012-13(Provisional) Report

With special reference to STEM education in India also, the gender gap is further more evident. The fields of Arts and Medicine show almost same trend with more than 80 females for 100 males in university education. The fields of science and commerce show almost same trend with the women representation falls between 60 and 70. When the attention falls on engineering and technical fields, it is less than 40 women per 100 men (Table 12.5).

Table 12.5: Number of Females per 100 Males in University Education in Major Disciplines, 2000-01 to 2008-09

Year	*Arts*	*Science*	*Commerce*	*Engineering & Technical*	*Medicine*
2000-01	81.40	61.40	55.30	28.7	68.20
2001-02	77.80	64.20	63.10	33.1	68.40
2002-03	82.24	60.55	57.95	29.17	71.19
2003-04	85.70	75.90	51.20	17.5	72.50
2004-05	87.30	84.30	51.60	31.1	53.10
2005-06	77.70	71.20	65.20	36.1	90.1*
2006-07	76.90	71.20	60.90	35.8	89.5*
2007-08	79.60	71.00	63.53	39.3	79.66
2008-09	86.80	66.90	65.30	39.7	88.31

Source: GoI (2015), Department of Secondary and Higher Education, MHRD

Table 12.6: Enrolment in different Programmes in Higher Education, 2015

Programme	*Male*	*Female*	*Total*
B.A.-Bachelor of Arts	28.22	37.84	32.55
B.Com.-Bachelor of Commerce	11.51	11.30	11.42
B.Sc.-Bachelor of Science	10.41	12.09	11.17
B.Tech.-Bachelor of Technology	9.10	4.46	7.01
B.E.-Bachelor of Engineering	8.07	4.06	6.26
B.Ed.-Bachelor of Education	1.34	2.84	2.01
L.L.B.-Bachelor of Law or Laws	0.86	0.48	0.69
M.A.-Master of Arts	3.45	5.42	4.34
M.Sc.-Master of Science	1.59	2.31	1.91
M.B.A.- Master of Business Administration	2.25	1.44	1.88
M.Com.-Master of Commerce	0.77	1.16	0.94
M.C.A. -Master of Computer Applications	0.92	0.75	0.84
M.B.B.S.-Bachelor of Medicine, Bachelor of Surgery	0.46	0.52	0.49
M.Tech. -Master of Technology	0.61	0.39	0.51
M.E.-Master of Engineering	0.25	0.22	0.24
Others	20.20	14.72	17.73

Source: GoI (2015) All India Survey on Higher Education, MHRD

Looking into the breakup of enrolment in different programmes in higher education, the participation of women in Arts education (both for B.A. and M.A.), is higher than that of men. In basic science and commerce too one can observe the same trend. In contrast to that, in applied fields of technology and engineering the enrolment is found to be only half of that of the males (Table 12.6).

STEM Participation by Gender in Kerala

Kerala tops in India in indicators like literacy rate, higher enrolment of students, percentage of girl students in school, schools and colleges in villages, low dropout rate among students, etc. Regional and gender disparities in literacy rates are the least in Kerala. Kerala leads other States in terms of women's enrolment as a percentage to total enrolment. The enrolment rate of girls at higher secondary level is 52.73 per cent. At degree level, girls' enrolment is 68.66 per cent. At postgraduate level it is 75.54 per cent. Among the degree courses, the percentage of girls is high in B.A. courses, closely followed by B.Sc. courses and B. Com. (Table 12.7). Up to 1970s, girls studying or applying for the technical and professional courses like Engineering, Agricultural and Veterinary Sciences were not in great numbers (Table 12.7). But the participation of women in technical and professional streams as well as in the Engineering Technology streams has shown marked increase. In the all India level, a total increase of 23 times is seen in enrolment in technical and professional streams; whereas the percentage of female students in Engineering and Technology streams increased from 0.3 per cent in 1950-51 to 13.1 per cent in 1993-94 (GoI, 1998). Kerala shows corresponding increase to this. The gender gap in engineering courses is

Table 12.7: Girls' Enrolment at Different Levels 2015-16

Courses	*Boys*	*Girls*	*Total*	*% of Girls*
School Education	1907811	1864910	3772721	49.43
Higher Secondary	168191	187606	355797	52.73
Graduation	226500	155520	70980	68.66
Post Graduation	14029	22883	30294	75.54
B. Tech	4022	2348	6370	36.86
M. Tech	607	768	1375	55.85
Total Engineering	4629	3116	7745	40.23
Polytechnic	10518	21587	32105	32.76

Source: Directorate of public instruction, Department of college education and Department of technical education, 2015

more when we compare it with other courses. For graduation in engineering the female intake is only 36.86 per cent whereas in the postgraduate level, it is 55.85 per cent. This means, in conventional courses girls outnumber and outperform boys. But boys still outnumber and outperform girls in the professional, engineering and technological courses. The total number of students enrolled in various Arts and Science colleges (excluding unaided colleges) under the four general universities in Kerala during 2014-15 is 2.27 lakh. Of this 1.56 lakh (68.66%) are girls.

Gender Participation in Scientific Research

An in depth enquiry on gender participation in STEM was conducted among the five universities of Kerala. In the first step, the number of research scholars enrolled in STEM fields in five different universities in Kerala were collected. In all universities, the number of female is high (Table 12.8). From the available data, it is perceived that Mahatma Gandhi University and CUSAT have an equal share of females along with males, but all the other universities under study showed more proportion of females in the enrolment list. This is due to more participation of females in research education in recent times. The females are always better in academics right from their school days and the same trend is observed in scientific research education too.

Table 12.8: Research Scholars in STEM in Universities of Kerala, Various Years

University	*Scholars*		*Total*	*Share*	
	Male	*Female*		*Males*	*Females*
University of Kerala (2015)	250	444	694	34.91	62.01
Mahatma Gandhi University (2015)	103	106	209	49.28	50.71
Cochin University of Science and Technology (2013)	386	425	811	47.59	52.40
Calicut University (2014)	185	286	471	39.27	60.72
Kannur University (2015)	24	45	69	34.78	65.21
Total	948	1303	2254	42.05	57. 95

Source: University Annual Reports, various years

For the specific purpose of the present study, a sample of ten per cent was selected. Thus, a total of 220 research scholars in STEM fields were interviewed across five different universities in Kerala. The majority of respondents (63%) were females. The academic departments of the universities were divided into four schools for the purpose of analysing the data. While comparing the percentage of respondents belonging to different schools, the highest (36.8

per cent) is seen in Life Sciences. Next highest number of respondents is from the conventional school – Physical and Mathematical School – 25 per cent (Table 12.9). The difference between the mean age of males is 28.08 and females 28.15 among STEM researches from different universities. The place of residence of STEM scholars is also examined. From the responses it is observed that 68.6 per cent of females and 77.5 per cent of males are coming from rural area and 31.4 per cent of females and 22.5 per cent of males are from urban areas.

Table 12.9: Number of STEM Scholars in different Universities

	Gender		**Total (n=220)**
	Female (n=140)	*Male (n=80)*	
School			
Earth System Sciences	62.5	37.5	21.8
Life Sciences	65.4	34.6	36.8
Physical and Mathematical Sciences	58.2	41.8	25
Technology	69.4	30.6	16.4
Age			
Mean	28.15	28.08	28.12
Standard deviation	3.232	2.642	3.025
Place of residence			
Rural	68.6	77.5	71.8
Urban	31.4	22.5	28.2

Source: Primary Survey, 2016

Innovation and Creativity

The significance of scientific research, innovation and its performance of advancement has been playing a pivotal role for the competitiveness and economic progress of nation. Looking into scholars' research work publication during their academic period, female scholars' annual publication is higher than men in percentage (Table 12.10). Scholars' participation in different academic programme during their research is explained in Table 12.11. Women participation is higher than male in seminars and conferences. But the participation of men scholars is higher in international workshops and short time courses. The women scholars' trend in participation of conferences and seminars is increasing over the years but in training and short time courses both women and men are participating less in number.

Table 12.10: Academic Publications of STEM Scholars

Scholars Academic Publication	*Gender*				*Total (n=220)*	
	Female (n=140)		*Male(n=80)*			
	Yes	*No*	*Yes*	*No*	*Yes*	*No*
I Year	7.85	92.14	6.25	93.75	7.2	92.8
II Year	10	90	8.75	91.25	9.5	90.5
III Year	7.85	96	7.5	92.5	7.7	92.3
IV Year	3.57	92.14	2.5	97.5	3.2	96.8
V Year	0.71	99.25			.5	99.5

Source: Primary Survey, 2016

Table 12.11: Participation of STEM Scholars in Various Academic Programmes

Scholars participation in various academic programmes		*I Year*	*II Year*	*III Year*	*IV Year*	*V Year*
International Conferences	Female	56.6	55.8	70.4	92.9	85.7
	Male	43.4	44.2	29.6	7.1	14.3
International Seminars	Female	63.2	57.1	70	80	100
	Male	36.8	42.9	30	20	--
National Conference	Female	66.7	64.7	62.8	71.4	71.4
	Male	33.3	35.3	37.2	28.6	28.6
National Seminars	Female	71.4	62	68	55.6	66.7
	Male	28.6	38	32	44.4	33.3
International Workshops	Female	26.8	57.1	40	100	100
	Male	71.4	42.9	60	--	--
National Workshops	Female	55	66.7	62.5	75	100
	Male	45	33.3	37.5	25	--
International Training Programmes	Female	--	40.0	--	--	--
	Male	--	60.0	--	--	--
National Training Programmes	Female	53.8	54.5	72.7	--	--
	Male	46.2	45.5	27.3	--	--
Short Time Courses	Female	37.5	50	33.3	--	--
	Male	62.5	50	66.7	--	--
Certificate Courses	Female	70	63.6	40	--	--
	Male	30	36.4	60	--	--

Source: Primary Survey, 2016

From scholars' response to financial support and academic achievements during their research period, it is clear that more than 95 per cent of scholars get financial support for doing their research (Table 12.12). With regard to attaining patents rights on the research work, none of the scholars from the entire five universities attained any patents on their work. In terms of scholars' membership in different professional bodies and other association dealing with the area of interest, male scholars (25%) are higher than female researchers (17.1%)

Tabl 12.12: Academic Performance of STEM Scholars

Scholars' academic achievements	*Gender*				*Total (n=220)*	
	Female (n=140)		*Male (n=80)*			
	Yes	*No*	*Yes*	*No*	*Yes*	*No*
Receipt of scholarships	94.3	5.7	92.5	7.5	6.4	93.6
Receipt of any grants	3.6	96.4	2.5	97.5	3.2	96.8
Receipt of any award	12.9	87.1	15	85	13.6	86.4
Patents rights	--	--	--	--	--	--
Own membership in professional bodies/ Associations	17.1	82.9	25	75	20	80

Source: Primary Survey, 2016

Table 12.13: Scholars Participation in STEM Communication Activities

Scholars participation in different activity		*Never*	*Once*	*2-3 times*	*4-5 times*	*5 times*
Lecture / Talk to school / college students	Female	74.3	12.1	7.1	.7	5.7
	Male	73.8	12.5	5.0	2.5	6.2
Lecture / Talk to a public group	Female	88.6	5.0	4.3	2.1	.0
	Male	81.2	7.5	3.8	3.8	3.8
Workshop with school students	Female	88.6	7.1	3.6	.7	.0
	Male	86.2	6.2	6.2	.0	1.2
Workshop with a public group	Female	90.0	5.7	4.3	.0	.0
	Male	88.8	5.0	5.0	1.2	.0
Drop-in activities	Female	82.9	12.1	4.3	.7	.0
	Male	85.0	8.8	5.0	1.2	.0
Public debate or discussion	Female	90.7	5.0	2.1	.7	1.4
	Male	93.8	3.8	.0	1.2	1.2

Source: Primary Survey, 2016

To understand the scholars' participation in different activities and to what percentage did it differ across genders, we asked a series of associated activities for them to respond (Table 12.13). Based on the percentage analysis of the responses, in all the activities scholars are expected to engage in, majority indicated that they have never participated in the activities. Within the scholars, more females indicated "never" than males, except in the case of "drop-in activities" (85%) and participation in "public debate or discussion" (93.80%) where more male scholars indicated "never" compared to females.

Perceptions on Employment Opportunities and Job Preferences

An independent sample t-test was carried out to determine if there were differences in the mean responses between female and male scholars for the listed statements. Regarding the perceptions on career opportunities, it is evident that there is significant difference in mean between female and male scholars in terms of their ease of finding a career opportunity in Kerala. Comparing the mean values, males found it more difficult than females to find career opportunities in Kerala. In terms of finding career opportunity abroad, there is a significant difference between the attitudes of female and male scholars. Comparing the mean values, which is slightly higher than t, it can be interpreted that females felt it was slightly easier than males in finding career opportunities abroad. However, interestingly, in terms of men getting career opportunities abroad, there was a significant difference between attitudes of female and male scholars, where females with a mean value of 3.49 suggest that they feel it is easier for men to get career opportunity abroad than for them.

Scientific Research and Gender: The way ahead

The reported challenges faced by the female research scholars regarding their contribution to the research are wide and varied. According to them, a married woman would not get much time to involve in the research activities. They also have a feeling that almost all job opportunities are naturally set apart to men compared to women because males have more field experience than women. There is a widely held belief that field work capability is low for women and the same is supported by the female research scholars as the scope for their field work and lab work is limited by their family issues. Family life and responsibility towards their children, lack of family support in research, inferiority complex related to family life are some other issues put forward by the female research scholars. Some female research scholars feel that there is a prejudice of some research guides towards female researchers regarding the quality of work they do.

In additional to that, the females feel that the male dominant society discourages the achievements of women. The male members in scientific field feel that the women candidates have some inherent problems. Lack of exposure to the opportunities outside the university, lack of confidence in pursuing the scientific research, always looking for an early job to settle in life as far as possible, lack of interest in genuine research, less time to work compared to male counterparts especially at night, leading a socially restricted life and family restriction in many things, find to keep a balance between work and personal life, are some of them.

Out of the statements on how to enhance STEM participation (Table 12.14) in graduate level, a higher percentage of male and female researchers were indicating on universities' resources, facility enhancement and collaboration with other higher educational institution. Other indicators such as employment assurance, academic and personal support were also rated high.

While discussing the major challenges on pursuing Ph.D by female candidates, majority feels that it is the family life. As the marriage age is synchronising with the period of study, there is a high chance for dropping the higher studies and look after the families. It is interesting to look into the aspect of accessibility. The accessibility issue in Kerala for higher education is not that much prevalent and could be seen in the data. In order to improve the participation of women in the STEM system various suggestions are also put forward. They include admission to the scientific research only if interested, awareness creation about the opportunities underlying STEM research, awareness creation to female candidates, guidance to handle family life and research simultaneously, moulding young students with good scientific knowledge to the scientific careers, creating awareness about the STEM system to women at early age itself, encourage late marriage which will help to free working environment, enhancing the number and amount of fellowship to genuine female researchers, ensuring security and creating good working atmosphere inside the university, provision of more government funds for empowerment programmes, encouragement and support from the part of family must be assured, enhancing facilities for women participation with sufficient care for them, improving the experimental analysis facility in university, improve the facilities of research centres, need support from family and society to share their ideas and self employment opportunities for women scientists.

Table 12.14: Participation of STEM Graduates in Economic Contribution

Enhance the participation of STEM graduates in economic contribution		*Strongly Disagree*	*Disagree*	*Undecided*	*Agree*	*Strongly Agree*
Collaboration with other higher education institutions	Female	7	3.5	4.3	35.5	56
	Male	0	0	4.9	33.3	61.7
Collaboration with other higher education institutions	Female	1.4	1.4	7	30.5	66
	Male	1.2	2.5	2.5	34.6	59.3
Research collaboration and links with other institutions	Female	7	5	1.4	36.9	56
	Malc	0	3.7	6.2	35.8	54.3
Better Learning environments	Female	0	3.5	3.5	43.3	49.6
	Male	0	2.5	9.9	42	45.7
Better Research environment	Female	7	5	2.1	44.7	47.5
	Male	0	3.7	6.2	37	53.1
Connection between teaching and research from school level	Female	1.4	3.5	7.1	45.4	42.6
	Male	1.2	2.5	6.2	46.9	43.2
Study structure to be revised	Female	.7	4.3	8.5	45.4	41.1
	Male	0	8.6	7.4	44.4	39.5
Curriculum / syllabus must link with innovation	Female	.7	4.3	6.4	40.4	48.2
	Male	0	2.5	8.6	45.7	43.2
Cooperation with other subjects, programmes inside university	Female	.7	3.5	6.4	45.4	44
	Male	0	0	7.4	42	50.6
Management and organisation of University must be improved	Female	1.4	0	6.4	49.6	42.6
	Male	1.2	2.5	4.9	39.5	51.9
Internationalisation of curriculum and research activities	Female	0	.7	4.3	48.2	46.8
	Male	2.5	1.2	8.6	34.6	53.1
Practical training periods	Female	1.4	.7	4.3	44.7	48.9
	Male	1.2	2.5	9.9	44.4	42
Appropriateness of the learning outcomes attained by graduates	Fsemale	.7	2.1	5	51.1	41.1
	Male	0	0	6	40.7	43.2
Employability of graduates must be enhanced	Female	.7	2.8	2.8	39.7	53.9
	Male	1.2	3.7	9.9	33.3	51.9
Academic and personal support for students	Female	.7	4.3	1.4	38.3	55.3
	Male	1.2	3.7	4.9	38.3	51.9

Source: Primary Survey, 2016

Conclusion

The study tried to find out the gender gap existing in research on STEM subjects on scholars in different universities of Kerala. From the analysis it is generally understood that the females in STEM system would like to contribute to the innovation and development of the nation as a whole. Even though there is not much problems in accessibility and recognition, there is a general perception among the people in the system that women cannot perform well due to family issues. Researchers who were involved in STEM communication activity focused on lectures, talks workshop and discussion among different section of society. Majority of scholars never participated any kind of STEM communication activities. The academic achievements of both men and women are not satisfactory none of them achieved any patents for their works and comparatively men scholars' performance and participation is better than women. The stereotyping of women in family role is a long held notion and that is still going on even if she is in higher education and she is capable of contributing back to the society.

It is found that updating of research area and scientific field through regular training and workshops is needed for improving the participation of women in STEM fields. Adequate support and encouragement is to be given for women entrepreneurs and those who are interested in science related industry. Enhancement of awareness through motivational programmes for women from school and degree level to participate in STEM related activities and programmes is needed. Above all, the perceptions and social change are inevitable for a meaningful addition to the nation's wealth by more than half of the population, especially that of knowledge workers on whom the economy has invested a lot.

References

Asian Development Bank. 2014. Innovative Asia: Advancing the Knowledge-Based Economy, Philippines.

Beede, David N., Tiffany A. Julian, David Langdon, George McKittrick, Beethika Khan, and Mark E. Doms. "Women in STEM: A gender gap to innovation." Economics and Statistics Administration Issue Brief 04-11 (2011)

Chappiyal, Himali. 2014. "In science, India invest far less than China, US, South Korea". *The Times of India*

DTI Competitiveness White Paper 1998. Building the knowledge-driven economy Retrieved from www.dti.gov.uk/comp/competitive/main.htm

Kok, W. et al. (2004) Facing the Challenge. The Lisbon Strategy for Growth and Employment. Report from the High level Group (Brussels: European Commission). Also available at http://europa.eu.int/ comm/lisbon_strategy/ index_en.html

Leadbeater, Bonnie J., Gabriel P. Kuperminc, Sidney J. Blatt, and Christopher Hertzog. 1999. "A multivariate model of gender differences in adolescents' internalizing and externalizing problems." *Developmental Psychology* 35 (5):1268.

OECD 1996. The Knowledge-based Economy retrieved from http://www.oecd.org/dataoecd/ 51/8/1913021.pdf

OECD. 1999. The Knowledge-Based Economy: A Set of Facts and Figures, OECD: Paris.

University Grants Commission (UGC). 2014. 60th Annual Report 20113-14, New Delhi.

van Langen, Annemarie and Dekkers, Hetty. 2005. 'Cross-National Differences in Participating in Tertiary Science, Technology, Engineering and Mathematics Education', *Comparative Education*, Vol. 41 No. 3 p329-350.

13.
Quality Issues and Trends in Teacher Education
An Alternative Perspective

Asha J.V.

Today humanity is undergoing a major transition in education, our most powerful instrument for conscious social evolution. In order to cope up with this transition, the future education must be made relevant to the rapidly changing needs of the society, the increasingly sophisticated demands of the labour market, the growing shortage of attitudes and skills needed to promote entrepreneurship and full employment and at the same time cater to the values needed for social harmony and problem solving. Thus, the new human capital paradigm is no longer just about having extended years of schooling to prepare students for industrial jobs; but about content mastery, deep disciplinary understanding as well as acquiring the soft skills of communication, initiative, resilience, group dynamics and problem-solving abilities, among others. The increasing mobility available to many young people, privately funded opportunities to study abroad, and a weakening attachment to state and nation in many countries, even the emergence of a "civic deficit" society, is alarming policy makers. With the growing recognition that teacher quality is critical in preparing students for a society undergoing far-reaching economic and social changes, the need for policies and strategies to strengthen teacher preparation, and as a consequence, teaching, is even greater.

Professionally, powerful teaching is very important and increasing in our contemporary society as a result of the demands of dynamic initiatives of human development and evolution. Due to these developments and evolution, standards of learning would be higher in the 21st century than it had been in the past centuries. However, both the methodology and content of teacher education remain largely unchanged even after a few successive revisions witnessed within the last two decades. Granted that the range of specialised subjects has increased enormously and the range of information available to instructors and students has grown exponentially, the basic conception of education and pedagogy still closely resembles what it was in the universities of old (Jacobs, 2014). The situation demands attention as teachers would need to acquire additional knowledge and skills, both general and specific, to be able to survive and be successful in the 21st century learning environment. Growing evidence demonstrates that, among all educational resources, teachers' abilities are especially critical contributors to students' learning and consequently the success of a nation to advance in its economic, social and political spheres (Darling-Hammond, 2006).

A considerable body of research has shown that pre-service teacher education has a significant impact on early-career of teachers' teaching skills and their philosophies of teaching (Carter, Carre, & Bennett, 1993; Darling-Hammond, 2000b; Iredale, 1996; Temmerman, 1997; Caena, 2014). The role of teachers has become the most challenging in the present millennium, for they had to respond to varied / special needs, deficiencies and aspirations of the taught. The teachers and educators need to experiment with various innovative methods to make teaching appropriate to ground realities in specific conditions that exist in different parts of the state and in different system of schooling. The constructivist teacher education practised elsewhere in the world has shown to have a positive impact on student teachers' perceptions of their own teaching competencies, leading to increased confidence and also improved teaching practice within schools (Brinda, 1998; Byo, 1999; Chen, 1996; Darling-Hammond, 2000a; Ghaith & Shaaban, 1999; Feuerstein, 2011). However, some writers maintain that teacher education has relatively little impact on classroom practice (Su, 1992; Lampert & Ball, 1999; Stuart & Thurlow, 2000; Anitha, 2001). Wherever teacher training has been shown to be ineffective, it can arguably be attributed to the *type* and *design* of teacher training being provided (Iredale, 1996; Kennedy, 1999; Erudyce, 2015). In general we do acknowledge the fact that it is not with the system but with the way it is imparted that its strengths and weaknesses are truly reflected.

Building a high-quality education system relevant to 21st century social and economic realities has become a top priority for most governments and nations. Reforming education systems within a context of ever-deepening globalisation without first understanding its present challenges is not judicious. The regulatory bodies responsible for the development, maintenance and upgradation of Teacher Education Institutions in India are the National Council for Teacher Education (NCTE), the University Grants Commission (UGC) and the Rehabilitation Council of India (RCI). The NCTE revised the curriculum for teacher education in 1978, 1988, 1998, 2009, 2014 whereas the UGC Curriculum Framework and syllabi for B.Ed & M.Ed. programme came in 1990, 2001 and 2015. The B.Ed and M.Ed. (special education) curriculum is designed by RCI in consultation of the Curricular frames of NCTE and UGC. Thus, most of the Teacher Education Institutions in India had been working as per the Curriculums designed by UGC-2001 and NCFTE-2009 till the two year frame introduced by NCTE in 2014. However, the recent efforts undertaken by the NCTE, to achieve planned and coordinated development of the teacher education system throughout the country, the regulation and proper maintenance of norms and standards in the teacher education system and for matters connected therewith is really laudable. The mandate given to the NCTE is very broad and covers the whole gamut of teacher education programmes including research and training of persons for equipping them to teach at pre-primary, primary, secondary and senior secondary stages in schools, and non-formal education, part-time education, adult education and distance (correspondence) education courses. In the context of curriculum revisions happened in the country as per NCTE norms, the present paper tries to find out whether the new direction tries to chisel out a workable quality assured teacher preparation scenario in the country.

Objectives and Methodology of the Study

1. To find out the opinion of teacher educators on the facts and factors responsible for the discrepancy in the practices adopted and expected outcomes of teacher education curriculum
2. To identify the major challenges experienced by the teacher educators in incorporating the three components of the curriculum – theory, practicum, internship within the semester frame work
3. From the opinion collected from teacher educators, suggest modifications in the curriculum for enhancing quality of teachers.

Since the present study attempts to bring out relevant details from teacher educators regarding the practices adopted and expected outcomes of the revised NCTE curriculum, Normative Survey method was found appropriate for this study.

Sample: A representative sample of 42 teacher educators was selected at random from those teaching at M.Ed, B.Ed and D.Ed levels in Thiruvananthapuram district of Kerala. There are 24 B.Ed / M.Ed Colleges and 28 teacher training D.Ed institutions in Thiruvananthapuram district. The sample represents 42 out of these 52 institutions. One teacher educator was selected from each institution. Teacher educators from 10 institutions did not respond. So the sample was limited to 42. A comprehensive questionnaire with open and closed items was given to the sample.

Variables and Items: The study has taken the resourcefulness of the teacher education curriculum in improving the quality of teachers as the variable. As per the recent reification and restructuring of teacher education curriculum, the NCTE Framework has highlighted the focus, specific objectives, broad areas of study in terms of theoretical and practical learning, and curricular transaction and assessment strategies for the various teacher education programmes. The Framework argues that it has been prepared in the background of the NCF, 2005 and the principles laid down in the Right of Children to Free and Compulsory Education Act, 2009. Some important dimensions have been articulated as the vision of teacher education, which is considered as the hallmark of the new approach to teacher education. They are:

1. Reflective practice to be the central aim of teacher education.
2. Student-teachers should be provided opportunities for self-learning, reflection, assimilation and articulation of new ideas.
3. Developing capacities for self-directed learning and ability to think, be critical and to work in groups.
4. Providing opportunities to student-teachers to observe and engage with children, communicate with and relate to children.

As envisaged by the curriculum-developers, these dimensions help transform the prospective teachers to be self directed and productive. The questionnaire had items for gathering reflections of teacher educators on the basic issues in implementing these dimensions for achieving planned and coordinated development of teacher education system. It had four sub areas: developing capacities for self-directed learning, developing capacities for providing autonomy in teaching, incorporating the three components of the curriculum – theory, practicum, internship within the semester frame work and the suggestions for improving the quality of future teachers. One part of it consisted of closed items in a Likert-type scale ranging from 1 to 5 ('strongly disagree' to 'strongly agree'). The questionnaire was subjected to a pilot test in a similar context and the content validation was performed by five experts and the contributions from these enabled to develop the final version of the questionnaire with 26 closed items and five open items.

Analysis and Discussion

The analysis was carried out finding out the average rating to each item in the questionnaire. Then, an inter-rater reliability analysis (Kappa statistic) was calculated to find out the consistency among the raters. Results showed that the degree of agreement among the raters is good, with Fleiss Kappa being 0.67. The items in the questionnaire gathered the perception rating of teacher educators on self regulated learning and autonomy in teaching leading to consolidate the factors responsible for the discrepancy in the practices adopted and expected outcomes of teacher education curriculum. Likewise the major challenges were experienced by teacher-educators in incorporating theory, practicum and internship within the semester framework also. The alternative perspectives were collected qualitatively and presented as the perception of teacher educators' suggestions for modification of teacher education curriculum.

Factors responsible for the discrepancy in the practices adopted and expected outcomes of teacher education curriculum

For moulding teachers who can take up the challenges in the changing scenario, the prospective teachers should develop capacities for self-directed learning and for developing this, the curriculum should give teacher autonomy. On the basis of literature review, the factors contributed to self directed learning included in the questionnaire were: positive attitude, teaching competency and content knowledge, applying innovations in teaching, realise the potentials of learners, understand ways of self development, develop intrinsic motivation, develop leadership quality. The items in the questionnaire pertaining to these factors probed the strength of curriculum in imparting self directed learning. The summary of rating done by teacher educators is presented in Figure 13.1. It is evident that the teacher educators agree (as the score lies between 3 and 4 in the five point scale) that the two year curriculum frame work has the potential of developing positive attitude (3.7) and teaching competency and content knowledge (3.8) among prospective teachers. Comparatively the curriculum is rated to have little room for applying innovation in teaching (3.1) and developing intrinsic motivation (3.2). The strength of the curriculum in developing leadership quality is rated as 3.3 and overall rating of self directed

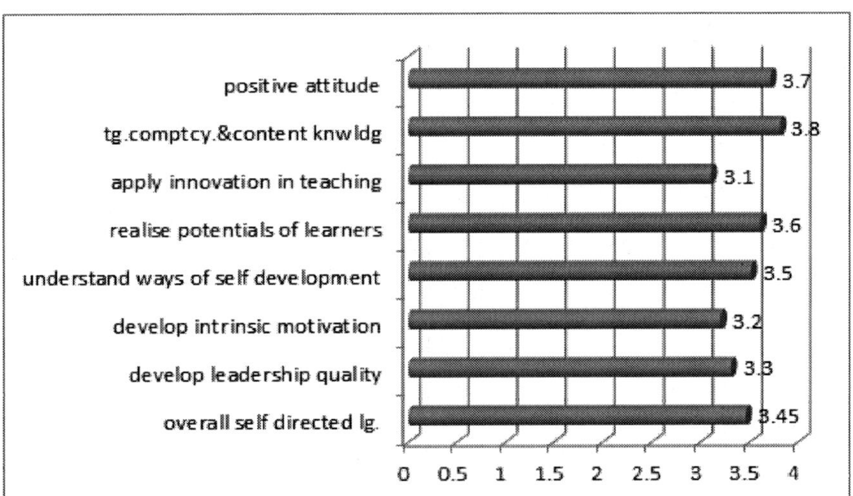

Figure 13.1 Rating on the Capacity of the Curriculum in Realising Self-directed Learning
Source: Prepared from the Primary data, 2016

learning is 3.45 in the five point scale (*see* Figure A). The opinion on 'positive attitude' and 'intrinsic motivation' seems to be contradictory even though the gap is negligible. In general, the teacher educators agree on the fact that the new curriculum for the two year teacher education courses – M.Ed, B.Ed and D.Ed. has the potential to develop self directed learning.

Another fact responsible for achieving planned and coordinated development of the teachers through the curriculum is the strength it has in the areas of teacher autonomy. The factors pertaining to the areas of teacher autonomy were analysed from the rating of teacher educators in autonomy to use their 'own methods for teaching', 'freedom to use collaborative learning environment', 'design ways to link theory and practice', 'using active learning strategies', 'use techno-pedagogy' in addition to 'achieving learning goals set by the curriculum'. The summary of ratings done by teacher educators is presented in Figure 13.2. It is evident that the teacher educators agree (as the score lies between 3 and 4 in the five point scale) that the two year curriculum framework is providing teacher autonomy (3.38) as per the overall rating whereas in the component factor 'achieving learning goal as per curriculum', the teacher educators disagree as per their rating 2.8 in the five point scale. This might be a hint to the content over load in the two year curriculum as suggested by majority of the teacher educators during personal discussions. The characteristics of the curriculum that received the highest rating by teachers was scored among items related to teacher autonomy are autonomy to use their own methodology (3.9), and the freedom to provide

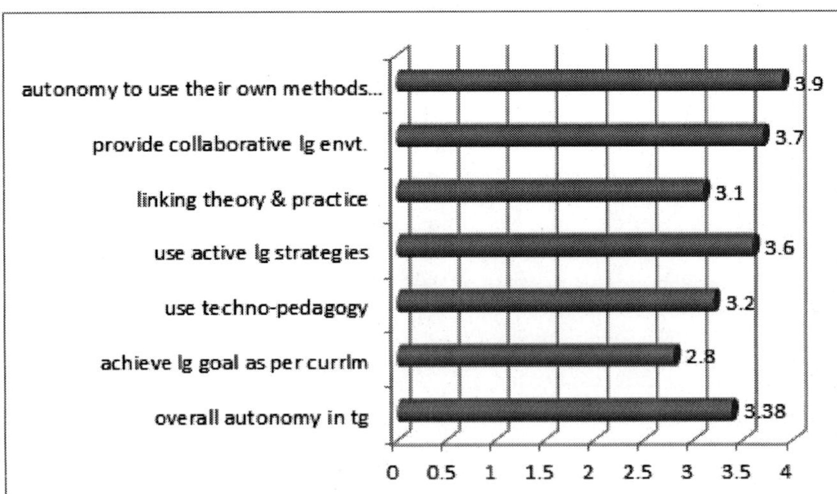

Figure 13.2. Rating on the Capacity of the Curriculum in Providing Autonomy in Teaching

collaborative learning environment (3.7) in the five point scale. The flexibility of the curriculum for linking theory, knowledge and experience (3.1) and provisions for using techno-pedagogy (3.2) are the factors that the teachers rated low. This hints at the fact that even though the curriculum gives teachers autonomy to use their own methodology, the curriculum is not that flexible in linking theory knowledge and experience. This is further evident when the teachers opine that the provision for using techno-pedagogy is low. This further suggests that even though changes have been effected, it is only tangential and the basic conception of education and pedagogy still closely resembles what it was in the universities of old (Jacobs, 2014).

Incorporating the three components of the curriculum – theory, practicum, internship within the semester framework

The divide between theory and practice in teacher education programmes builds up the rationale for arguing for a more effective, coherent, workable theory of action by way of practicum and internship. The opinion of Teacher Educators on incorporating theory, practicum and internship within the semester framework was crucial pertaining to the effective implementation of the curriculum. The key factors included in the curriculum such as reflection, practicum, recording the works, assignments, infusing techno-pedagogy,

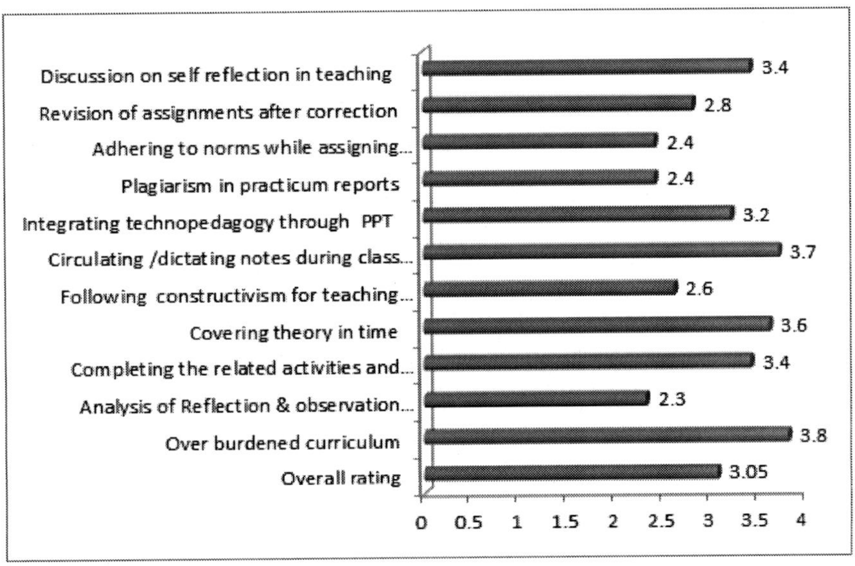

Figure 13.3. Rating of Teacher Educators on Incorporating Theory, Practicum and Internship within the Semester Framework

incorporating learning theories, etc., were analysed in this context. The rating of teachers on the use the reflective process to deepen their learning through a discussion of their self reflection, the average is 3.4 in the five point scale. The aspects in which the teacher's average rating fell in 'disagree' (the rating is between 2 and 3) are: revision of assignments after correction, adhering to norms while awarding internal marks, plagiarism check in practicum reports, following learning theories during classroom transaction and cross checking self reflection and observation during Internship (*see* Figure 13.3).

The fact 'over burdened curriculum' scored the highest rating 3.8 in the five point scale. The overall rating 3.05 shows that the teachers 'agree' that they could comply with incorporating theory, practicum and internship within the semester framework. In fact, a closer analysis makes it clear that the teachers use the same old way of dictating / circulating notes, cover the theory and complete the related written records in time for their claim. Integrating techno-pedagogy is done through PPTs whereas many other tools for effective teaching are available. This hints at the need for integrated orientation to be provided to teacher educators, especially for the young faculty members who have less experience. Research literature suggest that the experience and content mastery of teachers form the most important factors influencing student learning.

Suggestions for Modification in Curriculum for Enhancing Quality

The teacher education programme needs to provide for and facilitate prospective teachers deepening of understanding and critical reflection through both critical comprehensions of theory as well as hands-on reflective practice. A content analysis of the answers to the open ended question: 'Things that you would keep and change in the curriculum if asked to revise'. A total of 10 thematic units were analysed, of which six refer to maintaining the curriculum and methodology and three reflecting on things they would change. The major changes suggested were:

- The art education and work experience provided in the syllabus may be changed so as to meet the self development needs of teachers, such as developing skill of good calligraphy, improving the skills of expression during role plays and dramatisation of ideas, etc.
- The community living programme may be modified from the 'living together' for one day to 'living in the community' to identify the needs and deficits of the poor and needy in the society. This will help to develop a positive attitude towards the problems of the society.
- There is a need to provide cultural awareness to prospective teachers, and for this, performance of various folk arts and orientation of the folk literature through various activities may be included.

- For providing social orientation to the prospective teachers, they are to be encouraged through the curricular activities to organise clubs – either environmental, cultural, arts or sports and to monitor the works of the club for a period either simultaneously with internship or practice teaching.

The analysis of the personal interview with teachers hints at the fact that our system falls short of the characteristics of high quality teacher education in these 'new times'. To support the needs of a diverse student population, the teacher preparation programmes should:

- provide orientation to identify the needs and challenges of a pluralistic society so that the prospective teachers could better address the needs of minority ethnic and cultural groups, and support students who use a different language from the language of instruction, or who come from low socio-economic backgrounds;
- renovate the evaluation pattern from the traditional requirements of academic performance and results on standardised testing to include other relevant personal and experiential characteristics; and there should be a provision to grade the portfolios and records prepared by prospective teachers as a testimony to their innovation;
- encourage entry of a "non-traditional" pool of applicants like graduates from engineering, computer science, law and many other disciplines and provide room for training specialist teachers, who have proved their ability in different trades, art, music, etc. and have aptitude to become part of the education system.

Conclusion

There is an urgent need to recognise teachers' work as complex and demanding, and improvement in teacher quality requires a re-conceptualisation of how we prepare a new generation of teachers. The impact of teachers on the upcoming generation, i.e. their students, is very subtle and long-lasting and is therefore necessary that they should feel committed, contented and devoted to their noble professions. Many students who take admission see the course yet another alternative to secure a job and do not have the commitment or sincerity that is expected from a prospective teacher. Therefore, it is hoped that certain aspects which are characteristics of the new system, which accommodate and respond to the demands of the drift in time and technology, will improve our system and give an impetus to mould responsible teachers. These include a few alternative perspectives which have been emerged from the interaction with teacher educators. They are:

- Giving greater emphasis on teachers' values, skills and knowledge that are fundamental to good teaching. For realising this, instead of testing the theory through examinations only, the theories and principles may be integrated and linked through special intervention programmes and are to be spiralled in the two year curriculum.
- Expanding roles and responsibilities of teachers that can be shared collaboratively with other professionals. For this, there is a need to have successful partnerships which go beyond university faculties, schools and teachers to relevant outside stakeholders outside education. For example, tourism, disaster management, LSGIs, etc. The practicum for each course in the curriculum can have links which can be utilised by students as well as these agencies for the betterment of society.
- Setting up a section in every college of teacher education disseminating the different career options and opportunities for the degree holders of M.Ed / B.Ed / D.Ed pertaining to their expectations and aspirations resulting from changing teacher demographics and new job opportunities.
- "Personalising" learning for individual students to accommodate greater diversity in learning contexts. Adaptations and alteration to accommodate special learning needs, improvisation of assistive devices and soft tools for 'personalising' learning can be a good area which every teacher education institution can volunteer.

A special aspect which should be treated with priority highlighted by the teacher educators was that taking into consideration, the mushrooming of D.Ed / B.Ed / M.Ed colleges and the novice faculty handling the papers, there is a need to provide orientation course / faculty development programmes. Also it is advocated to introduce onsite support to teacher educators through discussion/ expert consultation forums. The universities, NCTE and the like the nodal agencies, have unleashed their powers for giving sanction to start teacher education colleges in a reckless way leading to the mushrooming of teacher education colleges in our nation. Hence, there is in fact no meaning in voicing on the lowering quality of the teachers produced through our system of teacher education. Being simply part of the system, it can only be avowed that a teacher is the fortune maker not only of an individual but also of the nation as a whole.

References

Byo, S. J. (1999). Classroom teachers' and music specialists' perceived ability to implement the national standards for music education. *Arts Education Policy Review,* 101(5), 30-35.

Caena, F. (2014). 'Teacher Competence Frameworks in Europe: policy-as-discourse practitioner research and students' learning', *Action in Teacher Education*, 31(2).

Carter, D. S. G., Carre, C. G., & Bennett, S. N. (1993). Student teachers' changing perceptions of their subject matter competence during an initial teacher training programme. *Educational Research*, 35(1), 89-95

Chen, C. Y. (1996). Factors affecting the self-fulfilment of secondary class music teachers in Western Australia: implications for pre-service and in-service music teacher education. Unpublished *Master of Music Education*, University of Western Australia, Perth.

Cochran-Smith, M., Barnatt, J., Friedman, A., & Pine, G. (2009). 'Inquiry on inquiry: and policy-as-practice', *European Journal of Education*, Vol: 49, Issue 3, 311-331.

Darling-Hammond, L. (2000a). How teacher education matters. *Journal of Teacher Education*, 51(3), 166-173.

Darling-Hammond, L. (2000b).Teacher quality and student achievement: A review of state policy evidence. Education Policy Analysis Archives, 8(1). Retrieved from http://epaa.asu.edu/epaa/v8nl.

Darling-Hammond, L. (2006). (In collaboration with Fickel, L., Koppich, J., Macdonald, M., Merseth, K., Miller, L., Ruscoe, G., Silvernail, D., Snyder, J., Whitford, B. L., & Zeichner, K.) Powerful teacher education: Lessons from exemplary programs. San Francisco: Jossey-Bass

Eurydice (2015). The Teaching Profession in Europe: Practices, Perceptions and Policies, Brussels: EACEA

Feuerstein, A. (2011). 'The Politics of Accountability and Teacher Preparation', *Action in Teacher Education*, 33, 3-23.

Ghaith, G., & Shaaban, K. (1999). The relationship between perceptions of teaching concerns, teacher efficacy, and selected teacher characteristics. *Teaching and Teacher Education, 15*, 487-496.

Iredale, R. (1996). The significance of teacher education for international education development. In C. Brock (Ed.), *Global perspectives on teacher education* (pp. 9-18). Oxfordshire: Triangle Books.

Jacobs, Garry (2014) Towards a New Paradigm in Education: Role of the World University Consortium *CADMUS*, Volume 2, No.2, May 2014, 116-125

Kennedy, M. M. (1999). The role of preservice teacher education. In L. Darling-Hammond & G. Sykes (Eds.), *Teaching as the learning profession: Handbook of policy and practice* (pp. 54-85). San Fransisco: Jossey-Bass.

Lampert, M., & Ball, D. L. (1999). Aligning teacher education with K-12 reform visions. In L. Darling-Hammond & G. Sykes (Eds.), *Teaching as the learning profession: Handbook of policy and practice* (pp. 33-53). San Fransisco: Jossey-Bass Inc.

Nair, Brinda. (1998) "Study of the opinion of Teachers Regarding DPEP Mathematics Curriculum Introduced in Standard III". *Unpublished M.Ed. Thesis*, University of Kerala, Thiruvananthapuram.

OECD (2009). PISA 2009 Results. Volume IV: *What Makes Schools Successful? Resources, Policies and Practices,* Paris: OECD Publishing.

Sharma, Anita, (2001). *A Study of Commitment among Teachers,* M.Ed. Dissertation, N.A.S. College, Meerut (C.C.S. University, Meerut).

Stuart, C., & Thurlow, D. (2000). Making it their own: Preservice teachers' experiences, beliefs, and classroom practices. *Journal of Teacher Education, 51*(2), 113-121.

Su, J. Z. X. (1992). Sources of influence in preservice teacher socialisation. *Journal of Education for Teaching, 18*(3), 239-259.

Temmerman, N. (1997). An investigation of undergraduate music education curriculum content in primary teacher education programmes in Australia. *International Journal of Music Education*, 30, 26-34.

Witmer, M. M. (2005). The fourth R in education: Relationships. *Clearing House: A Journal of Educational Strategies, Issues and Ideas, 78* (5), 224.

14.
Higher Education and Labour Market in India
Missing Linkages

G. L. Arunjilal

Theories on education and economic growth have established that human capital has a positive and significant effect on economic growth. Neoclassical economics has shown that economic growth could not only be explained by capital and labour increase but also by the contributions of the factors of production and the increase in technical progress (Solow, 1956). This has been further extended by the economists Mankiw, Romer and Weil (1992) through incorporating an explicit process of human capital accumulation. In a constantly changing growth environment, a discussion on the relationship between education, which provides human capital and the employers, specifically the labour market, who utilise the human capital is relevant. Globalisation has affected the employment situation via trade liberalisation, promotion of exports and imports and increasing incentives for investment and innovation. Routine cognitive tasks, mostly services, which were formerly almost non-traded across borders, are now easily traded necessitated by revolutionary advances in telecommunications and information technology. In the globalised world, education should certainly equip the citizens with necessary skills to succeed in the labour market, which is a key factor for improving economic growth and employment. Hence, practically, education can play an enabling role in faster economic growth only when the educated are gainfully employed. But there is evidence of growing educated unemployment and underemployment in India and across a wide range of countries. Learning at higher education level does not cater to skills and capabilities required for the emerging knowledge economy. Steady growth of educated labour force in India, and the emerging labour market changes during globalisation, call for an analysis of the relationship between the two sectors. The present discussion is an endeavour in this respect based on the following specific objectives:

1) To review the education sector in India with special emphasis on higher education.
2) To discuss the emerging changes in the labour market as a result of globalisation.

3) To analyse the missing linkages between higher education and the labour market.
4) To suggest strategies that would improve the link between higher education and labour market in India.

Overview of Education in India

Basically, primary education system in India has been supported by massive programmes to achieve the basic educational goals. But reports reveal otherwise. The Annual Status of Education Report (ASER), 2014, says only an average 48.1 per cent of V standard children across India can read a II standard level textbook. Even the basic readings in early grades reveal a pathetic situation in the report. It is seen that 32.5 per cent of the children in II standard cannot even identify letters. The current state of access to education indicated by the net attendance ratio (NAR) is also not satisfactory. Almost 89 per cent of kids attending primary school are from the richest fifth of the population both in the rural and urban areas, while that proportion drops to 79 per cent for kids in the poorest fifth of the population in rural areas and 78 per cent in urban areas. But NAR drops sharply when it comes to secondary school and becomes worse at the higher secondary level. The difference between the richest fifth and the poorest fifth in enrolment widens sharply from the primary section to the secondary and higher educational levels (NSSO, 71st round, July 2014).

Despite the problems at the primary and secondary education levels, higher education in India has made remarkable progress. It has grown steadily since 1990, placing India in a prominent position in the global higher education map. India's higher education system is the third largest in the world, next to the United States and China. It has the second highest higher education enrolment in the world and also the largest number of higher education institutes (*See* Table 14.1). By 2030, India will be amongst the youngest nations in the world. With nearly 140 million people in the college-going age group, one in every four graduates in the world will be a product of the Indian Higher Education system (Higher Education in India: Vision 2030).

However, in spite of the growth achieved in enrolment and in the number of institutions, only a few Indian Higher Education Institutions are globally ranked (*See* Table 14.2). Among the different criteria used for global ranking, India occupies a modest position in academic reputation, employer reputation and teaching (*See* Table 14.3). Most of the Indian institutions lag behind in research and citations. Limited numbers of Ph.Ds and very few international collaborations have led to low ranking of Indian institutions. Furthermore, only a handful of Indian B-schools have global accreditations such as AASCB, AMBA and EQUIS (FICCI Higher Education Summit, 2014).

Table 14.1: Country wise distribution of student enrolment in higher education (2012) and Number of higher education institutions (2013)

Country	*Student enrolment in higher education (2012) (million)*	*Number of higher education institutions by country (2013)*
India	26.7	33723
US	21.0	4140
Brazil	7.2	-
UK	2.5	-
China	32.6	2484

Source: UNESCO, 2013

Table 14.2: Global Ranking of Indian Higher Education Institutions

Country	*Number of institutes by country in QS World University Rankings (top 500) 2014/15*	*Number of institutions by country in Times Higher Education World University Rankings (top 400) 2014/15*
US	97	102
UK	48	46
Australia	23	21
China	18	11
Russia	10	-
Brazil	7	-
India	6	4

Source: FICCI Higher Education Summit, 2014

Table 14.3: India's Position in different ranking criteria

Criteria for ranking	*India's position*
Academic reputation	Moderate
Employer reputation	Moderate
Faculty-student ratio	Lags behind
Citations per faculty	Lags behind
International student ratio	Lags behind
International staff ratio	Lags behind
Research	Lags behind
Citations	Lags behind
Teaching	Moderate
International diversity	Lags behind

Source: FICCI Higher Education Summit, 2014

Globalisation has increased the wave of internationalisation of higher education marked by an increased flow of students and programmes across national boundaries. A significant number of Indian students go abroad for seeking quality education. However, incoming foreign students are limited in number. Number of Indian students studying in higher education institutions abroad had increased by 45 per cent during the period between 2006 and 2012. In 2012, only 31,000 foreign students came to India to study in higher education institutions. Few high ranked institutes, poor perception of education offered by Indian higher education institutions, lifestyle compromise and limited high quality placements are the primary reasons that discourage foreign students from developed countries coming to India. Indian higher education institutions have very few international campuses. During 2013, India had only 10 institutions at UAE, four at Mauritius and another four at Singapore and Malaysia (FICCI Higher Education Summit, 2014). Similarly foreign higher education institutions have not set up branch campuses in India due to the challenging regulatory environment in the country. International higher education institutions have low number of collaborations with Indian higher education institutions due to various academic difficulties like managing collaborations with Indian higher education institutions and lack of professional management in Indian higher education institutions. Thus, an assessment of the current state of the Indian higher education system indicates that India is prominently placed on the global higher education map on account of student enrolment and number of institutions. But it lags behind in terms of global ranking of higher education institutions, performance indicators and collaborations with foreign education institutions.

Emerging Labour Market Changes

Emergence of a Global Labour Market

The nature and pattern of economic growth has considerable impact on the labour market globally and regionally. Globalisation has resulted in the emergence of a global labour market. Over the past three decades, industrialisation of developing countries, rising trade and immigration, have all helped to bring about a more integrated labour market (McKinsey Global Institute, 2012). Structural shifts in global economy, productivity enhancement and technological progress are driving the demand for highly skilled workers, innovators and knowledge workers.

The world today is at the beginning of a fourth Industrial Revolution. We stand on the brink of a technological revolution that will fundamentally alter the way we live, work, and relate to one another (Klaus Schwab, 2016).

Developments in genetics, artificial intelligence, robotics, nanotechnology, 3D printing and biotechnology, to name just a few, are all building on and amplifying one another. The future of jobs report by the World Economic Forum specified the major drivers of change in employment and skills across industries and regions. This report was based on an extensive survey among Chief Human Resources and Strategy Officers (CHRSO) and other senior talent and strategy executives of leading global employers, representing more than 13 million employees across nine broad industry sectors in 15 major developed and emerging economies and regional economic areas. The report classified the drivers of change under demographic and socio-economic and technological aspects.

Table 14.4 Drivers of Change in the Skill and Employment Front

Rank	*Demographic and Socio-Economic drivers of change*	*Technological drivers of change*
1	Changing work environments and flexible working arrangements	Mobile Internet and cloud technology
2	Rise of the middle class in emerging markets	Advances in computing power and Big Data
3	Climate change, natural resource constraints and the transition to a greener economy	New energy supplies and technologies
4	Rising geopolitical volatility	The Internet of things
5	New consumer concerns about ethical and privacy issues	Crowd sourcing, the sharing economy and peer-to-peer platforms
6	Longevity and ageing societies	Advanced robotics and autonomous transport
7	Young demographics in emerging markets	Artificial intelligence and machine learning
8	Women's rising aspirations and economic power	Advanced manufacturing and 3D printing
9	Rapid urbanisation	Advanced materials, biotechnology and genomics

Source: Future of Jobs Report 2016, World Economic Forum.

The major industry drivers of change and disruptions to labour market are identified and ranked according to the share of respondents who expected each trend to be among the top trends impacting their industry by the year 2020. Collectively, technological disruptions are seen as very significant drivers of industrial change by the respondents relative to socio-economic drivers. Among these, growth in cheap computing power and the ubiquity of the mobile Internet have already had widespread impact on the labour market. Technological trends such as 3D printing, artificial intelligence and the Internet of things are expected to be well underway in specific industries in the years leading up to 2020. Demographic and socio-economic shifts are expected to have nearly as strong an impact on business models and organisational structures as technological change. Technological change gives way to work practices of the digital age, including remote work, flexible work and on-demand work. The rising middle class in emerging markets, the need for transition towards an environmentally sustainable economy and increased geopolitical volatility are all seen as major organisational drivers of change. The rising role and importance of women in the economy is transforming the composition of the talent pool and the skill profiles of the jobs required (World Economic Forum, The Future of Jobs, 2016).

Changing Nature of Employment: Gaps in Labour Demand and Supply

Today changes in labour demand and supply are evident in advanced and developing economies. According to McKinsey Global Institute, the global labour force will grow to 3.5 billion by 2030. Almost 90 per cent of the labour force growth will be in developing economies including China and India stimulated by demographics and rising labour force participation where a massive 'farm-to-factory' shift took place that raised the proportion of non-farm jobs. Increasing use of technology and the drive for productivity have all raised demand for high skill workers, while depressing job growth for workers with lower skills. These have caused imbalances in the labour market through changes in supply, demand and wages. The most significant imbalances identified by the McKinsey Global Institute include:

i) A potential shortage of about 38 to 40 million high-skill workers, or 13 per cent of demand for such workers.
ii) A potential shortage of nearly 45 million medium-skill workers, or about 15 per cent of demand for such workers.
iii) A potential surplus of 90 to 95 million low-skill workers around the world or 10 per cent of the supply of such workers.

India is placed in the last category where the proportion of low-skill workers in the labour force has been growing. During the period from 2000 to 2010, India added 67 million non-farm jobs. The distribution of labour force by skill level revealed that about 27 per cent of the labour force was illiterates and about 40 per cent had below secondary level of education. More significantly, only about 11 per cent among the non-agricultural workforce within the age group 15 to 59 years had either received formal or vocational training in India during 2009-10 (Mehrotra et al., 2013). India has also lagged behind China in raising the skills of its workforce. While it has comparable numbers of workers with a tertiary education, the share of people with secondary education in India is less than half the ratio in China and many other developing economies. The result of the slower evolution in India's labour force is reflected in its growth and productivity record (McKinsey Global Institute, 2012).

Declining Share of Labour Income: Rising Inequality

Two sorts of income inequality have been mentioned by scholars. The first is the growing gap between top earners and those in the middle and at the bottom. The second is the gap between labour on the one hand, and capital (such as profits, interest and rent) on the other. The first is rise of income inequality in advanced economies associated with the erosion of labour market institutions. The rise of top income shares and less redistribution due to erosion of minimum wages have considerably increased the overall inequality (IMF, 2015). The second is the inequality associated with rise in the share of capital. Thomas Piketty in his book *Capital in the Twenty First Century* cited the rise in capital's share of income in rich countries between 1970 and 2010 as proof of his thesis that rising wealth and inequality are inherent to modern Capitalism. The Global Wage Report 2012-13 released by the International Labour Organisation (ILO) showed that there is a long-term trend of a falling share of wage and a rising share of profits in many countries across the world. The average share of labour income in national income dropped from 69 per cent in the early 1990s to 64 per cent in the years just before the global financial crisis. Also downward trend in labour income has been observed in select G20 countries since 1990s by other international institutions (IMF, 2007; European Commission, 2007; BIS, 2006). In advanced economies, while demand for low-skill labour remains weak, income inequality is growing as lower-skill workers including 75 million young people experience unemployment, underemployment, and stagnating wages.

For most of the emerging economies in the global south, the share of wages in gross value added is lower than the developing economy average of 52 per cent. Among them, India fares the worst. The Government of India estimates too reveal that the share of wages in national income fell from 40 per cent at the start of the 1990s to 34 per cent by 2009-10 and much sharply in the organised sector, from 69 per cent to 51 per cent in the same period (NSSO & CSI, Govt. of India).

Thus, the labour market of both advanced and developing nations has undergone tremendous changes. Globalisation has witnessed the emergence of a global labour market driven by demographic, socio-economic and technological drivers of change. Increasing use of technology and the drive for productivity have changed the skill component of jobs. These have caused imbalances in the labour market through changes in supply, demand and wages. The shift from low and medium skill labour to capital goods and knowledge industries have reduced the labourer's share of income and increased inequality.

Missing Linkages between Higher Education and Labour Market

Mismatch between Graduate Skills and Labour Market Needs: Growing Unemployability of Educated Labour Force

There is some disconnect between the labour market and the choices that students are making when they go in for higher education. As a result, the youth are not gaining the educational skills that the labour market needs and they are excluded from meaningful employment opportunities. By 2025, India's demographic dividend is expected to contribute 25 per cent of global workforce. Thirty lakh graduates will join the Indian job market every year but only about five lakhs will be considered employable. According to National Skill Development Corporation (NSDC), the growing skill gap in India is estimated to be more than 25 crore workers by 2022. The skill gap appears to be staggering among some disciplines. Ninty per cent of Indian engineering graduates, 75 per cent of IT graduates, 55 per cent in manufacturing, 55 per cent in healthcare and 50 per cent in banking and insurance are deemed 'unemployable' (Higher Education in India: Vision 2030).

The structural transformation of the workforce with slow growth in the non-agricultural sectors on the one hand and a large output of graduates with general education having low skill will create a great imbalance in the economy and labour market. Over production of college graduates are compounded by increasingly hostile labour markets in which degree holders are forced to work in poorly paid, unskilled positions. India could raise the number of college graduates in its labour force by 36 million in the coming decade (World Economic Forum, 2016). But today companies are increasingly looking for competencies at multiple levels. Also persons having higher education are more selective with regard to employment, whether they are adequately skilled or not. This imbalance will generate more unemployed general education graduates. Reports on employment and unemployment by the NSSO show that India has been witnessing a situation where the proportion of unemployed has been increasing among those with higher education while the same has been decreasing among those with lower educational achievement in the working age group of 15-59 (*See* Table 14.5).

Table 14.5: Distribution of Unemployed Population Aged 15-59 Years across General Education Levels

General Education Level	*2004-05*	*2009-10*	*2011-12*
Not literate	31.22	24.44	21.24
Literate: below primary	8.23	8.41	8.47
Primary	13.35	15.27	12.25
Middle	17.22	18.16	17.58
Secondary	9.91	10.78	12.07
Higher secondary	6.17	8.20	8.56
Diploma / certificate course	2.95	2.38	3.12
Graduate	7.06	9.19	12.08
Postgraduate and above	2.07	2.93	4.44
Others	1.83	0.24	0.18
Total	100.00	100.00	100.00

Source: Employment and unemployment rounds of NSS: 61st, 66th and 68th, National Sample Survey Organisation

Missing Industry-Academia Linkages

With globalisation taking place, the job market has become highly competitive. Now, a person not only has to compete for a job with the people from his own community or country but also with the people from other countries. So apart from degrees, it is the additional skills and knowledge that distinguish one from other competitors. Indeed, many of the Indian universities have failed to fulfil this purpose. Good academia-industry interface is characterised by the interactive and collaborative programmes between academic institutions and industrial sectors. Collaboration between academia and industry is increasingly a critical component of efficient national innovation systems. It is useful to examine the experience of developed countries to better understand the different types of university-industry collaboration, motivations to form these agreements and barriers to cooperation, as well as the role of public policy in fostering such linkages. Developing countries face even greater barriers to such alliances, calling for a differentiated approach to promoting university-industry collaboration (Jose Guimon, World Bank, 2013). A few collaborations that are possible in the Indian scenario are:

i) *Producer-Consumer Interaction*: The common interaction model between academia and industry is that of producer-consumer. This relationship necessitates some collaboration as the consumer has to ensure that the output of the producer satisfies the needs to a large extent. Hence, one form of collaboration, which is more in the nature of a feedback loop, is for the industry to provide inputs back to the academic institutions regarding their perception or evaluation of their products. Interestingly, this kind of interaction does not occur in a structured manner, as both the sides maintain some distance with each other.

There is another possible area of collaboration. In India, the engineering education system, the way it has evolved, is currently not in the best of shape, and will require a lot of help to improve. And it is also clear that, though traditionally the Government was responsible for higher education, relying on the Government alone will not solve the problem fast enough. So, the industry and the established education players will have to pitch in. Some companies and institutes have started some initiatives of their own on this front. But this seems like a very viable area for collaboration, where joint programmes have a better chance of success. However, not much seems to be happening in this area, even though both sides can gain substantially from it.

ii) *Collaboration in Continuing Education*: One of the core competencies of academic institutions is teaching. And many institutes engaged in high end education, have courses and ability to provide training for high-end manpower development. Many of these topics are of interest to industry. Therefore, a natural collaboration possibility is for the academic faculty and institutes to conduct training in topics of interest for industry.

iii) *Collaboration in Research:* Today in a world driven by Intellectual Property, there is an increased interest in collaboration in the area of research. For the purposes of our discussion, research can be considered as the activity of creating new knowledge. Though academicians in most good institutes engage in research, collaboration in this area is possible only if the industry has a need for research. Research is typically not a business or a profit centre but a long term investment, which helps a company to generate more revenue and profits. In India, till recently there was no need for research in most companies — the knowledge that existed in the public domain was sufficient for the business that the company was engaged in. But that seems to be changing now. Thus, the missing linkages between higher education and labour market in India can be viewed from growing unemployability owing to the mismatch between graduate skills and labour market needs, prevalence of labour market imbalances and growing incidence of unemployment among the educated and the lack of industry-academia linkages.

Strengthening the Link between Higher Education and Labour Market-- Strategies to Follow

Indian economy has witnessed impressive rates of growth in recent years. In 2015-16 growth rate reached 7.6 per cent. The challenge continues to be to ensure that economic growth translates into better labour market conditions (ILO, 2016). Following strategies can help to improve the relationship between higher education and labour market in the Indian context.

i) *Move Towards a Student Demand-Driven System*: It has been felt that India requires a higher education system that is adaptive to the needs of a modern society and the consequent challenges of a global economy. This includes Government's commitment to ensure that India's higher education system better meets the future requirements. The Higher education system must become more efficient, responding to market needs, employers and government. The existence of a demand-led system with employers and individuals having a strong and coherent voice will dramatically improve and accelerate the engagement and relationship between higher education and employers. This involves increasing volumes of employer co-funding being brought to support skills development. Additional funding should support high quality teaching and learning, and improve access and outcomes for students from low socio economic backgrounds.

ii) *Need for a Globally Relevant and Competitive Higher Education System:* The vision should be to build a 21st century model for higher education that is of high-quality, equitable and affordable. It should be exemplary and be a model for a higher education system that is not just the best in the world but the best for the world. The period has also been characterised by a transformation from 'the world of knowledge' to 'the world of work.' The main purpose of university education should be 'work readiness'. Employability has to be considered as a key factor in the curriculum design. There is a need for embedding employability in the student life cycle and training programmes.

iii) *Strengthen Industry-Academia Linkages*: The importance of collaboration between academia and industry in the modern day world has direct implications on country's growth prospects. The procedure and periodicity of such an interaction needs to be streamlined to realise our demographic dividend. India is home to some of the most respected higher education institutions, and, it is imperative that the corporate and academia should set up a permanent channel of dialogue to ensure that the human capital providers and utilisers work in tandem. The requirements of industry are changing day by day and thus we need to improvise on the curricula and training in order to make our youth more employable and stay relevant.

iv) *New Endeavours of Training Programmes*: Novel ventures are required to make the labour force relevant. One such endeavour is Bridge to Employment (BTE) programme. Bridge to Employment is a pre-employment training programme that helps companies to recruit unemployed people whatever be their experience of work. The main objective is to provide customised training to equip unemployed people, with necessary skills to compete for new employment opportunities on an equal basis with others. Training courses are tailored to meet the skill requirements of the job. Bridge to Employment (BTE) programme is being run very successfully in UK by universities in collaboration with industry, civic society, etc.

v) *Initiatives for Skill Development and Entrepreneurship*: Recently new initiatives for skill development and entrepreneurship are provided by the Ministry of Skill Development and Entrepreneurship. The ministry is responsible for co-ordination of all skill development efforts across the country, removal of disconnect between demand and supply of skilled manpower, building the vocational and technical training framework, skill up-gradation, building of new skills, and innovative thinking not only for existing jobs but also for jobs that are to be created. Government took the initiative in setting up of the National Skill Development Corporation India (NSDC), National Skill Development Agency (NSDA) and the National Skill Development Fund. The draft report of the Education Policy, 2016 has made a series of programmes for skill development. First, skill development programmes in school and higher education system will be reoriented. Second, a detailed plan for the creation of skill schools for improving employment opportunities for secondary school students in special focus districts will be prepared. Third, joint certificates by the Sector Skill Council and the School / College authorities to help students take up wage-employment or start their own enterprise. All the above programmes should give wide coverage to include more students and the low skilled and the unemployed towards work orientation.

Summary and Conclusions

Education can play an enabling role in faster economic growth only when the educated are gainfully employed. But there is evidence of growing educated unemployment and underemployment in India and across a wide range of countries. Learning at higher education level does not cater to skills and capabilities required for the emerging knowledge economy. Many countries including India face the paradox of mounting skilled labour shortages co-existing with rising graduate unemployment and underemployment. Thus, in a constantly changing world driven by socio-economic and technological factors, the sync between providers and utilisers of human capital is essential for constituting growth.

Though India is significantly placed in the global higher education map on account of student enrolment and number of institutions, in terms of global ranking it lags behind advanced countries and other developing nations. The labour market of both advanced and developing nations has undergone tremendous changes. Globalisation has witnessed the emergence of a global labour market driven by demographic, socio-economic and technological drivers of change. Increasing use of technology and the drive for productivity have changed the skill component of jobs. These have caused imbalances in the labour market through changes in supply, demand and wages. The shift from low and medium skill labour to capital goods and knowledge industries have reduced the labourer's share of income and increased inequality. Growing unemployability owing to the mismatch between graduate skills and labour market needs, prevalence of labour market imbalances and growing incidence of unemployment among the educated and the lack of industry-academia linkages are clear evidences of the missing relationship between education and employment.

A major challenge is the translation of the impressive rates of growth in India into better labour market conditions. A few strategies including the introduction of student demand-driven system, globally relevant and competitive higher education system, strengthening of industry-higher education linkages and practice of new endeavours of training programmes and skill development initiatives will have strong implications in maintaining the link between education and employment. Universities and industry can come together to meet national challenges. Across the world, higher education is linked to higher levels of employment and life evaluation, making it the proverbial ticket to a better job and a better life.

References

Bhalla (2008): 'Gobalisation and Employment Trends in India', *The Indian Journal of Labour Economics*, Vol. 51, No. 1

Centre for Higher Education Policy Studies (2011): 'Perspectives on Higher Education and the Labour Market Review of International Policy Developments' *IHEM/CHEPS Thematic Report*, Egbert de Weert C11EW158.

Federation of Indian Chambers of Commerce and Industry (2014): 'Higher education in India: Moving towards Global Relevance and Competitiveness', *FICCI Higher Education Summit 2014.*

Federation of Indian Chambers of Commerce and Industry (2015): 'State-Focused Roadmap to India's Vision 2030', *FICCI Higher Education Summit 2015*, Ernst & Young Global Limited.

Florence Jaumotte and Carolina Osorio Buitron (2015): 'Inequality and Labour Market Institutions', *Research Department, International Monetary Fund.*

Government of India (2014): 'Educational Statistics at a Glance', *Ministry of Human Resource Development*, Bureau of Planning, Monitoring and Statistics, New Delhi

Government of India (2015): 'All India Survey on Higher Education', *Ministry of Human Resource Development*, Department of Education, New Delhi.

International Labour Organization (2015): 'The Labour Share in G20 Economies, Report Prepared for the G20 Employment' *Working Group Antalya*, Turkey.

International Labour Organization (2016): 'World Employment Social Outlook, Trends 2016', *International Labour Office*, Geneva.

International Labour Organization (2016): 'India labour Market Update', *International Labour Office*, Geneva.

Institute for Human Development (2014): 'India Labour and Employment Report 2014', Academic foundation, *The Indian Society of Labour Economics*, New Delhi.

Jose Guimon, (2013), 'Promoting University-Industry Collaboration in Developing Countries', The Innovation Policy Platform, World Bank.

Mantz Yorke ( ): 'Employability in Higher Education: What it is –What it is not', Learning and Employability Series 1and 2, *The Higher Education Academy*, UK.

World Economic Forum (2016): 'Report on the Future of Jobs, Employment, Skills and Workforce Strategy for the Fourth Industrial Revolution', World Economic Forum.

15.
Bridging the Industry — Academia Gap
The Way Ahead for Higher Education in Kerala

P.S. Deva Kumar

The whole education-employment eco-system in India has been under the scanner for the last one decade for obvious reasons. It is almost seven decades after we got independence, still not even a single higher learning institution of this great country is figuring in the top 100 listing available globally. To continue its growth story and achieve the long cherished vision of India becoming the human resource hub for the whole world by cashing on the demographic dividend it is blessed with, we have a long way to go. As per a study conducted by Aspiring Mind (2016), an agency engaged in assessing the employability trends in Engineering Education in India, only 17.91 per cent of engineers were employable for the software services sector, 3.67 per cent for software products and 40.57 per cent for a non-functional role such as Business Process Outsourcing. This being the case with a discipline taught with the potential employment opportunities in mind, we can think about the plight of Arts and Science education in our country. Always, there used to be a hue and cry on the part of the industry citing that the academic output produced by the so called prestigious and caveated institutions of this country could not be absorbed in their respective domains as majority of them are short of employable skills. The stalwarts of industry in this part of the world expressed their concern and worries about the academic output of these pioneer institutions not even acquiring the skill set of a trainable class. This phenomenon can be observed across disciplines like basic science, engineering and technology, commerce, management, economics, language studies and other arts and science disciplines.

Of late the policy makers of this country have found it extremely vital to venture for a slogan like "Skill India". This is perhaps a 360^0 shift from the long cherished dream of mass education through enhanced Gross Enrolment Ratio (GER), pursued by the country since independence. Skill development and entrepreneurship efforts across the country have been highly fragmented so far. As opposed to developed countries, where the percentage of skilled workforce is between 60 per cent and 90 per cent of the total workforce, India records a low 5 per cent of workforce (under the age group of 20-24 years) with formal vocational skills. There is a need for speedy reorganisation of the ecosystem of skill development and entrepreneurship promotion in the country to suit the needs of the industry and enable decent quality of life to its population. Today, more than 20 Ministries / Departments run 70 plus schemes for skill development in the country. However, there are gaps in the capacity and quality of training infrastructure as well as outputs, insufficient focus on workforce aspirations, lack of certification and common standards and the lack of focus on the unorganised sector. The doyens of modern day industry went one step further in commenting that the academic output of the so called triumphant institutions are not even possessing the traits of a trainable class. There is no exception to this across disciplines like basic science, engineering and technology, commerce, management, economics and other arts and science disciplines.

The role of institutional players in the knowledge based higher education sector has changed from that of a mere disseminator of knowledge to a knowledge producer in the global economy where stakeholders always expect graduates to satisfy the emerging demands and requirements of the skill markets. A similar kind of pressure is experienced by the educational institutions in this part of the globe also. As former President Mr. Pranab Mukherjee had rightly pointed out, the Make in India initiative which is aimed at making our country a manufacturing hub, depends to a large extent on the deepening of the academia-industry alliance. The statement highlights the importance of collaboration between academia and industry in the modern-day world, which in the long run may even have direct implications on the country's prospects. Given India's ambitious target of becoming a global superpower, the procedure and periodicity of such an interaction needs to be streamlined to truly realise our demographic dividend. The requirements of industry are changing day by day and we thus need to improvise on the curricula and training in order to make our youth more employable and stay relevant.

Medical Education System — A Model to be Emulated

Barring medical education, our country could not project a bright spot to emulate in meeting the industry expectations. It requires no rocket science technology to understand why medical graduates are standing out among the lot. The curriculum design of the medical discipline is so evolved in this country to enable a student to have a real time connect of what he is learning in the classrooms with the demand of the health care industry. This process is further strengthened up by providing the students with the privilege of working as an understudy by way of house surgency-ship. This in turn empowers the student to choose the right kind of specialisation in which he / she is required to build on the higher order skills as demanded by health care sector. A striking difference medical education stream is possessing over other streams can be cited in the number and longitude of the interactive spells a student is having with the servicing industry of his discipline.

Skilling India Dynamics

The government has finally decided to address the skill deficiency syndrome spotted by the industry consistently in the past. As part of this, a Ministry of Skill Development and Entrepreneurship has been set up in the Centre. It has identified 24 broad areas for skill enrichment. It is planning to set up 50,000 skill development centres across the country. States are also directed to set up Skill Development Centres considering the geographical nature of respective skill requirement. The Central Bill provides accreditation agencies to certify the various skill programmes to make it acceptable for the industry. This is in line with making India one of the economic powers by 2025, by capitalising on the demographic advantage of its human capital.

University Education System — Need for Revamping

In the above discussed skilling philosophy, the role of universities is ill defined. The bits and part measures taken at the various universities (a total of 749 in all in India) are astonishingly short of the industry expectations. Even at the university level a proper mapping of the potential employers the curriculum is supposed to cater is not available, less to talk about the affiliated institutions with the universities in this regard. It can be construed that a preset curriculum for a term of 5 to 10 years on a trot and delivered to the students using the traditional tools of teaching learning exercise stood as the major culprit. Many a programme could introduce a project study for the fulfillment of the course undergone to ensure a real feel of the industry to which the discipline is associated. The Indian experience in this regard is again far away from the industry expectations owing to so many reasons. The universities are offering the projects to be pursued along with the regular semesters, which are already packed with academic programmes. Only a few institutions and disciplines are offering summer internships. This has made the project assignments a mere ritual for a great majority of disciplines and students. A very few of the projects are selected for further funding by the industry concerned. Project assignments are offered as at the fag end of the academic programmes which delineates a student from further exploring the possibility of linking the academic inputs with industry applications / observations made as part of project assignment.

Enigma with University Curriculum

There is an accepted practice among the academicians to frame their curriculum by ensuring utmost balance for the comprehensive development of the student. However, this often has resulted in the student learning a wide variety of disciplines, which majority will not be practising in real life. This aspect requires urgent attention as university education is generally provided to the masses in the age group of 17 to 23, which is ideal age for imparting core specialised streams. This eventually has resulted in student acquiring domain strength imbalances beyond repair in the future, if required. This is the major cause behind the industry's contention that majority of the university trained are not further trainable. This eventually is forcing the graduates and post graduates to be accommodated in job situations with any "degree tagging".

Any Degree Tagging — Story of Misnomers

The Indian job market is characterised by the presence of substantially large enough employment opportunities requiring no specific specialisations at all. For example, an office clerk, bus conductor, police constable, bank clerk (even a bank officer), most of other government jobs barring a few exceptions, etc. fall under the above category which is an asylum for majority of the university output. Though many of the above job positions require specific skill sets which unfortunately the established university education is not capable of ensuring through their respective disciplines. Like in the case of a store keeper who is supposed to possess locating skills, posting skills, counting skills and verification skills can be chosen from a discipline like Philosophy, Hindi or even Psychology. The kind of resources and time utilised by the university and the student in learning his / her domain of interest and the extent to which such skills are applied in practice is still a daunting question in this part of the world. Gone are the days the students are supposed to learn a preset curriculum which has virtually no remote connection to the skill set requirements of the employer.

Multi-disciplinary orientation practices followed by the educational institutions in the country are also dragged into controversy recently. Most often these practices turned out to be a platform for creating counter opportunities with regard to complementary disciplines, without regarding the true demand of the respective industry. For Example, if Economics is made as a complementary subject for History main students, a similar counter offer will be made to Economics main students in the form of History by neglecting the design the industry exactly want in the form of multi-disciplinary and complimentary domain development with their academic output.

R & D Initiatives of University Institutions

Time and again quality of research taking place in the universities has taken a beating from the industry. The average annual number of patents registered in the country stood a paltry less than 900 in number. This trend is not going to improve in the near future, with the kind of priorities being placed by the Universities in this regard. Within the patented inventions, the proportion of commercially exploited ones is still not up to the mark, when compared to universities in the West and European countries. Erosion of faith and dependence from the part of industry including farmers is declining at fast pace. Lack of university-industry interaction at the desired level and frequency of such interactions are again the culprits doing the damage.

Objectives of the Study

Following are the broad objectives set for the present study:

(i) To analyse whether there exist any distinguishing deviations in practices while finalising curriculum across various disciplines.
(ii) To identify whether there exist significant difference in the criteria followed in admitting the students across disciplines.
(iii) To identify the gaps in quality of deliverables and industry expectations with regard to various disciplines.
(iv) To verify whether the academic output coming out of the universities are settling in jobs carrying any degree-tagging.
(v) To provide suggestions for strengthening partnership between academia and industry based on the findings of the study.

Analysis

Criteria of Students Selection — Aptitude in the Relevant Discipline

Selection of students for the academic programmes needs to be done after ensuring his / her aptitude towards the discipline. Table 15.1 shows that across disciplines, viz. Arts, Business and Commerce, Language and Science streams there exists much variation in this regard. Where Language streams ensure 10 per cent aptitude compliance, only 25.7 per cent and 58.8 per cent are ensuring the same in Arts stream and Science streams respectively. Under Commerce and Business Stream it is only 85 per cent. Overall it shows that only 37 per cent are selecting a programme based on their sheer aptitude towards the discipline.

Table 15.1: Criteria of Students Selection — Aptitude in the Relevant Discipline (%)

Whether Student selection is based on aptitude test or not	*Discipline of faculty*				
	Arts Stream	*Business and Commerce Stream*	*Language Stream*	*Science Stream*	*Total*
Yes	25.7	85.0	10.0	58.8	37.0
No	74.6	15.0	90.0	41.2	63.0
Total	100	100	100	100	100

Mapping of the relevant industries in which students can be employed

The first step towards making the discipline and curriculum industry savvy is to map the potential employers with whom academic output can be accommodated. Analysis as highlighted in the Table 15.2 shows that only 44.3 per cent of the programmes delivered through our universities have gone for listing the potential employers for the respective disciplines. Barring Commerce and Science where 50 per cent and 44.4 per cent of the programmes map the potential employers respectively, the efforts done in Arts stream and Language streams are not up to the mark. In the case of Arts stream it is only 14.3 per cent and Languages lagging behind with only 10 per cent of the programmes going for the mapping exercise.

Table 15.2: Mapping of Potential Employment Opportunities (%)

Whether Mapping of potential employers are done with regard to the discipline	*Discipline of faculty*				
	Arts Stream	*Business and Commerce Stream*	*Language Stream*	*Science Stream*	*Total*
Yes	14.3	50.0	10.0	44.4	44.3
No	85.7	50.0	90.0	55.6	55.7
Total	100	100	100	100	100

Feedback about Where Students are Getting Placed

The practice of keeping track of where the academic output of the respective disciplines were reviewed and it was found that only 77.4 per cent of respondents are keeping any kind of record as to this. Once again Arts and Language disciplines are lagging behind with 57 per cent and 69 per cent of the respondents keeping track of placement records. With regard to Science, Commerce and Business domains 80 per cent and 75 per cent of the respondents are keeping the kind of records regarding placement status of their respective students.

Chi-square results show that more or less all the teaching faculties are maintaining the placement records intact and there exists no significant difference among the disciplines in this regard. So the null hypothesis stood accepted with a p value of 0.015.

Students Settling with Jobs Requiring any Degree Tagging

Another astonishing factor which drags our higher learning institutions is about the academic output of our universities settling with jobs requiring any degree-tagging. Nearly 79 per cent of the respondents opined that their output is settling with jobs requiring any degree criteria. Barring Business and Commerce stream, only 17 per cent settling with any degree tags, the desirability of performance in this count on account of Arts, Language and Science streams are not up to the mark, with Arts recording 85.7 per cent, Language stream with 93 per cent and Science discipline with 61.1 per cent settling with any degree tagged employment.

Chi-square results again supplement the above observation with a p value of 0.066 which allows the acceptance of the null hypothesis that disciplines are almost in the same line with regard to their academic output settling with employment opportunities demanding any degree requirement.

Industry feedback about academic output

With regard to the extent of feedback obtained from employers of the academic output of the respective domains, the story is really pathetic altogether. All the four major streams have found it not so important to have industry feedback about the quality of the academic output the employers are receiving. Eighty seven per cent of the departments are neither seeking the industry feedback nor provided with the industry feedback. Chi-square results in this regard reveal that there exists no significant difference among the four disciplines with regard to eliciting feedback about the quality of input the industry is getting from the university system. Therefore, the null hypothesis is rejected.

Chi-square results confirmed this. There exists no significant differences among the various disciplines in bringing in the industry expertise in revising the curriculum to make it more relevant and current.

Benchmarking Curriculum with Reputed Institutions at National Level

Only 46.5 per cent of the respondents believe that there is any benefit available in benchmarking their respective curriculum with that offered at National Level Institutions. The practice being followed by Arts stream and Language stream needs immediate attention.

The result is confirmed by chi-square tests. There exists no significant difference among the various disciplines with regard to benchmarking exercise with national level reputed Universities and Institutions.

Findings

Overall it shows that only 37 per cent of the respondents are selecting a programme based on their sheer aptitude towards the discipline. Only 44.3 per cent of the programmes delivered through our universities have gone for listing the potential employers for the respective disciplines. The practice of keeping track of where the academic output of the respective disciplines was reviewed and it was found that only 77.4 per cent of respondents are keeping any kind of record as to this. Another astonishing factor which drags our higher learning institutions is about the academic output of our universities settling with jobs requiring any degree tagging. 78.6 per cent of the respondents opined that their output is settling with jobs requiring any degree criteria.

With regard to the extent of feedback obtained from employers of the academic output of the respective domains shows a really pathetic story altogether. All the four major streams have found it not so important to have industry feedback about the quality of the academic output the employers are receiving. 87 per cent of the respondents never received any kind of feedbacks from the employers where their students are placed. Barring Business and Commerce stream no other disciplines could bring in industry experts while designing their respective curriculum with 45.7 per cent of the respondents found it not necessary to have the experts while designing the curriculum content of their respective disciplines. Only 46.5 per cent of the respondents believe that there is any benefit available in benchmarking their respective curriculum with that offered at National Level Institutions. The practice being followed by Arts stream and Language stream needs immediate attention.

Suggestions

Though constrained by misfired practices, adequate funding, quality faculty, autonomy in true sense, political interventions, etc., still hope is left on these institutions to do wonders, if not miracles. The core solution lies in evolving a dynamic platform for a real time interaction with the respective industry stakeholders by the academia. To enable this, the stakeholders' needs are to be identified with objectivity. There should be frequent cross overs from industry to academics and vice versa. The industry participation should not end up with the curriculum finalisation phase alone. They should be provided with ample opportunities during the deliverance phase also. In other words, they should be invited to handle sessions, especially in areas where dynamic changes have taken place as well as while finalising project topics by the students and faculty members. Their regular and frequent feedbacks on the curriculum and the student performance need to be documented for future guidance. Selected projects can be pursued at financial and technical assistance from the respective industry stakeholders, if they are willing. Students shall be facilitated with real life exposure in the respective industries, once they receive 20 to 30 per cent of the total curriculum intake of the programme. The projects need to be got completed along with the student acquiring 70 to 80 per cent of the total curriculum under offer. This will enable the student to counter verify what he has absorbed in the industry with his academic counterpart so as to make the learning process more meaningful. Academic seminars and workshops need to be arranged on such selected industry themes so that more industry contributions can be facilitated. The project themes and seminar/ workshop outcomes can be incorporated as case study for completing the remaining 20 per cent of the academic programme.

Similarly, there should be university-industry tie-ups in place so that faculty members can be placed with industry openings by way of exchange programmes. This in turn will facilitate the game to be beneficial to both the players. Patent registration and commercial exploitation options need to be exploited. In fact, they need to be reckoned as one of the performance evaluation norms in the respective disciplines. For developing a culture of creating commercially exploitable patents budget allocations shall be made by the university with ample support sought from the industry partners identified in this regard. To start with, the academic autonomy shall permit at least 20 per cent of the curriculum to be framed in each programme according to the choice made by the individual student after submission of the project report. Multi-disciplinary choice shall also be provided at this level for ensuring maximum benefit to the students in this regard. Campus placement initiatives can be phased at this stage.

As we know skilling is not a one time process in itself, it encompasses lifelong learning in the sense that the learner, wherever he / she identifies a skill gap requiring academic intervention needs to be provided with the right kind of academic support throughout his / her productive career. To facilitate this, campus infrastructure, beyond the regular hours shall be utilised. Skill courses on demand need to be structured on a dynamic basis under proper accreditation and certification. Inter-university network platforms can be developed to make such short duration industry specific modules to be cost effective.

Conclusion

Opening the flood gates of ideas by spreading the red carpet for the industry stakeholders to the university campuses will definitely make our university education more and more skill oriented and nothing less than this. To stand relevant in the age of skilling initiatives and institutions, our universities cannot miss the last bus in their domain of expertise once they were the pioneers. If the universities are not going to consider it as a signaling event, for many of the programmes currently they are offering, no takers will be there in the immediate future.

References

Bercovitz, J., Feldman, M., Feller, I. & Burton, R. (2001). Organizational structure as a determinant of academic patent and licensing behavior: An exploratory study of Duke, Johns Hopkins, and Pennsylvania State universities. *The Journal of Technology Transfer, 26,* 21-35.

Chesbrough, H. (2003). *Open Innovation: The New Imperative for Creating and Profiting from Technology.* Boston: Harvard Business School Press.

Dill, D. and & Vught, F. (2010) *National Innovation and the Academic Research Enterprise.* Baltimore, MD: John Hopkins University Press.

Geiger, R. & Sá, C. (2009). *Tapping the Riches of Science: Universities and the Promise of Economic Growth.* Cambridge: Harvard University Press.

Perkmann, M. & Walsh, K. (2007). University-industry relationships and open innovation: towards a research agenda. *International Journal of Management Reviews, 9*(4), *259-280.*

Vedovello, C. (1997). Science parks and university-industry interaction: geographical proximity between agents as a driving force. *Technovation,* 17(9), 491-502.

Welch, A. (2005). Challenge and change: The academic profession in uncertain times. *Higher Education Dynamics,* 7, 1-19.

Aspiring Minds Employability Report on Indian Graduates 2013.

Contributors

Dr. N.V. Varghese, Director, Centre for Policy Research in Higher Education, NUEPA, New Delhi. nv.varghese@nuepa.org

Dr. Dato'morshidi Sirat, Founding Director, Commonwealth Tertiary Education Facility (CTEF), c/o National Higher Education Research Institute (IPPTN), UniversitiSains Malaysia, Penang, Malaysia.

Dr N. Varaprasad, Adjunct Professor, National University of Singapore and SIM University.

Dr Radhakrishnan Pillai, Center of Excellence in Interdisciplinary Studies and Research, University of Calicut, Calicut - 673 635. pillai_radhakrishna@hotmail.com

Dr M. Kunhaman, Professor, Tata Institute of Social Sciences, Tuljapur Campus. mkunhaman@rediffmail.com

Dr. C. M. Malish, Centre for Policy Research in Higher Education, NUEPA, New Delhi.

Dr. Nidhi S. Sabharwal, Centre for Policy Research in Higher Education, NUEPA, New Delhi.

Aishna Sharma, Ph.D. Student, Zakir Husain Centre for Educational Studies, School of Social Sciences, Jawaharlal Nehru University, New Delhi-110067. aishnas@gmail.com.

Dr Saumen Chattopadhyay Professor at Zakir Hussain Centre for Educational Studies, Jawaharlal Nehru University, New Delhi.

Dr. C. Krishnan, Associate professor of Economics, Government College Kodanchery, Calicut -673 580. ckcalicut@rediffmail.com

Dr Rajan Varughese, Former Pro Vice Chancellor, Mahatma Gandhi University, Kottayam, Kerala.

Dr. S. R. Sheeja, Assistant Professor of Economics, SDE, University of Kerala, Thiruvananthapuram.

Dr Christabell P J, Department of Futures Studies, University of Kerala, Thiruvananthapuram, christabell@keralauniversity.ac.in.

Rajeev B, Assistant Professor, Department of Futures Studies, University of Kerala, Thiruvananthapuram. rajmaveli@gmail.com.

Dr J.V. Asha, Assistant Professor & Hon. Director, Curriculum Development Centre, Department of Education, University of Kerala, Thiruvananthapuram

Dr G. L. Arunjilal, Head, Dept of Economics, Government Arts College, Trivandrum.

Dr P. S. Deva Kumar, Asst. Professor of Commerce, Govt. College for Women, Thiruvananthapuram.

Index

Academic adjustments, 89
Academic Ranking, 15
Accelerated pace of technological development, 50
Access and equity, 154
Access to quality, vii, 157
Accessible, 13, 74, 156
Admission and examination processes, 60
Affirmative action, 159, 163
Affordable, 74, 203
Africa, 3-5, 7, 8, 15, 18, 21, 56
Age group of 17 to 23, 210
Agenda for global exchange, 54
Alternative development, 72
APJ Abdul Kalam Kerala Technological University, 55
Arab states, 5, 7
Artificial intelligence, 197, 198
Asia, 3- 5, 11, 17-19, 24, 44, 68, 179
Aspiring Mind, 207
Assessment and Accreditation Agencies, influence of, 149
Award of additional grant, 118

Bangladesh, 6, 38
Barriers, 157
Bihar, 76, 77, 85, 89, 159
BRICS, 157
Budget cuts, 18
Build, Operate and Transfer, 150
Building a high-quality education system, 182

Cambodia, 7, 22
Case study institutions, 85
Case study states, 85
Caste stereotypes, 88
Caste/ Community Based Disparities, 158
Caste system, 64
Catholic Church, 8
Change maker, 154
Changing investment pattern, 49
Changing Nature of Employment, 198
Character of education, 49
China's gross domestic product, 22
Chinese higher education, largest system, 59
Chinese investment in ASEAN countries, 22
Christian churches, 145
Clarity in development literature, 71
Collaboration, academia and industry, 201
College cluster, 152
Commercialisation of University System, 149
Commonwealth of Independent States, 18
Competing for ideas, skills and knowledge, 50
Competitive global environment, 154
Comprehensive development of the student, 209
Contribution to development, 2
Corporate Social Responsibility (CSR), 152
Cost recovery measures, 7
Cross border mobility, 8
Cross-border research partnerships, 62
Cross-border students in India, 60
Curriculum to match industrial requirements, 157

Decade of decline, 1980s, 3
Declining trend, developed countries from 1980s, 3
Delhi, 13, 20, 69, 85, 112, 140, 163, 180, 217
Demand for skilled workers, 48
Demand-supply gap, vii
Developing countries, viii, ix, 2-4, 7, 18, 21, 49, 51, 53-56, 63, 79, 130, 157, 196
Developing world class universities, 16
Dissemination of specialised knowledge, vii
Disadvantaged groups, x, 87, 88, 91, 157, 158, 159
Discrimination, ix, xiii, 85
Diversification of study programmes, 2
Draft report of the Education Policy, 2016, 204

East Asia, 3, 4, 5, 7, 21, 22, 56
Economic crisis, 17, 21
and Higher Education, 17
Economic interest and investment, 2
Economic Stability and Academic Performance, 61
Economic value of knowledge, 2, 18
Education and Employability, 39
Education Hubs, 8, 10, 20
Education, key to equity, 157
Education-employment eco-system, 207
Educational inequality, 50
Effect of Large Population, 59
Eleventh Plan, 116, 156
Elite Universities, Best Talents, 53
Emerging economies, 27, 197, 199
Asia, 22
Knowledge economy, 53, 193, 204
Emerging Labour Market Changes, 196
Employability of graduates, vii
Employment abroad, 52
Engineering colleges, 142
English Oxbridge model, 38
Environment for development, 32
Equitable, 23, 74, 203
Equitable, vii
Equity in higher education, 154
Equal Opportunity Cell, 160
Ethiopia, 5, 6
Exchange of doctoral students, 62
Expanding access, important challenge, 157
Expansion across countries, 3
Expansion in higher education sector, viii, 84, 155
Expansion of enrolment, 5
External Quality Assurance (EQA), mechanisms, 14, 19

Faculty Regulatory Framework, 64
Feudal minds, 74
Financial assistance to weaker sections, 157
Fiscal deficit, 132
Foreign educational providers, 59
Foreign students, viii, 23, 52, 58, 196
Foreign training by offering fellowships, 61
Friedman, Milton, 122

Gaps in Labour Demand and Supply, 198
GATS, 8, 20, 51
Gender disparity, 158
Gender inequality in STEM education, 166
Gender parity, 5
Gender Participation in Scientific Research, 172
Gender-wise GER, 5, 158
Geographical Inequalities, 158
GER, xv, 3, 4, 5, 6, 84, 115,156, 157, 158, 159, 169, 207
Global
Citizenship, 51
Economic crisis of 2008, 18
Economy, 24, 48, 50, 166, 196, 203, 208
Enrolment in higher education, 3, 18
GER, 3, 4
Industry attracting billions of dollars and millions of students, 8
Knowledge economy, 52, 154
Revival, 2
Standards, 2, 19, 59
Superpower, 208
Globalisation of education, 8, 48
Government Colleges, 142
Graduate Skills and Labour Market Needs, 200
Gross enrolment ratios, 3
Growing educated unemployment and underemployment, 193, 204
Growth in 1970s and 1980s, 3

Higher Education Funding Agency (HEFA), 123, 127
High income countries, 3
High quality placements, 196
High skills leading to high wages, 49
Household investment, 2
Human Capital Theory, 48
Human capital, 116
effect on economic growth, 193

ILO, 17, 21, 199
Impact of Globalisation on Indian Education System, 65

Imparting skills and education, vii
Inclusive, x, 73, 74, 84, 154, 157, 159
  Growth strategy formulated, 156
Inclusiveness of higher education, 155, 162
Increase in enrolment in developing countries, 3
Inculcation of citizenship, 116
India's human resource potential, 154
Indian B-schools, 194
Indian Universities depend on the grant, 140
Indira Gandhi Scholarship for Single Girl Child, 160
Individual discrimination, 86, 88
Indonesia, 5-7, 22, 24
Inequities in the distribution, 71
Infrastructure development, 157
Innovation-driven economy, 24
Innovative education, 52
Input based funding, x
Institutional discrimination, 86, 88
Inter-regional disparities, 4
Inter-university network platforms, 215
Internal quality assurance cells (IQACs), 19
Internal resource generation, 138
International Benchmarking, 43
International comparison, 156
International Monetary Fund (IMF), 50, 56, 116
International student community, 58
Issue of Inclusiveness, 157
  increasing access, 162
  Low quality education and research, 116
  Subsidisation, 115

Kannur University, xvi, 130, 137, 172
Karnataka, 85
Kenya, 6
Kerala, x, xiv, 55, 76, 85, 89, 129-151, 166-172, 176, 183, 191, 207, 217
  College education scenario, 143
  Expansion of Higher Education, 142
  Financing of colleges, 143
Kerala State Higher Education Council, 152
Knowledge and skills, 13, 17, 49-51, 65, 181
Knowledge based higher education sector, 208
Knowledge economy, 73, 75
Knowledge, Key Asset of New Economies, 51
Knowledge society, 73, 75, 164
Knowledge transfer, 62
Knowledge workers, 50, 73, 75, 179, 196
Knowledge, driving force, 2
Knowledge-based economy, 27, 38, 164, 166

Largest education systems, 154, 157
Largest higher education systems, vii
Latin America, 4, 8, 63
Lessons for Developing Nations, 46
Liberal higher education policy, 142

Magnet economies, 50
Maharashtra, 76, 85, 89
Mahatma Gandhi University, 130, 133, 136, 148, 172, 217
Makerere University, Uganda, 7
Malaysia, ix, 7, 9-11, 16, 22-28, 32-37, 51, 54, 56, 217
  Education Blueprint, 2015-2025 (Higher Education), 28, 29
  Vision 2020, 26
Massive Open Online Courses (MOOC), viii, xv, 8, 12, 13, 19, 20, 48, 118, 161
Medical Education System, 208
Middle income countries, 3
Ministry of Skill Development and Entrepreneurship, 204, 209
Mode of funding, 101, 115-127
  Analysis of, 103
  and Governance, 115
  Private, 103
  Reforms, 126
Model Degree Colleges, 160
Modi, Prime Minister, 124
MOOCs, *see* Massive Open Online Courses
Moving towards sustaining universities, 138
Multiple campus Universities, 152

NAAC, 149, 150
National Commission for Minority Educational Institutions, 160
National competitiveness, 2
National Council for Teacher Education, 182
National Education Policy of 1986, 160
National Knowledge Commission, 112
National Monitoring Committee for Education of SCs, STs, 160
National Qualification Frameworks, 16, 21
National Skill Development Corporation, 200, 204
National Skill Development Fund, 204
NCFTE-2009, 182
Negative effects of global economic crisis, 19
Neo-liberalism post 1990s, 111
Neoliberal ideology, 23, 26, 35
New Forms of Globalization, 8
New generation of teachers, xi, 189
New public management (NPM), 32, 52, 100, 125
NGOs, 71
Non-academic matters, 54
Non-institutional sources of financing, 146
Novel start-up eco-system, 73
NQF, 17

OECD, 2, 8, 17, 20, 38, 54, 69, 164, 180, 192
Off-campus Courses in Aided colleges, 148
Open and Distance Learning, alternative approach, 161
Opportunities for doctoral degree holders, 59
Opportunities to Indian Higher Education System, 64
Own campuses in foreign nations, 63

People's struggles, 71
Plagiarism, 188
Policy makers, 15, 142, 181, 207
Post-Doctoral Fellowships for Women, 160
Post-Second World War period, 72
Powerful teaching, 181
Pre-service teacher education, 182
Private Aided Colleges, 142
Private higher education, 5, 7, 8, 32, 33
Professionalisation of teaching, 79
Proliferation of institutions, 2
Public funding support, 2
Public Higher Education institutions, 7, 117
  Funding for, 26
  Model for, 33
  Privatisation of, 117
Public Private Partnership, viii, 125, 142, 152
Public universities as agent, 23, 35
Puducherry, 159
Punnayya Committee, 112, 141

Quality higher education, 13-15, 74, 81, 117, 125
Quantitative and qualitative challenges, vii

Rashtriya Uchchatar Shiksha Abhiyan (RUSA), 152, 161
Redesigning education with employment, 52
Reforming education systems, 182
Reframing of educational policies, 50
Regional Qualification Frameworks, 17
Rehabilitation Council of India, 182
Relationship, education and economic development, vii
Religion-based universities, 38
Religious minorities, 157
Republic of Korea, 5, 8
Research funding, 66
Reservation in higher education institutions, 160
Resources allocated, 3, 30
Market needs, 203
Revival, higher education worldwide, 18
Role in national development process, 26
Role of Research in Institutional Success, 55

Scheme of Interest Subsidy on Educational Loans, 160
Science, Technology, Engineering and Mathematics (STEM) Education, xi, 164
Scientists of India, 54
Self-financing courses, 147, 149
  Aided Colleges, 147
Share of public expenditure, 3
Singapore, spending on Education, 41
Skill Development and Entrepreneurship, 204
Skilled workforce, 24, 165, 207
Skilling India dynamics, 209
Social garbage, 82
Social life of campus, 88
Social mobility, 154, 157
Society oriented to job oriented, 49
Socio-economic backwardness, 160
Stakeholders, higher education institutions, 58
State funding, 6, 111
Strengthening of industry-higher education linkages, 205
Strengths and Weaknesses of Indian Higher Education System, 63
Strong research base, 54
Structural adjustment policies (SAP), 116
Student Demand-Driven System, 203
Student-friendly administrative system, 60
Sub-Saharan Africa, 7
Suitably skilled employees, 49
SWOT Analysis, 63
System of franchising, 50

Takshila, Nalanda and Vikramashila, 38
Teacher quality, xi, 181, 189
Tertiary education, 6, 32, 38, 56, 59, 62, 63, 66, 69, 199
Thailand, 22, 24, 37, 61
Threats of Higher Education System, 64
Times ranking, 15
Top 500 research institutions in the world, 55
Top ten institutions, 16
Trade liberalisation, 50, 193
Trained and qualified faculty, 157
Transformation of the education system, 48
Trends and tendencies, 75

U.R. Anathamurthy Committee Report (2010), 153
Unauthorised fund collection, 148
Under privileged sections, 157
UNESCO Convention against Discrimination in Education, 86
University Grants Commission (UGC), 56, 62, 118, 180, 182
University of Calicut, 130, 133, 134, 135, 217
University of Kerala, 130, 133
University-eligible age group children, 156
University-eligible age group students are not getting enrolled, 157
Upskilling attitude among the working population, 46
Uttar Pradesh, 85

Vedic learning, 38
Vision 2020, 23, 24, 28
Vision 2030, 194, 200
Voucher system, 115, 122

White Paper (2001) of Kerala Government, 147
World Bank, 6, 17, 19-21, 24, 29, 37, 51, 54, 69, 139, 141, 156, 201
  Database, 41
World Trade Organisation, 32, 50
World University Ranking, 15
WTO, 32, 50, 51

Youth, 3, 38, 81, 200, 204, 208
  Population, 3